The Truth About
Supply-Side Economics

The Truth About Supply-Side Economics

MICHAEL K. EVANS

Basic Books, Inc., Publishers   New York

Library of Congress Cataloging in Publication Data

Evans, Michael K.
  The truth about supply-side economics.

  Includes index.
  1. Supply-side economics. 2. United States—Economic
policy—1981–   . I. Title.
HB241.E93   1983   338.973   82-72392
ISBN 0-465-08778-7

To E.D., D.R., and R.I.

You visionary of hell, never have I had fair play in your forecasts. Calamity is all you care about, or see, no happy portents; and you bring to pass nothing agreeable.

The Iliad

It is often said that happy countries have no history, and no historians. It may also be pointed out that prosperous nations have no economists.

CHRISTIAN STOFFAËS,
Reaganomics in Perspective

CONTENTS

Part I

Introduction

Part II

The Myths of Supply-Side Economics

Part III

The Enduring Truths of Supply-Side Economics

Part IV

Policy Implications

Part I

Introduction

CHAPTER 1

Supply-Side Economics: Myths and

Realities

Where the Reagan Program Went Wrong

Supply-side economics came of age on July 31, 1981, the day that Congress sent President Ronald Reagan an unprecedented five-year $749 billion tax cut. From the unconventional scribblings of virtually unknown academics, a small but determined coterie of economists and politicians had in seven years forged a program that was on the brink of being accepted by a majority of the American public. The economy stood poised, they contended, to experience the nirvana of more rapid growth and declining unemployment simultaneously with lower inflation and interest rates. In addition, the federal government would end twenty years of deficit spending and return to a balanced budget in the face of unprecedented tax cuts and massive increases in defense spending. Such were the claims offered by Reagan administration economists.

To be sure, one did not need 20/20 vision to spot the skeptics in the crowd. Cries of "voodoo economics" still resounded in the air, as did the claim that the budget could be balanced only "with mirrors." Humorists gibed that the budget could be balanced by keeping two sets of books, or by buying our new weapons from Taiwan. But for the most part the general public, wearied and disturbed by fifteen years of almost steadily increasing inflation and declining living standards, and buttressed by a new president then at the peak of his popularity, were more than willing to give the new program a try. They were to be sorely disappointed.

Judged by any reasonably unbiased criteria, including the administration's own forecast, the program *as actually implemented* was an egregious failure. When Wall Street heard the news of the tax cut, the stock market plunged almost 20 percent in a two-month period, and the economy promptly entered a recession which was to send unemployment soaring to postwar highs and profit margins and capacity utilization to postwar lows. Whereas the rate of inflation was indeed cut in half, interest rates initially failed to decline; and some yields, particularly mortgage rates, moved to new all-time peaks. The so-called real rate of interest—the nominal rate less the rate of inflation—reached levels unmatched since the early 1930s. The financial position of the federal government made a hollow mockery of the claim to return to a balanced budget as the deficit soared from $60 billion in fiscal year (FY) 1981 to $110 billion in FY 1982 and appeared headed toward $180 billion in FY 1983.

Many of the original supply siders continued to claim that the program that had failed so miserably was not the one originally designed by the Reagan administration. To be sure, personal income tax rates were cut 5 percent on October 1, 1981, and 10 percent on July 1, 1982, instead of 10 percent at the beginning of both years. Furthermore, government spending was not curtailed nearly as rapidly as originally planned. Certainly these deviations had serious repercussions on the economy. However, to stake one's defense of supply-side economics solely on these disparities is to ignore, if not completely misunderstand, the underlying dynamics that doomed the Reagan program to failure even as the president was appending his signature to this historic legislation.

The Reagan program, as it was structured, asked the economy to perform not one but three unnatural acts. The first was for the gross national product (GNP) to grow faster at the same time that the money supply growth was being severely restricted. The second was for the rate of real growth to increase from 1 percent to 5 percent at the same time that the rate of inflation was cut in half, from 10 percent to 5 percent. The third was to balance the budget by 1984 in spite of massive increases in defense spending and unprecedented tax cuts. These inconsistencies are examined in greater detail in chapter 2.

The difficulty of accomplishing even one of these three estimable goals can be demonstrated with the aid of a few simple graphs and charts. Figure 1.1 shows the behavior of the velocity of money—defined as GNP in current dollars divided by the so-called narrow money supply, which is basically currency plus checking accounts—over the past thirty years. The predicted money supply growth rates used for this forecast are the *maximum* increases that Paul Volcker, chairman of the Federal Reserve Board of Governors, stated that he would allow; and for 1981 and most of 1982 he kept his word, at least on an annual basis. Although the year-to-year changes in velocity over the postwar period are quite substantial, it is clear from figure 1.1 that even in peak years velocity never rose as fast as the *minimum* increase that the Reagan program had assumed. Hence either the monetary targets were set far too low or, if they were not, the expected growth of GNP was far too optimistic.

The projected combination of faster growth and lower inflation is slightly more plausible, since gains in productivity could conceivably offset the inflationary pressures generated by the sharp improvement in demand. However, this would require an unprecedented improvement in productivity over a relatively short period of time. Furthermore, it would be completely antithetical to previous postwar experience, since each of the past five postwar recoveries has been accompanied by an increase in inflation which has averaged about 2 percent during the expansionary phase of the business cycle.

The forecast of the return to a balanced budget by 1984 represented the most astounding optimism of all. The deficit in FY 1981 was $58 billion, the difference between $657 billion in outlays and $599 billion in tax receipts. According to the official Reagan administration estimates, the tax cuts for FY 1984 alone were to be $150 billion. If the Reagan administration's own estimated growth rate of nominal GNP from 1981 to 1984—which is actually far in excess of what occurred in 1981 and 1982—is applied and the tax cuts are subtracted, estimated receipts would increase only from $657 to $692 billion.

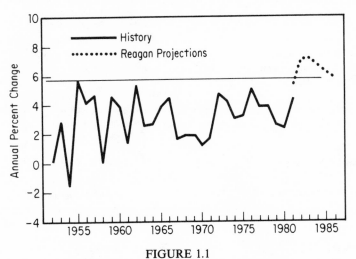

FIGURE 1.1

Historical and Projected Change in Velocity

SOURCES: 1951–70: *Long-Term Economic Growth, 1860–1979,* U.S. Department of Commerce (Washington, D.C.: U.S. Government Printing Office), p. 61; 1970–80: Department of Commerce and Federal Reserve Bank; 1981–85: Calculated from *America's New Beginning: A Program for Economic Recovery* (Washington, D.C.: U.S. Government Printing Office, February 18, 1981), p. S-1.

Now let us see what that implies for government spending. Here we take the Reagan defense estimates verbatim and assume the same increase in the social safety net programs contained in the original February 18, 1981, budget. As shown in table 1.1, balancing the budget would thus have required a reduction in all other expenditures from $258 billion in FY 1981 to $129 billion in FY 1984—a virtual impossibility. If, on the other hand, all those other expenditures were to remain constant in real terms—that is, to increase by the rate of inflation estimated in the Reagan forecasts—the budget deficit for FY 1984 would be approximately $200 billion, which is likely to be close to the actual figure.

Even David Stockman never thought that all government spending excluding defense and social safety net programs could be cut in half; someone obviously committed a major error in estimating tax receipts. During periods of increasing inflation, tax receipts have tended to grow about one and one-half times as fast than GNP; in other words, if GNP were to rise 10 percent per

TABLE 1.1

Balancing the Budget, Reagan Style

	1981	1984	
(1) Total budget receipts estimated before tax cuts	$ 599	$ 842	Assuming GNP growth contained in official Reagan administration forecast, and assuming taxes and GNP grow at the same rate.
(2) Less: tax cuts		150	
(3) Equals: total receipts projected under the Reagan program	599	692	(1)–(2)
(4) Defense outlays	160	250	From Reagan budget.
(5) Plus: Social safety net programs	239	313	Same as (1) above.
(6) Plus: All other expenditures	258	129	Calculated as a residual—for 1984, the amount necessary to balance the budget by 1984. Equals (7)−(4)−(5).
(7) Equals: total outlays	657	692	

SOURCES: Expenditures: *America's New Beginning,* February 18, 1981, budget. Tax cuts: Joint Committee on Taxation Staff, December 29, 1981. Other calculations by Evans Economics, Inc.
NOTE: All figures in billions of current dollars.

year, taxes would increase 15 percent. The two major reasons for this are as follows. First, book profits, although not economic profits, rise faster than GNP during periods of inflation. Because they are taxed at a much higher rate than personal income, total tax receipts increase more than proportionately. Second, inflation pushes individuals into higher tax brackets—the phenomenon known as bracket creep—so that personal income tax receipts also rise faster than GNP during periods of inflation.

Yet when inflation is decreasing, as the Reagan administration had projected, the relationship between taxes and GNP moves in the other direction. Profits decline as a proportion of GNP, and although bracket creep is still present as long as prices are rising at all, it becomes a much less important revenue generator. Thus in these calculations taxes rise only at the same rate as GNP, although with the sharp increase in tax avoidance even that may be an overestimate. The Reagan estimates of tax receipts thus turn out to be severely overstated.

Hence, to succeed in reaching its goals of higher growth, lower inflation, and a balanced budget by 1984, the Reagan program would have required: (1) an unprecedented increase in velocity over a five-year period; (2) an extraordinary improvement in the rate of productivity growth; and (3) more than a 50 percent reduction in all government spending excluding defense and social safety net programs.

Given the logical inconsistencies inherent in the Reagan forecast and the severe recession that did indeed develop, one may well presume that only a small minority of economists really expected that such miracles could come to pass. Yet at least initially that was not at all the case. While most economists did not believe that inflation could be reduced as quickly as was projected by the Reagan forecast, they did accept the predictions that the economy would soon enter a prolonged boom and that the budget could be balanced by 1984.

To be more specific, in March 1981 a survey conducted by Eggert Economic Enterprises, Inc. showed that, of forty-four leading economists, virtually none of whom had any ties to the administration, a strong majority expected the Reagan program to work.[1] The average growth rate expected for real GNP in 1982 was 3.7 percent, compared to the decline of 1.8 percent which actually occurred.* The rate of inflation projected by those economists for 1982 was 9.6 percent; the actual figure turned out to be a substantially lower 6.0 percent because of the effects of the recession. Perhaps most surprising, in view of subsequent events, was that fully 67 percent of the economists surveyed expected that the federal budget would indeed be balanced by 1984.

---

*All 1982 figures used in this book are preliminary and subject to substantial revision by the U.S. Department of Commerce in July 1983.

The same survey was conducted again in September 1981, right after the tax cut had been passed and economists had presumably taken the opportunity to readjust their forecasts. To be sure, only 11 percent instead of 67 percent thought the budget could be balanced by 1984, but their overall view of the economy was almost as optimistic. Real growth for 1982 was still expected to be 2.6 percent, whereas the forecast for the rate of inflation had declined by 9.6 percent to 8.1 percent. How could the collective economics profession—the same group that had predicted the change in real GNP with an average error of only 0.5 percent per year over the past five years[2]—have come so unglued?

First, few if any economists thought that Paul Volcker and other members of the Federal Reserve Board of Governors would so single-mindedly pursue their goal of reducing money supply growth in the face of a prolonged period of economic stagnation and record postwar unemployment rates, although Volcker did repeatedly broadcast his planned course of action and frequently warned that further budget cuts would be necessary if interest rates were to decline.

Second, the tax cut passed in August 1981 contained far more tax reductions and loopholes than was generally expected even a few days earlier. In addition, the degree to which tax collections were being sliced by both legal and illegal tax avoidance was not generally understood. Hence the standard budget projections far overestimated the revenue growth during the 1980s.

Third, most economists failed to gauge how much difficulty Congress would have in cutting government spending. Only a handful of economists ever believed that economic health could be restored by cutting taxes without also cutting government spending. For if that were not the case, if tax cuts alone were sufficient, why bother with any taxes at all? We could simply eliminate all taxes and live happily ever after with a $750 billion budget deficit instead of a mere $180 billion. Obviously the problems of the economy are much more intractable than those that can be solved merely by cutting taxes without offsetting reductions in spending.

In defense of the economic forecasts at the time, the two previous major attempts at broad-based tax cuts—the Mellon reductions of the 1920s and the Kennedy-Johnson tax cut of the early 1960s, mainly in 1964—had indeed provided faster growth and balanced budgets without higher inflation. Hence it was perhaps not wholly unreasonable to expect that the same performance could once again be generated by the Reagan tax cuts.

The Mellon tax cuts, which have been praised by some economists and journalists as spearheading the dynamic growth of the 1920s, consisted of a number of broad-based reductions in the personal income tax rate schedule that reversed the sharp increase in tax rates pressed into service during World War

I. Whereas there is little question that these tax reductions did improve the economic health of the nation, they are not directly relevant to present conditions because federal taxes then represented such a minuscule proportion of GNP. Indeed, during the 1920s federal personal income taxes averaged less than 2 percent of personal income.

Thus the direct focus of comparison is properly with the Kennedy-Johnson tax cuts. For those not familiar with this landmark legislation, it superficially appears to have been quite similar to the Reagan tax cuts of 1981. Personal income tax rates were reduced by 20 percent over two years. Corporate income tax rates were lowered through (a) the introduction of a 7 percent investment tax credit, (b) a reduction in depreciation lives by 30 percent to 40 percent, and (c) a cut in the top corporate income tax rate from 52 percent to 48 percent. We need only to compare, however, the underlying economic circumstances and the structure of fiscal and monetary policy in 1964 and 1981 to understand why the Kennedy-Johnson tax cut worked and the Reagan tax cut did not. This point is discussed in detail in chapter 2; but the salient points can be briefly summarized here.

First, the federal budget was virtually in balance and the rate of inflation was only 1.2 percent in 1963. This permitted the Fed to validate the increase in economic activity without worsening inflationary pressures. Second, the Kennedy-Johnson tax cut did tighten up on a number of tax loopholes and raised some tax rates. Congress made a belated effort to accomplish this in August 1982, but the original 1981 tax legislation contained no such attempts. Third, and most important, federal government spending increased only 1 percent in FY 1965, compared to the 11 percent gain in FY 1982. Hence the underlying state of the economy, the reaction of the monetary authorities, and the structure of fiscal policy were dramatically different in 1964 and 1981.

The Need for Supply-Side Programs: The Deterioration of the U.S. Economy

It is thus clear, both from theoretical constructs and unbiased empirical evidence, that the Reagan program that was put into place was doomed to failure. Yet it would have been an egregious error, far worse even than the one committed by the Reagan architects, to assume that the essential planks of the Reagan program were not necessary. For as the 1980 elections approached, the U.S. economy was already well into a period of prolonged deterioration which would have intensified if the Johnson-Nixon-Ford-Carter policies had remained in place.

Now that inflation has been largely—if temporarily—brought under control, it is all too easy to forget how close the economy was edging toward runaway inflation. While the U.S. economy had undergone several periods of rapid inflation in its history, notably during and shortly after wartime, these had without exception been followed by periods of price stability or even deflation. Thus in 1940 the average price level in the United States was actually about 20 percent lower than it had been in 1800. Even the inflation engendered by World War II was followed by a period in which the price level rose less than 2 percent per year. Yet from 1965 to 1982 the consumer price index more than tripled, and double-digit inflation was beginning to be accepted as commonplace.

Another dimension of the deterioration in the economy can be glimpsed from the pattern of long-term interest rates since 1860, as shown in figure 1.2. From that date until 1969, they had fluctuated within a narrow band from 3½ percent* to 7½ percent. Starting in 1970, however, they rose to 8 percent and then continued to increase fairly steadily, reaching peak levels of over 15 percent in 1981. Even during years of 20 percent inflation, long-term rates had not previously risen above 7½ percent because bondholders correctly perceived that these bursts of inflation would be temporary. During the past decade that has obviously no longer been the case.

Indeed, the record of the U.S. economy since 1965 had been one long story of impaired performance. From 1947 to 1965, productivity increased slightly more than 3 percent per year, while from 1977 through 1981 it actually declined. The rate of inflation for that earlier period averaged 1.9 percent—including the commodity inflation at the beginning of the Korean War. The inflation rate then increased to 4.1 percent for the 1966–72 period and 9.0 percent for the 1973–81 period. The unemployment rate, which had averaged 4.8 percent from 1947 to 1965, rose to an average of 6.7 percent from 1975 through 1980 and surpassed 10 percent by late 1982. Even the once highly valued dollar had lost more than half of its purchasing power by 1980 relative to now-strong foreign currencies such as the deutsche mark, the Swiss franc, and the Japanese yen. These figures are summarized in table 1.2.

This serious degradation of U.S. economic performance can be directly tied to declining productivity, as already mentioned and as illustrated in figure 1.3. The following factors contributed to this sharp decline in productivity:

1. A sharp increase in both the average and marginal tax rates on personal income took place in the years following the Kennedy-Johnson tax cut. Indeed,

---

*Whenever a fractional percentage is cited, a general range is implied. A decimal percentage indicates an exact figure.

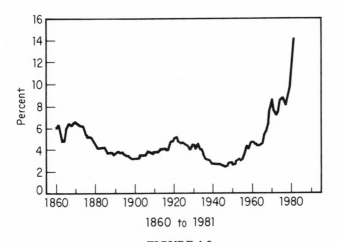

FIGURE 1.2

Long-term Interest Rate

SOURCE: *Long-term Economic Growth,* 1860–1970, U.S. Department of Commerce (Washington, D.C.: U.S. Government Printing Office), p. 224.

TABLE 1.2

Relative Performance of U.S. Economy, 1947–82

	Real Growth	Unemployment Rate	Produc- tivity	Consumer Price Index	Value of Dollar[a]	Prime Rate
1947–65	3.9	4.8	3.3	1.9	100.0	3.5
1966–72	3.5	4.4	2.4	4.1	98.0	6.3
1973–81	2.7	6.7	0.9	9.0	69.5	10.7
1982–	−1.8	9.7	0.4	6.2	82.1	14.9

SOURCE: *Economic Report of the President,* (Washington, D.C.: U.S. Government Printing Office, February 1982), "Value of Dollar," calculated by Evans Economics, Inc.
[a]Index, 1947–65 = 100.0, relative to strong foreign currencies (£, DM, FFr, SFr, BFr, DFl, and ¥)

as shown in figure 1.4, if the Carter performance of the economy had continued throughout the 1980s, *the marginal tax rate of the median American worker, including federal, state, and local taxes, would have reached 60 percent by 1990.* Tax avoidance would have become rife, while individual incentive, work effort, and labor productivity would have been even more severely penalized.

2. A sharp increase occurred in the rate of inflation that tilted investment away from productive assets toward so-called fixed supply assets—land, gold and silver, Old Masters, and so forth—which added not one iota to the productive capability of the U.S. economy. The increase in inflation also penalized savers, with the result that the total net national saving rate fell to postwar lows and interest rates rose to all-time peaks.

3. The maximum rate on capital gains taxes doubled, which had the effect

11

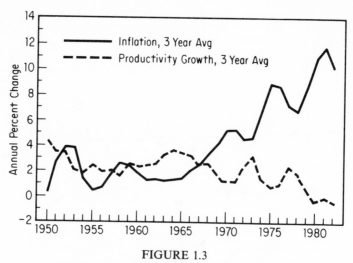

FIGURE 1.3

Change in Inflation and Productivity, 1950–1982

SOURCES: *Economic Report of the President* (Washington, D.C.: U.S. Government Printing Office, February 1982) and Evans Economics, Inc.

of crushing the stock market and reducing the size of the venture capital industry and public underwritings of small companies by 99 percent (!) from 1969 to 1975.[3] In addition, federal funding and support of research and development projects were sharply curtailed. While improvements in existing technology continued to advance, new developments were reduced to a trickle.

4. Government regulatory activity underwent a massive increase during the 1970s, so that by 1982 the cost of meeting government regulations borne by the private sector amounted to $150 billion per year. The additional cost of a 1982 model new car due to fuel economy, safety, and anti-pollution regulations rose by an average of $1,600.[4]

5. The energy "policy" implemented was so convoluted that efficient oil companies had to subsidize those who were less efficient, and the major beneficiaries of domestic tax policy and controls were not American consumers at all but rather Arab sheikhs.

To a certain extent these have been listed in reverse order of difficulty of solution. President Reagan ended the controls on domestic oil prices almost immediately; much to the amazement of his critics this produced an actual decline in petroleum prices. His administration also cut back the cost of government regulation, reversing many of the most costly and unproductive restrictions. Capital gains taxes had been sharply reduced in 1978, and further reductions were incorporated into the 1981 Tax Reduction Act. However, the problems of reducing inflation and cutting marginal tax rates required radical surgery on the American economy, surgery which President Rea-

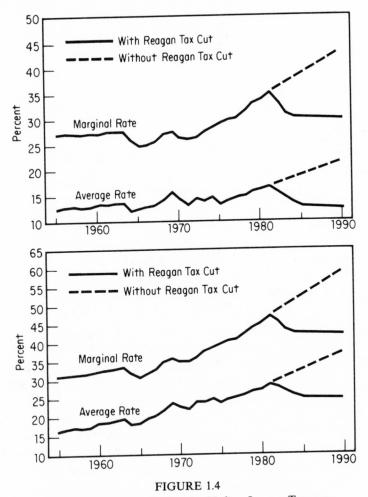

FIGURE 1.4

Federal Income Tax Burden for Median Income Taxpayer
Total Tax Burden for Median Income Taxpayer

SOURCES: *Economic Report of the President* (February 1982) and Evans Economics, Inc.

gan—and a majority of supply-side economists—thought could be successfully performed.

Maintaining Equilibrium Between Demand and Supply

Several editions of Paul Samuelson's best-selling textbook *Economics* contain the line that "You can make even a parrot into a learned political economist—all he must learn are the two words 'supply' and 'demand.' "[5] Yet the

13

sad fact of the matter is that between 1965 and 1980 many of our brightest economists and government planners unlearned even that first elementary lesson of economics. Pretending that the equilibrium between demand and supply had somehow been suspended, they substituted the belief that an increase in demand would somehow be matched by an equal expansion in supply, and thus all that was needed to spur the economy to greater heights was to increase private and public sector consumption. The result, of course, was that demand exceeded supply, which lead to ever-increasing rates of inflation and reductions in productivity growth. This was the cancer that had to be reversed by the economic policies of the 1980s before it consumed the entire increase in economic activity for the coming years.

There was no precedent for this theory of economics. In fact, before the Great Depression of the 1930s, the primary emphasis of mainstream economics was placed on the supply side rather than the demand side. Economic policy was designed to provide the maximum increase in production, based on the belief that the more goods and services that an economy could produce, the better off its inhabitants would be. This line of economic thought, which indeed carries all the way back to Adam Smith, replaced the earlier doctrine of the Mercantilists who believed that sterile supplies of gold and silver, rather than the production of goods and services, represented the wealth of nations.[6]

Once Smith's views on the importance of the productive capability of an economy became generally accepted, mainstream economics then appropriately focused on the factors that determined the equilibrium of aggregate demand and supply. Once the industrialization of society was under way, the problem of recurrent business cycles began to appear as an important feature of the economic landscape. Periods of recession and even brief depression occurred throughout the industrialized world, and it was clear that an enlargement of economic theory was needed to deal with this dimension.

The mainstream thought that emerged during the nineteenth and early twentieth century held that supply created its own demand. This principle came to be known as Say's Law after Jean Baptiste Say, a nineteenth-century French economist,[7] but it was actually embraced by most of the major economists of his time, notably James S. Mill and David Ricardo. In fact, the supply-side view, as stated by Say's Law, came to "dominate economic thinking" and remained "largely unchallenged" through the 1920s.[8] As might be expected, Say's Law sold at a heavy discount during the Great Depression and has never really recovered.

Before Say is dismissed as a complete crank, it may be worthwhile to explore briefly the logic that did lie behind his "law." Say stated that in order to produce goods it was necessary to purchase materials, hire labor, and invest in plant and equipment. The money spent for these factor inputs would in turn be used by its recipients to purchase the goods and services they desired. If more workers were hired, labor income and hence consumption would rise. If consumers decided to save a greater proportion of their income, those savings would be translated into investment, which would also generate more jobs and income. If planned saving was greater than planned investment, the rate of interest would fall until these two quantities were brought into equilibrium. In other words, individuals worked either to purchase consumer goods and services or to invest the money they had saved, which meant that someone else would use the funds for productive purposes. Hoarding was not considered a realistic alternative—nor has that ever been the cause of recessions or depressions.

As mentioned above, nineteenth-century economists considered business cycle activity to be a normal, if disagreeable, part of economic activity. Nothing in Say's Law implies that an economy cannot undergo periodic imbalances; only that if they do occur, interest rates, wages, and prices will adjust and return the economy to equilibrium in a relatively short period of time—usually a year or less. When the economy does recover, the total productive capability determines the amount of goods and services that are produced, not the amount that people want to buy. For with a given amount of labor, capital, raw materials, education of the labor force, and level of technology, only a certain amount can be produced at any given time. Simply printing more money for people to spend without improving the productive capacity of the economy will not raise the amount of available goods and services in the marketplace.

Stated this way, Say's Law does not seem like such an outlandish theory, and yet we know that the U.S. economy remained mired in the Great Depression for almost an entire decade and was rescued from this stagnation, not by planned government policy, but only by World War II. The fatal flaw in Say's Law occurred in the assumption that demand would always rise to equal the increase in supply; whereas in fact several autonomous, or exogenous, developments could distort this relationship and plunge the economy into a prolonged period of underutilization of existing resources. Between 1929 and 1933 several such events occurred.

1. Consumer purchasing power was drastically curtailed by the collapse of the stock market as well as a one-third reduction in the money supply, due in part to wholesale bank failures. Thus consumers found that virtually billions of dollars of their savings had "disappeared" and hence their purchasing power no longer matched the production of goods and services.

2. In an unbelievably ill-timed attempt to balance the budget, the Hoover administration and the Republican Congress combined to pass a bill which quadrupled the bottom tax rate and raised the top rate from 25 percent to 61

15

percent. Worse yet, this bill, which was passed on June 6, 1932, was made retroactive to the first of the year. Because withholding had not yet been invented, most of the increase in taxes was due on March 15, 1933, and the withdrawal of funds to pay the increased taxes was the final act which drove many banks to close their doors at that time.[9]

3. Ordinarily, a decline in planned investment activity relative to saving would cause interest rates to drop, thus helping to restore equilibrium. However, in spite of the sharp reduction in economic activity, long-term rates moved even higher after the stock market crash of 1929. Highest-rated Aaa corporate bond rates rose from 4.7 percent in 1929 to 5.0 percent in 1932, while Baa rates rose from 5.9 percent all the way to 9.3 percent—an impossible rate to pay during a period when prices were falling 10 percent a year. This short-circuited a crucial link necessary to move the economy back toward full capacity and employment.

4. The passage of the Hawley-Smoot Tariff Act, designed to exclude imports and hence divert production to domestic sources, had the unintended but entirely predictable result of actually diminishing the U.S. net foreign balance. While imports did indeed decline, exports fell much faster, thus reducing net exports by 64 percent between 1929 and 1933.

Many conservatives have pointed to the Roosevelt era as the beginning of the sharp upward drift in the ratio of government spending to GNP, but the facts do not support this hypothesis. While Roosevelt did increase the involvement of the federal government in the affairs of the average citizen and corporation, this was not accomplished by any massive rise in spending. In FY 1933, which was half over by the time Roosevelt was sworn into office, total federal government spending represented 8.2 percent of GNP. By FY 1940, the last peacetime year, this proportion had risen only to 9.5 percent, whereas the budget deficit as a proportion of GNP had declined from 4.7 percent to 3.1 percent. One can perhaps argue that the programs put in place by the Roosevelt administration later led to the huge growth in government spending, but even this is not very accurate, and in any case the government spending/GNP ratio did not increase significantly during the 1930s.

Indeed, the inability of either the U.S. or the British economies to extricate themselves from this massive and prolonged depression led John Maynard Keynes, who had heretofore been in the mainstream of economic orthodoxy, to suggest that if the private sector could not bridge the gap between demand and production, the public sector ought to accomplish this through higher spending. Keynes even went so far as to suggest that the world would be better off if one group of unemployed dug holes and another group filled them up, for that would increase employment, income, output, and sales.[10] Although we have no definitive record of that particular activity occurring, Brown University (and presumably others) still has tables of the logarithmic and trigono-metric functions to 100 decimal places, hand-calculated by unemployed math-ematicians and scientists during the 1930s. Mechanical calculators were not allowed, of course, for that would have speeded up the process and returned those scientists to the unemployment lines sooner.

The above does not really do justice to Keynes, one of the most imaginative economists of the twentieth century whose plan for international currency re-form at Bretton Woods in 1944 laid the groundwork for two decades of unpar-alleled worldwide economic expansion. Keynes understood the insidious ef-fects of inflation precisely. He wrote in one well-known essay, "There is no subtler, no surer means of overturning the existing basis of Society than to debauch the currency . . . as inflation proceeds and the real value of the cur-rency fluctuates wildly from month to month, all permanent relations between debtors and creditors, which form the ultimate foundation of capitalism, be-come so utterly disordered as to be almost meaningless."[11] Keynes suggested an increase in government spending only as a method for extricating the econ-omy from the Great Depression—a situation which, he believed, would other-wise lead to the end of capitalism and its replacement by either socialism or fascism. It is most unlikely that he would have endorsed higher government spending during periods of double-digit inflation.

Although Roosevelt allegedly planned to increase social welfare spending after economic activity declined again in 1938, not much was done before World War II began. That soon brought the U.S. economy to peak production levels, and it continued to run near full employment for more than a decade after the end of the war. The 1958 recession jolted this complacency and brought forth a plethora of suggestions to spur the economy through higher government spending or lower taxes, but Eisenhower rejected all of them in favor of a balanced budget. Though the Kennedy-Johnson tax cut appeared to be following Keynesian principles, it was in fact a carefully crafted sup-ply-side tax cut, balanced by slower rates of growth in government spending, although admittedly that is not how it was sold to the public.

Thus for the first twenty years of the postwar period, the increase in aggre-gate demand closely paralleled the increase in supply. Whereas this can to a certain extent be regarded as a happy coincidence, it was in large part the result of a federal government budget that remained in balance during this period,* a rate of inflation low enough not to distort decisions affecting saving and in-vestment, and a tax code which, while far from perfect, did not actively dis-courage saving, investment, and entrepreneurship.

*The actual budget deficit for the 1947–1965 period averaged $1.2 billion per year. The so-called national income and product account (NIPA) budget, which more closely measures the effect of the budget on the economy, actually showed an average annual surplus of $0.6 billion over the same period.

Nineteen sixty-five marked the end of this era. Whereas government policy of the previous twenty years had been even-handed toward its goals of increasing both consumption and production, the scale tilted dramatically under the Johnson administration. Trying to fight both the Vietnam War abroad and the War Against Poverty at home, Johnson succeeded in winning neither. In addition, the new government policy of massive increases in transfer payments, coupled with higher interest rates, a 10 percent income surtax, and two suspensions of the investment tax credit in three years shifted the mix of GNP from capital formation toward consumption. As a result, aggregate demand began to outstrip aggregate supply: the classic story of too many dollars chasing too few goods.

Under these circumstances, it was inevitable that the rate of inflation would eventually increase. However, neither Johnson nor Nixon could accept this fact. Refusing to admit that the increase in inflation was a sign that the economy was dangerously out of balance, they tried to short-circuit the problem by imposing wage/price guidelines and controls. These controls, while offering a temporary respite, merely reduced productivity even further, thereby virtually guaranteeing that inflation would reach new heights once the controls were removed.

The latter-day supporters and apologists of Keynesian economics did not see it that way, however, preferring to believe that untramelled growth in demand could coexist with stable prices if only wage/price guidelines could be enforced; even today, Walter Heller continues to call for such guidelines.[12] In order to maintain the appearances of any semblance of economic theory, these supporters invented what became known as Keynes's Law, namely that demand creates its own supply. According to this convoluted attempt at logic, it is necessary for individuals, businesses, or governments merely to spend enough, and somehow increases in productive capacity will automatically occur. Any temporary increase in inflation that might take place before the new equilibrium position is reached can be handled by using guidelines to limit wage or price increases.

The logic behind Keynes's Law is that as demand rises, stimulated perhaps by higher government spending or an increase in handouts to the private sector, the rate of return on invested capital will rise apace because firms will be producing more goods per unit of capital. As this happens, they will expand their productive facilities and thus increase total capacity. More labor can be obtained from the ranks of the unemployed, or from those not currently in the labor force but ready and willing to work if they know that jobs are available. Thus growth in productive capacity will match the increase in demand, and equilibrium will be maintained.

It should be immediately apparent that Keynes's Law is as intellectually bankrupt as the outmoded Say's Law which it essentially replaced. However, that was not what policymakers of the 1965–75 decade believed. Almost a dozen new-fangled econometric models were built by the academic community and flourished, all designed to predict that an increase in demand could be accomplished without worrying about higher inflation.

The best known of these models included those constructed by the Brookings Institution, the Wharton School, the Federal Reserve Board, the University of Michigan, and Harvard University (later Data Resources, Inc.), and indeed this author participated in the estimation of several of these models. While model builders at the time genuinely believed that demand-driven models containing rudimentary or no supply-side variables would generate the most accurate predictions, they just happened to tell the politicians exactly what they wanted to hear: more government spending will help rather than harm the economy. Virtually all models of the time gave the result that the so-called balanced budget multiplier was positive, which means that an equal increase in both government spending and taxes would raise GNP and not increase inflation.

It is thus no surprise that the policies of the Johnson, Nixon, Ford, and Carter administrations were aimed primarily at stimulating consumption while providing little or no aid for investment or productivity. Even when double-digit inflation reared its ugly head in 1974, the recommended policy was not to stimulate investment and productivity, but rather to increase consumption through the purest demand-side tax cut of all, a rebate. When this author wrote in 1975 that none of the problems of the economy had been solved by the severe recession of the previous year and that inflation and interest rates at the peak of the next business cycle would be even higher than the levels reached in 1974,[13] many observers wrote off these forecasts as the work of a crank, or, in somewhat kinder language, an "iconoclast." Official government policy, under Republicans and Democrats alike, was to keep consumption high enough to reach full employment and assume that investment, productivity, and total capacity would all take care of themselves.

Balanced—and Unbalanced—Approaches to Supply-Side Economics

It was against this background that the concept of supply-side economics emerged. Supply-side economics can be formally defined as the branch of economics that deals with those factors affecting the productive capacity of the economy. Most of the emphasis of supply-side economics under the Reagan administration has focused on tax cuts, but these are only a means to an end. The desired end is higher productivity which permits more rapid growth and lower inflation to occur simultaneously.

Under a balanced supply-side program, which includes personal income tax rate cuts, corporate income tax rate cuts, government spending cuts, and a decrease in the amount of government regulation, the U.S. economy would have eventually regained its earlier posture of balanced growth with significantly lower inflation. One of the primary purposes of this book is to enumerate and describe these conditions and to provide empirical evidence indicating not only the magnitude but also the response of the economy to such programs.

However, the supply-side program that was actually implemented was clearly not a balanced one. The optimal supply-side program can be likened to a three-legged stool: personal tax cuts, business tax cuts, and government spending cuts. Remove any one of the three legs, and the stool collapses. That is what happened with the Reagan program. Taxes were cut by an unprecedented amount but government spending in FY 1982 rose 4.6 percent in real terms—an amount *greater* than the average increase during those so-called big spending decades of the 1960s and 1970s.

For it must be kept in mind at all times that tax reduction is a two-edged sword. Whereas reducing tax rates will increase the productive capacity of the economy—that is, aggregate supply—it will also increase aggregate demand. Equally critical, the demand side of the tax cuts becomes effective long before the supply-side elements click into place. This is particularly true for personal income tax rate reduction. Some of the additional money will be spent, and some will be saved. The amount that is spent will raise consumption and aggregate demand immediately. The part that is saved, however, while it will eventually be transformed into higher investment and productivity, will in general not become fully productive for two to three years. Similarly, the incentive effects will emerge only slowly over time. Thus a timing problem initially arises; during the first two years of a tax cut, the demand-side effects overwhelm the supply-side effects.

If the economy is in a position of substantial unutilized capacity, little or no inflation, and a balanced budget, then an increase in aggregate demand in advance of the rise in aggregate supply may well be in order. Demand will increase initially, and by the time the economy begins to approach full employment, the additional capacity will permit further expansion without higher inflation. This is precisely the way the Kennedy-Johnson tax cut worked before it was derailed by the Vietnam War and the Great Society programs.

However, the situation is quite different if inflation is already at double-digit rates, inflationary expectations are running rampant, and the budget deficit is substantial. In these cases, the tax cuts will create more inflation, bigger deficits, and higher interest rates *unless* they are offset by a reduction in aggregate demand elsewhere in the system.

Successful reduction could come from two main sources. First, Congress could vote to reduce government spending, in particular transfer payments. Second, taxes that do not adversely affect saving and investment or hamper work effort and incentives could be increased, the major examples being an excise tax on energy, a consumption tax, or a flat-rate income tax. Monetary policy could also be tightened, but this invariably hurts investment far more than consumption, thereby reducing the investment/consumption ratio and hampering future growth in productivity.

To summarize, given the disequilibrium situation that the Reagan administration inherited, the proposed tax cuts had to be offset by either massive spending cuts or other tax increases. If neither option was chosen, the only remaining alternatives were higher inflation or prolonged recession.

This is not the end of the story, though. For even if the Reagan tax cuts had been offset by government spending cuts or appropriate tax hikes elsewhere, the economy could not have grown as fast as predicted by Reagan economists so long as the monetary constraint remained in place. Just as supply-side tax cuts do not become effective quickly, it is illogical to expect a massive gain in productivity in the period of a year or two. Consequently even with an optimal fiscal policy, the economy would have had to undergo a recession in order to reduce inflation quickly. If it did not, the underlying rate of inflation would have declined much more slowly, probably about 1 percent per year, until a new equilibrium was reached.

Thus even under the optimal supply-side program, the available choices still would have been limited to either an initial recession or a much more drawn-out decline in inflation. Given existing institutional constraints and rigidities, it simply was not possible to move immediately from the disequilibrium position of 1980 to balanced non-inflationary growth.

This is hardly a criticism of supply-side economics. Indeed, it is patently ridiculous to expect any economic program to cure the ills of the past fifteen years overnight. Either the economy must undergo a recession to wipe out the abuses that have become embedded in an inflation-oriented economy, or the rate of inflation can be reduced only gradually. Yet this logic escaped the architects of the Reagan program.

Hence the economic program offered by President Reagan to the American public contained two critical mistakes. First, it was far too lopsided—cutting taxes without cutting spending. Second, it promised too much too soon. Any unbiased observer should have conceded that the advantages of the program would not become apparent for at least two years following implementation. But of course that is not the way politicians of any persuasion sell their programs.

The unbalanced approach that was taken, however, hurtled the economy into a far more serious recession than was necessary. In this situation we have learned another unpleasant truth about supply-side economics: all those inducements to higher investment, greater productivity, increased work effort, and improved individual incentives simply do not work at the trough of a recession. Few will invest in plant and equipment, no matter how favorable the tax treatment, if existing capacity is being utilized at 50 percent or 60 percent. A more diligent search for employment is bound to end in failure if the number of available jobs is shrinking. The drive toward higher productivity, longer hours, and less absenteeism means little if the worker has just received a pink slip in his last paycheck. Thus the advantages of supply-side economics are always nullified by deep and prolonged recessions.

Because of the unprecedented severity of the 1981–82 recession in terms of unemployment, profit margins, and capacity utilization, it has become fashionable to denigrate everything that supply-side economics incorporates, especially the broad-based tax cuts. It is now clear that Reagan's program was not implemented properly, and that the economic recovery, even after being postponed so long, will still be much more anemic than the Reagan forecasters originally anticipated.

Yet it would indeed be a grave error to write off supply-side economics completely now that we have suffered through the worst of the battle. In every single postwar recovery through 1979, inflation at the peak of the business cycle has been higher than that at the peak of the previous cycle. This has time and again resulted from an increase in aggregate demand that exceeds the gain in aggregate supply. It is this pattern that must be defeated—a reversal that can be accomplished only through lower tax rates and a reduction in the relative size of the government sector. For a return to the old pattern of stimulating consumption while neglecting or inhibiting investment will, if repeated yet another time, lead to even more serious economic consequences than have heretofore been witnessed. To that end we must strive even harder to retain the essential elements of supply-side economics so that as the economy finally does recover, the benefits that sprout during periods of expansion will not have been trampled to death in the rush to escape supply-side economics altogether.

The remainder of this book explores in greater detail the benefits and disadvantages, the myths and realities, and seeks to discover, at least in this author's opinion, the truth about supply-side economics.

Part II

*The Myths of
Supply-Side
Economics*

CHAPTER 2

Myth 1: Interest Rates Would Decline as Soon as the Reagan Program Was Announced

The Cutting Edge of the Reagan Program

The first myth packaged by the merchandisers of the Reagan supply-side program was the claim that the financial markets would rally dramatically the moment the program was being announced, well before Congress had passed any new legislation. Though the original tax cut was to be retroactive to the first of the year, the spending cuts could not be, and hence the markets were supposed to take them on faith.

According to the doctrine of January 1981, the immediate plunge in interest rates would lower inflation for two reasons. First, the consumer price index (CPI) would increase less rapidly, since the mortgage rate is an important component of the CPI. Second, business costs in general would diminish, since interest is clearly one of the costs of doing business, although not usually one which is passed along to the consumer in the short run.

Once these factors had initially diminished inflation, the entire virtuous cycle would be set into motion. Lower inflation would moderate wage gains because of smaller cost-of-living allowances, both formal and informal. Smaller wage gains would translate immediately into lesser increases in unit labor costs, which would then be reflected in lower price increases for all goods and services.

The lower rate of inflation would then reduce interest rates even further. First, interest rates would decline *pari passu* with inflation, thus keeping the real rate of interest intact. Next, the real rate of interest itself would diminish as investors came to realize that the long-term trend in inflation was reversing. Hence, long-term bonds would become a much more attractive investment because of the likelihood of capital gains as well as substantial yields.

The architects of the Reagan economic program honestly believed that this initial reduction in interest rates and inflation would be the cutting edge of supply-side economics. Indeed, the Reagan projections incorporated in his initial budget estimates show that inflation as measured by the implicit GNP deflator* would decline from 9.2 percent in 1980 to 5.4 percent in 1985, with the three-month Treasury bill rate falling from 14 percent to 6 percent over the same time frame. Real growth would increase at an average rate of 4.6 percent over the 1982–84 period, with the ratio of government spending to GNP falling from 23.0 percent to 19.2 percent.

One of the major reasons that the Reagan economists thought interest rates would decline so rapidly is that they were unusually high relative to the rate of inflation at the beginning of 1981. The real rate of interest had averaged from 0 percent to 1 percent for short-term rates and from 2 percent to 3 percent for long-term rates over the past twenty-five years. Yet in the latter half of 1980, interest rates had overcompensated for the rise in inflation; real rates also continued to climb rapidly throughout much of 1981 and the first half of 1982, reaching as high as 10 percent.

The underlying rate of inflation, usually measured by economists as the change in unit labor costs,† declined from about 10 percent in 1980 to about 4½ percent by 1982. If interest rates had remained faithful to their pattern of the past twenty-five years, by mid-1982 the federal funds rate would have fallen to 6 percent, the prime rate to 8 percent, and the long-term Aaa corporate bond yield to 9 percent. Instead, in mid-1982 these figures were approximately 14 percent, 16½ percent, and 15 percent respectively, although they did decline in the second half.

---

*This is the most comprehensive measure of inflation since it includes the prices of capital goods, net exports, and government purchases as well as consumption. The more common measure of inflation, the consumer price index was projected to decline even more sharply, from 13.5 percent in 1980 to 4.7 percent in 1985.

†Defined as the change in wage rates (including fringe benefits) minus the change in productivity.

Myth 1: Immediate Decline in Interest Rates

It is not far-fetched to claim that if interest rates had somehow managed to decline to these lower levels promptly, the economy under Reagan would have indeed entered a period of prolonged prosperity with gradually declining rates of inflation. Reaganomics did indeed founder on the shoals of high real rates of interest. Furthermore, the question of why real rates, after remaining negative for several years, suddenly jumped to a range of between 5 percent and 10 percent is one that baffled the economic forecasting profession. Well-known economists of all persuasions, including Milton Friedman, expressed surprise and confusion over the devastating increase in real interest rates in 1981 and 1982. Forecasts prepared by this author early in 1981 also showed real rates declining, although not as fast as the Reagan estimates.

The reasons that real interest rates increased so dramatically in the first eighteen months of the Reagan administration are many and varied. However, they all revolve around the same central theme—the low level of the national saving rate, which intensified the competition for existing funds. Furthermore, this rate was expected to decline even further, primarily because of fears over a mushrooming budget deficit.

If Paul Volcker and his colleagues on the Federal Reserve Board of Governors actually carried out their stated intentions of gradually reducing the growth rate of the money supply each year, the real growth targets projected by the Reagan administration would be virtually unattainable. Yet with a much slower rate of growth, the chances of balancing the budget under the Reagan fiscal policy assumptions by 1984, or for that matter any time in the 1980s, were nil. Hence, public sector borrowing would increase much faster than private sector saving, thus diminishing total saving and keeping interest rates high. This would further diminish the chances of rapid economic growth, and the vicious cycle would intensify. Moreover, the resulting decline in economic activity would generate additional increases in government spending, thus making a hollow mockery of the spending cuts contained in the Reagan budgets.

As a result, financial market participants never believed a word of the balanced budget promise; they indeed expected that the increased deficit would be monetized, leading to a return of double-digit inflation. They were wrong in the sense that they underestimated the resolve of the Fed and therefore got less inflation and more recession than expected, but the results of this combination made the deficit figures even larger and total national saving even smaller.

A more detailed explanation of why real interest rates rose so much during the opening months of the Reagan administration rests on an understanding of the moods and beliefs, the worries and fears of financial markets. Their beliefs that the Reagan five-year projections contained crucial inconsistencies led them to foresee huge budget deficits in future years. Their worries about these budget deficits were intensified by the sensitization of financial markets after fifteen years of rising government spending and larger deficits. Their fears were heightened by the fact that private sector saving had also declined markedly in the past five years; given a generally sluggish economy, they saw little chance for improvement in that area either.

The claims by Reagan administration stalwarts that the tax cut package would increase total national saving were dismissed out of hand. Whereas the Kennedy-Johnson tax cut had been a sparkling success, it had been preceded by a balanced budget and stable prices, and it had been accompanied by virtually no growth in government spending—a near-impossibility given the outsize increases in defense projected in the Reagan budget. Hence financial markets never believed the Reagan scenario and viewed any enlargement of tax cuts not accompanied by offsetting spending reductions in government spending as a signal to sell rather than buy.

The Inconsistencies of the Reagan Projections

The Reagan administration's economic projections for the 1982–86 period are given in table 2.1. These forecasts are remarkable for at least three reasons. First, as already shown in chapter 1, they imply an unprecedented increase in velocity (the ratio of GNP to M1), given that the monetary constraint remained in place. Second, they assume that inflation would decline significantly at the same time that real growth is rapidly increasing. Third, the projections that show a deficit being transformed into a surplus by 1984 in spite of the massive tax cuts conceal either the most remarkable spending cuts in history or an unprecedented increase in taxes per dollar of GNP, once the tax cuts have been subtracted.

The most obvious inconsistency in the forecasts is to be found in the implied increases in velocity, given in column 3 of table 2.1. An increase of approximately 12 percent in nominal GNP has usually occurred only with an increase of 7 percent to 8 percent in M1, but both the administration and the Fed agreed this was far too high a growth rate for money supply and that the maximum target growth should gradually be lowered.

The only other time that velocity has ever grown at an average rate of 6 percent or better for five years or more was during the 1946–51 period, when

Myth 1: Immediate Decline in Interest Rates

TABLE 2.1
Reagan Administration Economic Assumptions

	Nominal GNP	Maximum Growth in Ml	Minimum Growth in Velocity	Real GNP	Implicit GNP Deflator	Percentage Unemployment	Surplus or Deficit[a]	Treasury Bill Rate
1980[b]	8.9	6.7	2.2	−0.1	9.0	7.2	−59.6	11.5
1981	11.1	6.0	5.1	1.1	9.9	7.8	−54.5	11.1
1982	12.8	5.5	7.3	4.2	8.3	7.2	−45.0	8.9
1983	12.4	5.0	7.4	5.0	7.0	6.6	−23.0	7.8
1984	10.8	4.5	6.3	4.5	6.0	6.4	0.5	7.0
1985	9.8	4.0	5.8	4.2	5.4	6.0	7.0	6.0
1986	9.3	3.5	5.8	4.2	4.9	5.6	30.0	5.6

SOURCE: *America's New Beginning,* p. S-1.
NOTE: All figures are calendar-year basis except the deficit. Columns 1–5 indicate percent of change; columns 6 and 8 are percent; column 7 is billions of dollars.
[a]Fiscal year basis (p. 12)
[b]actual

the annual increase did average 7.4 percent per year. However, that increase was the mirror image of a 9.2 percent annual *decline* in velocity during the 1942–45 period, when people saved record amounts of money because wartime restrictions and price controls left little that could legally be bought with the extra dollars. Indeed, velocity actually declined from 1915 (the first year for which figures are available) through 1951. From 1951 to 1981, velocity increased an average of 3.0 percent per year. Yet the Reagan forecasts assumed that this long-term trend growth rate could somehow magically be doubled during the next five years.

The odds that inflation would decline at the same time the economy was booming can best be put in context by the figures given in table 2.2, which shows the pattern of inflation rates during the beginning years of recovery in previous postwar upturns. Inflation has increased an average of about 2 percent during this phase of the recovery, whereas the Reagan projections expected a 5 percent *decline.* Clearly this pattern would be directly contradictory to previous evidence.

However, this result is not quite as bizarre as the one that projected record increases in velocity, for lower inflation could be accomplished by a dramatic rise in productivity. During periods of boom and depression alike, the rate of inflation has been virtually identical to the increase in unit labor costs. Hence, reducing the rate of inflation to 5 percent implies that, one way or another, the growth in unit labor costs must also be reduced to 5 percent per year.

During the postwar period, the rate of increase in wage rates has been ap-

29

TABLE 2.2

Inflation Rates During Recovery

Initial Year of Recovery	Rate of Inflation*			Percentage Change in Inflation
	Initial Year	1 Year Later	2 Years Later	
1955	−0.4	1.5	3.6	4.0
1959	0.8	1.6	b	—
1961	1.0	1.1	1.2	0.2
1971	4.3	3.3a	6.2	1.9
1976	5.8	6.5	7.7	1.9
1981†	11.1	8.3	6.2	−4.9

SOURCE: Calculated by Evans Economics, Inc.
aYear of wage and price controls
bNew recession began
*Percentage change in the consumer price index
†Projected by the Reagan administration

proximately equal to the rate of inflation minus the difference between the actual unemployment rate and 7½ percent. In other words, if unemployment was 7½ percent, wage rates and inflation rose by the same amount. If unemployment declined to 4 percent, wage rates rose 3½ percent faster than inflation, and so on.

According to the official Reagan economic forecasts summarized in table 2.1, the unemployment rate was projected to decline to 5.6 percent by 1986. This implies that wage rates would increase 2 percent faster than the rate of inflation. Since fringe benefits usually add an additional 1 percent per year to the rise in labor costs, this could be accomplished only if productivity growth were to return to 3 percent. That was indeed the average rate posted during the 1947–65 period, but productivity growth has steadily declined since then and was actually negative from 1977 through 1981. While not impossible, the Reagan program would have required a complete reversal of those factors which had retarded productivity during the past fifteen years. With the monetary constraint inhibiting investment, that would have been a truly Herculean feat.

For the financial markets, the forecast of a balanced budget by 1984 was undoubtedly the single least believable projection made by the Reagan administration. As already mentioned in chapter 1, those figures, taken at face value, implied a 50 percent reduction in all government expenditures except defense and safety net programs—an obvious impossibility. Yet the financial markets had lived through large budget deficits before without so much as turning a hair. To clearly understand why market psychology was so different this time, we will now examine the factors that caused such an allergic reaction to the Reagan plans.

Myth 1: Immediate Decline in Interest Rates

The Sensitization of Financial Markets

In previous recessions large budget deficits had no measurable effect on interest rates. Budget deficits have always proliferated during periods of slack economic activity; and the deficit exceeded 4 percent of GNP in FY 1976—substantially higher than the 1981 or even 1982 deficit ratios—yet at the same time the Treasury bill rate dropped below 5 percent and the prime rate fell below 7 percent.

One reason for this low level of interest rates was clearly accommodative monetary policy. The Fed pushed interest rates down sharply as soon as it became clear that a severe recession was underway and then kept them down by permitting rapid growth in the money supply during the early stages of the recovery. This was not unusual; indeed, for the entire postwar period money supply growth during the first year of recovery averaged 3 percent higher than during the previous recession. Yet it is clear that much more than Fed easing was at work here. Specifically, the financial markets never would have acquiesced in permitting interest rates to decline below 5 percent in 1976 if they had thought that a budget deficit equal to 4 percent of GNP was even close to becoming permanent.

Hence, the major reason that financial markets had previously been lulled into a false sense of security was the general belief that the deficits were temporary; when the economy returned to full employment and full capacity, the budget would then be balanced. This hypothesis generally masqueraded under the rubric of the "full-employment" (later changed to "high-employment") budget.

This concept first became widespread in the 1958 recession when liberal economists wished to stress that even though the deficit for FY 1959 was 3.6 percent of GNP, the budget would have remained in balance if the economy had remained at full employment. The idea was used again in the early years of the Kennedy administration and then corrupted, like so many other economic principles, by Richard Nixon.

Even before Nixon, however, the full employment budget was always an inferior concept for two reasons—one technical and one economic. On a technical basis, it is impossible to know revenue levels at full employment—they are always estimated with standard rule-of-thumb approximations—and thus the tendency by incumbent politicians invariably exists to paint the picture a little rosier than is actually the case. However, this point is minor, and could always have been modified by asking some congenital pessimist to work on the numbers. The other objection is much more serious, namely that financial market pressures caused by the deficit might preclude the economy from ever reaching full employment and the balanced budget. In sort of an economic Zeno's paradox, the real deficits that occurred while the economy was below full employment would push interest rates high enough to choke off economic growth, and hence the mythical balanced budget at full employment would never be reached at all. This is essentially what happened in the aftermath of the Nixon wage-price controls and again to Jimmy Carter in 1979 and 1980.

This paradox had been discussed as early as 1972 by several economists, including Don Conlan, then of Dean Witter, whose "Everything You Wanted to Know About Fiscal Policy . . . But Were Afraid to Ask"[1] still remains a classic. A few others predicted a sharp increase in interest rates in 1973 and 1974 based on this logic. However, such accuracy was as rare then as it is now. For the most part the economic community was comforted during both the Nixon and Ford administrations by the idyllic belief that since the budget was to be balanced at full employment, deficits didn't matter.

As long as Ford and Greenspan ran the economic affairs of the country, the financial markets were quiescent, as noted by the 5 percent interest rate during 1976. However, when Carter took the wraps off spending—still never running a deficit at full employment, mind you—more and more people began to realize that the economy was being subjected to the same hoax that had occurred under Nixon, and that interest rates would match and then exceed previous highs. This time they were not going to be caught unaware. This author had forecast in 1975 that the prime would hit 15 percent at the peak of the next business cycle,[2] but this prediction received very little credibility, partly because the timing was off, thereby violating one of the cardinal rules of forecasting (which is never to provide a number and a date at the same time.) Forecasters who started predicting in 1977 that interest rates would rise indefinitely without giving any clear time/date sequence have obviously had much the better of it.

Foremost among the economists supplying such forecasts were two New York financial analysts, Henry Kaufman of Salomon Brothers, and Al Wojnilower of First Boston (actually located on Wall Street). From 1977 until mid-1982 these two economists steadily predicted that interest rates would continue rising virtually without exception. Because the trend of interest rates during this period was overwhelmingly in the upward direction, they received great renown at the expense of more conventional forecasters who were wont to predict declines in interest rates which never occurred.

Although the forecasts of these two are fairly similar, Kaufman is by far the better known of the two, partly because of his greater enthusiasm and adeptness with the financial press and partly because his interest rate forecasts often are supported with detailed tables showing the flow of funds among various sectors of the economy, which invariably support the position that interest

Myth 1: Immediate Decline in Interest Rates

rates will have to move higher in order for the government to attract sufficient funds from the private sector. Wojnilower takes a less detailed and somewhat more philosophical view. In December 1977 he startled an audience of fellow economists, including this author, by starting a speech with "the world as we know it is coming to an end." After this attention-grabbing opener, he went on to say that whereas previously the financial markets had adjusted to what they considered in general to be a non-inflationary environment, events had changed so much that lenders would now start to demand ever-increasing premiums for higher inflation—a forecast which for at least the following four years proved to be essentially correct. Fortified with this kind of track record, and preying on a financial community so completely demoralized that it was willing to believe the worst, Wojnilower and Kaufman were able to influence Wall Street thinking to such an extent that the opposing Reagan views received only lip service.

The interest rate picked up markedly early in 1980. During FY 1980 Jimmy Carter had the unparalleled effrontery—or bemusement—to offer the country a new budget for every season of the year. He originally offered a FY 1980 budget that was fairly similar to his earlier proposals in that it made no attempt to cut back on existing programs but also did not contain any major expansions. However, as high interest rates pushed the economy to the brink of recession, Carter reconsidered. Having ignored the advice of those cynical but professional politicians who told him to take the recession in 1979 so that he could campaign in the midst of a strong recovery, he now found himself in a bind. In January 1980 few could predict that the weak economy would begin to improve by July, so Carter plumped for a much more expansive budget. The five-year projections from this budget showed a much higher level of government spending throughout the entire period and the likelihood of continuing deficits even during periods of economic recovery.

In fact, this was probably the only honest budget prepared for the years on either side, but the financial community was generally unprepared for this and received the news with great trepidation. As Alan Greenspan, at that time representative of much of the thinking of the New York financial community, put it:

Unlike many other nations in this hemisphere and elsewhere, the United States cannot for any length of time successfully function above, or even at current levels of interest rates. . . . We have developed a very complex financial infrastructure based upon the assumption that for the American economy, inflation when it occurs, is temporary and reflective of extraordinary circumstances. . . . Up until very recently the markets assumed that a noninflationary environment was always just beyond the horizon.[3]

Greenspan then pointed out that the inflation premiums demanded by financial markets in 1980 were unique in American history. The blame for this, he felt, could be placed squarely on the shoulders of President Carter.

It was President Carter's January 1980 budget message which apparently triggered the final explosion. The budget revised fiscal 1984 expenditures upward by $165 billion from estimates made only a year earlier. From this the markets concluded finally that the federal budget was now truly out of control. In effect, for the first time in American history, the financial community based its investment strategy on the expectation that inflation had become a deep seated, long-term problem.[4]

Interest rates, which had been drifting upward in any case, spurted anew in early 1980, with short-term rates up 4 percent and long-term rates up 2 percent, at that time an uncommonly big jump in only three months. Once Carter realized what had happened, he abruptly recalled his most recent budget estimates and submitted an entirely new set showing that government spending was well under control and the budget would run a substantial surplus by 1985. But it was of no use. The news was out, and the financial markets had seen a glimpse of what was really in store for the future.

Indeed, Greenspan commented that the financial community would "insist" on seeing much lower growth rates of government spending before these inflation premiums would disappear. He called for "extraordinary" cutbacks in nondefense spending relative to projected levels, none of which were forthcoming under either Carter or Reagan. He then concluded by stating:

Monetary policy has become increasingly a hostage of fiscal policy in recent years. Until we reduce the aggregate drains on the credit markets created by federal policy, direct, and indirect, the Federal Reserve will have little leeway to pursue a discretionary monetary policy. . . . Unless we apply strong restraining policies, both on the fiscal and the monetary side, we risk being unable to subdue, and ultimately defuse, the inflationary pressures which undercut the productiveness of the American economy.[5]

Greenspan's comments are noteworthy for two reasons. First, he illustrated how upset members of the financial community were about the Carter experience of 1980, and why they would not be likely to change their minds one year later without some fairly compelling evidence. Reagan was somewhat naïve when he expected the grizzled veterans of the financial community to accept his budget policies on faith before he had even submitted them to Congress, let alone shepherd them through the maze of committees and eleventh-hour traps that substantially increased spending or cut taxes without appearing on the surface to change anything.

Second, Greenspan stressed that it would be virtually impossible for the economy to grow at the rates contained in the Reagan budget estimates, and yet this growth is essential to provide the additional revenues that would balance the budget by 1984 (recall the 4.6 percent projected growth in real GNP for the 1982–84 period). Greenspan points out that the economy could not grow rapidly at current high interest rates, yet he called on the Fed to continue to provide strong restraint—which is clearly the formula for even higher rates and lower growth. In the face of determined monetary restraint the stimulatory effects of tax cuts will always come to naught—a point which is discussed in greater detail in chapter 3.

The Wall Street economists were not the only ones or even the most important element who thought that the Reagan program would lead to higher interest rates. The Fed board members themselves, especially Paul Volcker, expressed much the same sentiment. Volcker had to be somewhat more circumspect in his pronouncements for he could not easily come out directly and say that the Reagan plan would fail even before it was tried. Yet he made it quite clear that unless government spending was reduced proportionately with the tax cuts, the Fed itself would have to step in and pull the reins on money supply growth through rigorous enforcement of the target growth rates. In essence, if fiscal policy would not or could not do the job, monetary policy would take over by default. The Fed would not legitimize the creation of what it perceived to be overly inflationary budget policies on Capitol Hill.

Many economists and politicians have claimed that the tight monetary policies of the Fed were ultimately the cause of the higher interest rates and strangled economic growth. For in previous recessions rapid increases in the money supply had led to lower interest rates and economic recovery. These improvements, however, were based on financial market expectations that inflation and the federal budget could be kept under control: as has been made clear, since 1980 that was no longer the case. Hence the Fed's earlier ability to spur recovery through easier monetary policies now became strictly circumscribed, and the answer to whether the Fed could have spurred economic recovery through lower interest rates rests critically on the issue of financial market expectations and faster money supply growth, a topic complicated enough to be examined separately in chapter 3.

However, given the sensitization of the financial markets, it is doubtful whether the procedures of the past would have worked. In addition to the change in expectations, both private and public sector saving were abnormally low—another important reason why rates stayed high. Faced with this loss of saving, the Fed probably could not have pushed rates lower before mid-1981 even if it had pursued the easy money policies of an earlier day.

The Declining Rate of Saving in the U.S. Economy

The large budget deficits of 1981 and 1982 were only the culmination of a long series of events which had reduced the amount of saving available for capital formation. Four years of negative real rates of interest had severely impacted private sector saving. The personal saving rate, for example, had declined from 8.6 percent in 1975 (and 8.0 percent during the 1970–75 period) to 5.8 percent by 1980, as shown in table 2.3. The corporate saving rate, particularly when adjusted for the phony profits stemming from inflation, was also near postwar lows in 1980. This shortage of saving clearly contributed to the rise in interest rates.

The sharp decline in the net national saving rate from 6.9 percent in 1979 to 4.3 percent in 1980 was particularly harmful because it came at a time when inflation was intensifying and the need for borrowed funds was hence rising in tandem with the higher value of transactions.

The reported rate of saving usually rises during periods of inflation for several reasons. The government deficit narrows because the increase in tax receipts from higher inflation is initially greater than the increase in spending, which is based on last year's inflation rate. Reported corporate profits rise be-

TABLE 2.3

Net National Saving Rate

	Personal Saving Rate, %	Profits[a] Adjusted for Inflation/GNP, %	Federal Budget Deficit (in billions of dollars)	Net National Saving Rate, %
1976	6.9	2.1	−53	4.9
1977	5.9	2.8	−46	5.9
1978	6.1	2.9	−29	7.1
1979	5.9	2.3	−16	6.9
1980	5.8	1.5	−61	4.3
1981	6.4	1.5	−60	5.0
1982	6.5	1.0	−148	1.9

NOTE: All figures on National Income and Product Accounts (NIPA) basis.
[a]Undistributed profits after taxes plus inventory valuation adjustment plus capital consumption adjustment.

cause fixed costs have not yet been revalued at today's higher prices. Finally, people used to save more with higher inflation because they realized it is best to save a little more for the squall that will occur as the economy shifts back to normalcy.

However, none of these events transpired in 1980. The budget deficit continued to rise, due in part to the decline in economic activity and in part to the runaway budgets previously mentioned. Corporate profits declined as energy and interest costs rose faster than prices, and sales declined. Consumers, far from saving more because of recession, decided that with inflation rates above the prevailing rate of interest, they might as well take advantage of the "free lunch" and borrow just as much as they could.

In fact, even these reported declines probably understated the true reduction in personal saving occurring in the economy. The Federal Reserve Board prepared estimates of the amount of money that consumers had converted from fixed assets, such as real estate, into liquid assets—much of which they then spent. For 1978 the amount of funds converted in this way was estimated to approach $90 billion. Consumers obtained second or third mortgages on their houses and then used the money for purchases of goods and services; in some cases cash was obtained from selling gold and silver at vastly inflated prices. Of course the money that was lent to consumers by financial institutions had to come from somewhere; these institutions had to borrow it in the market-place by offering ever-higher interest rates. Alan Greenspan has argued that this method permitted consumers to offset the initial effects of high interest rates that would ordinarily have dampened consumer demand.

Moreover, consumers put what little saving they did, not into the traditional financial market instruments—savings accounts, bonds, and stocks—but into assets that were fixed in supply. In addition to real estate, these covered a wide range of additional assets: gold and silver, Oriental rugs and ceramics, objets d'art, and so forth. Money tied up in such assets was completely sterile in the sense that it did not flow back into the productive sector of the economy. As a result, the pool of available funds shrank even more.

Of course, this is true only up to a point since the money paid for gold or silver, for example, went to someone else who presumably put it back into circulation. While in the literal sense this must be true, unless the funds went to some Arab sheikh who buried them in the desert, quite often the money was circulated outside the United States, thereby reducing the funds available in this country for investment. This is not the place to enter into a comprehensive explanation of world financial flows; suffice it to say that in many cases the money was recycled back to large banks that lent the sums to Third World countries, who then could not repay the loans. As a result, exports rose but the pool of savings diminished, thus putting further upward pressure on interest rates.

Though such a policy was detrimental to the overall U.S. economy, individual investors could hardly be faulted for seeking out the highest rate of return. As is shown in table 2.4, during the 1970s the rate of return on fixed assets surpassed the rate of return on financial market instruments by phenomenal margins. The outsized gains in these fixed assets were well advertised, and as success stories proliferated, more and more funds were drawn out of the existing pool of savings in financial assets. This shifting of asset preference was unprecedented in the postwar period and correlates well with the sharp rise in interest rates from 1977 through 1980.

Even after inflation subsided and consumers were no longer able to borrow at interest rates below the rate of inflation, the total net national saving rate continued to decline. In 1981 and 1982 the main culprit was the increase in the federal budget deficit. While even the most pessimistic members of the financial community would not have foreseen early in 1981 that the budget deficit would rise to $110 billion in FY 1982 and at least $180 billion in FY 1983, they were aware that the net saving rate was clearly trending downward for at least the next two years. Such a development meant, in the unlikely chance that the economy did try to mount a significant recovery, that the increased competition for the shrunken supply of funds would invariably drive interest rates skyward, thereby aborting any sustained upturn.

TABLE 2.4

Relative Ranking of Return on Investments

	10 Years	Rank	5 Years	Rank	1 Year	Rank
Oil	29.9%	1	21.2%	4	6.3%	3
U.S. Coins	22.5	2	21.4	3	−27.8	13
U.S. Stamps	21.9	3	26.6	1	−3.0	9
Oriental Rugs	19.1	4	17.1	6	−16.2	11
Gold	18.6	5	17.3	5	−34.0	14
Chinese Ceramics	15.3	6	23.7	2	−0.5	6
Farmland	13.7	7	10.7	9	−0.9	7
Silver	13.6	8	5.5	13	−44.5	15
Diamonds	13.3	9	13.7	7	0.0	5
Housing	9.9	10	10.0	10	3.4	4
Old Masters	9.0	11	13.7	8	−22.0	12
CPI	8.6	12	9.6	11	6.6	2
Stocks	3.9	13	7.7	12	−10.5	10
Foreign Exchange	3.6	14	1.6	14	−1.9	8
Bonds	3.6	15	0.6	15	11.4	1

SOURCE: Reprinted by permission of Salomon Brothers Inc., "Bonds May Still Be the Only Bargains Left," by R. S. Saloman, Jr. (June 8, 1982).
NOTE: All returns are for the period ending June 1, 1982, based on latest available data.
Table prepared by Samuel G. Liss.

Myth 1: Immediate Decline in Interest Rates

The Differences Between the Kennedy-Johnson and Reagan Tax Cuts

The quotes from Wojnilower and Greenspan make it eminently clear that Wall Street pundits did not expect Reagan to be able to balance the budget; they thought that his tax cuts would lead to ever-increasing deficits. Yet the Reagan team supply siders argued vigorously that the Kennedy-Johnson tax cuts, while similar in nature, had produced a balanced budget in the very year after the tax cut, and that a similar performance could be expected from the Reagan policies.

The devout supply siders would have people believe that the two bills were fundamentally equivalent. It is true that they did contain similar across-the-board reductions in personal income tax rates and significant and meaningful business tax cuts. However, we need only to compare the underlying economic circumstances and the nature of the two bills to understand why the Kennedy-Johnson tax cut worked and the Reagan tax cut did not.

First, the federal budget was virtually in balance and the rate of inflation was only 1.2 percent in 1963. Hence, the Treasury was not saddled with the burden of excessive interest payments and the Fed did not need to worry about an acceleration in inflationary expectations. Even optimists would concede that introducing the Reagan program from a disequilibrium position was much more difficult than a situation when the budget was already in balance and inflation was close to zero.

Second, the Fed validated the increase in economic activity that occurred during the two years following the tax cut. Real GNP growth rose from 4.0 percent in 1963 to 5.3 percent in 1964 and to 6.0 percent in both 1965 and 1966. Money supply growth rose from an average of 2.6 percent in 1962 and 1963 to 4.5 percent in 1964 to 4.3 percent in 1965. It then declined to 2.9 percent in 1966 as the first credit crunch occurred, which was largely responsible for reducing real GNP growth in 1967 to 2.7 percent.

Third, while the Kennedy-Johnson tax cut did include a 20 percent across-the-board reduction in personal income tax rates and several tax breaks for business, it did not include any further long-term tax reductions, in sharp contrast to the indexation of the personal income tax rate schedule included in the final Reagan package. In addition, the Kennedy-Johnson tax bill tightened up on some methods of tax avoidance, accelerated corporate tax payments, and was followed by a major boost in social security taxes in 1966.

Fourth, inflation did increase slightly from 1.3 percent in 1964 to 2.9 percent

39

in 1966, which made balancing the budget somewhat easier. Hence, the return to a balanced budget was partially accomplished by a small increase in the rate of inflation.

Fifth, and most important of all, government spending increased only 1 percent in FY 1965, the year after the major portion of the Kennedy-Johnson tax cut was passed. We are so accustomed to think of Lyndon Johnson as the big spender incarnate—with the Vietnam War, the Great Society, and Medicare—that it is sometimes difficult to recall that government spending grew only 1 percent his first full year as president. Had spending grown only 1 percent in FY 1982 instead of the 11 percent actually recorded, I have absolutely no doubt that the Reagan fiscal policy would have been much more successful. Indeed, when Johnson turned on the spending taps in FY 1966 and government spending rose 12 percent, inflation accelerated, interest rates rose, the first credit crunch ensued, productivity growth declined, and the economy never did regain the spark of rapid growth that had initially followed the tax cut.

What is generally referred to as the Kennedy-Johnson tax cut actually includes several different reductions from 1962 through 1965. The major tax reduction was the 20 percent across-the-board reduction in personal income tax rates. The reduction was actually flared slightly at both ends and squeezed in the middle; the lowest marginal rate fell from 20 percent to 14 percent and the highest rate from 91 percent to 70 percent, while the 50 percent marginal rate was cut only to 42 percent. This decline took place over a two-year period, with about two thirds of the reduction in rates occurring in 1964. The corporate income tax rate was also reduced from 52 percent to 48 percent in two steps.

In addition, Kennedy had already reduced business taxes as early as 1962. That year marked the introduction of a 7 percent investment tax credit and a reduction in depreciation lives on new capital plant and equipment by 30 percent to 40 percent. As shown in table 2.5, the three business tax cuts accounted for precisely one third of the total tax reduction. Finally, in 1965 Johnson reduced excise taxes on a number of goods and services, including telephone calls, household appliances, and a large number of other items originally taxed to raise revenues during World War II. These tax reductions amounted to approximately $2½ billion per year when fully phased in. While these are technically part of the overall Kennedy-Johnson tax cutting legacy, they are not usually included in the general definition of this measure and are mentioned here only for purposes of clarification.

The figures presented in table 2.5 illustrate three different facets of the Kennedy-Johnson tax cut, both in comparison with the Reagan tax cut and by itself. First, the personal income tax cuts were only half as large relative to

Myth 1: Immediate Decline in Interest Rates

GNP as the Reagan tax cuts; the close equivalency implied by some ideological supply siders is fiction. Second, one third of the Kennedy-Johnson tax cut was received by corporations, as opposed to one fourth under the Reagan tax cut; indeed, when the 1982 rescindments are added back in, *only 10 percent* of the Reagan tax cut accrued to corporations. Third, and perhaps most revealing, the federal budget actually returned to a surplus position in the year following the Kennedy-Johnson tax cut.

It is this surplus that has so endeared this tax cut to the hearts of the supply siders, providing those lyric outbursts assuring everyone that the Reagan tax cut could do no worse. Yet an understanding of how the budget managed to post a surplus in 1965 is critical if we are to understand the failures of the latter-day Reagan muddle.

It is impressive enough that the budget deficit did not increase in 1963 or 1964 in spite of tax cuts of $2.4 and $2.8 billion respectively—far better than the Treasury could manage today. The truly amazing figure, however, belongs to FY 1965. Not only were taxes cut an additional $8.1 billion, but the surplus position actually increased by $3 billion, for a total improvement of $11.1 billion. Hence it is 1965 that we examine in detail.

First, nominal GNP increased 8.4 percent in 1965. Thus if taxes had grown proportionately with GNP, they would have increased $9.7 billion. Ordinarily such an increase would be offset by the rise in government spending, which generally grows at about the same rate as GNP, if not a little faster. FY 1965, however, was unique in this regard because total federal spending rose only

TABLE 2.5

Kennedy-Johnson Tax Cut

	1963	1964	1965	1966
Personal tax cuts		$2.4	8.7	12.4
as a percentage of GNP		0.4	1.3	1.7
Corporate tax cuts	$2.4	2.8	4.6	6.4
as a percentage of GNP	0.4	0.5	0.7	0.9
Surplus or deficit, NIPA basis	$−1.7	−1.5	1.4	0.0
	Reagan Tax Cut			
	1982	1983	1984	1985
Personal tax cuts	$27.2	76.4	119.5	146.9
as a percentage of GNP	0.9	2.2	3.1	3.3
Corporate tax cuts	$8.6	20.8	33.4	47.0
As a percentage of GNP	0.3	0.6	0.9	1.1

SOURCE: Reprinted by permission of the publisher from *Reaganomics: Supply Side Economics in Action*, by Bruce Bartlett (Westport, Conn: Arlington House), p. 214.
NOTE: All figures in billions of dollars, except percentages.

41

$1.3 billion that year. This was clearly a one-year oasis; it then rose $14, $22, and $18 billion in each of the next three fiscal years. In examining the 1965 budget "miracle," however, it is well advised to keep this unique pause in spending clearly in mind. Hence the gap between the proportional increase in taxes and the actual rise in government spending that year amounted to $8.4 billion, or a full 75 percent of the $11.1 improvement given above.

Let us put these figures in today's perspective. Federal government spending increased $76 billion in FY 1982, while the government budget was approximately six times as big as it was in 1964. Thus applying the same growth rate that occurred in 1965 would mean that government spending would have increased only $8 billion instead of $76 billion in 1982. Financial markets would have been ecstatic about the Reagan tax cuts if government spending increased only $8 billion.

The additional $3 billion gap is accounted for by two other factors. First, the Kennedy-Johnson tax cut included some slight tax increases. It removed the 4 percent tax credit for dividend income, a regulation Eisenhower placed in the tax code as the first step toward the end of double taxation. Second, corporate income tax payments were speeded up in 1964, and several other timing adjustments were also instituted. In addition, the inflation rate increased approximately 1 percent in 1965, and profits rose more than proportionately, which also increased Treasury receipts.

We now return to the fact that nominal GNP grew 8.4 percent in 1965. Of this only 2.2 percent was due to higher inflation, so that real growth was 6.0 percent. The Kennedy-Johnson tax cut was unquestionably a major cause behind this superheated growth rate. But as recent experience has shown, this could not have happened unless the monetary authorities permitted it with their blessings. In 1964 and 1965 the prime rate remained constant at 4.5 percent, the mortgage rate stayed constant at 5.8 percent, and both corporate and government bond yields rose by less than 0.1 percent. Because the budget was in balance and inflation was not a problem, tight monetary policy was not needed to offset the beneficial effects of expansionary fiscal policy.

Since 1965 was a one-year period of stability in government spending, an explanation is needed to explain how the budget remained balanced in 1966 in the face of a $14.2 billion increase in government spending. Nominal GNP increased 9.4 percent in 1966, which implies an $11.3 billion increase in taxes if rates are proportional. Taxes were cut an additional $5.5 billion in 1966, so the gap left to be explained by faster-than-proportional tax increases and other factors is $8.4 billion.

The surplus was reduced by $1.4 billion and social security taxes rose $4.4 billion because of an increase in the income base from $4,800 to $6,600 and in the rate from 3.625 percent to 4.2 percent. This leaves only $2.6 billion of

increased tax revenues not yet explained. That figure is just about 2 percent of total taxes in 1966 and is due to an additional 1 percent rise in inflation, bracket creep, and another disproportionate increase in corporate profits.

By mid-1966 the economy began to overheat, however, and monetary policy could no longer serve as a benevolent bystander. Interest rates rose sharply and the economy contracted. As a result, the federal budget deficit in the next two fiscal years zoomed to $9 and $12 billion, respectively, figures that would be equivalent to $45 and $60 billion at 1981–82 levels of GNP. It took the 1968–69 surtax to restore budget balance, but by then the economy was heading into the first recession in almost ten years and the temporary budget deficits became permanent.

Yet none of this should detract from the fact that the Kennedy-Johnson tax cut provided a near-perfect example of how enlightened supply-side economics can work under optimal conditions. Stripped to its bare essentials, the tightwire act of balancing the budget in the two years following the Kennedy-Johnson tax cut was due to:

1. A pause in government spending, followed by an increase which was partially offset by tax hikes.
2. Monetary policy which was able to encourage unhampered growth because of virtually no inflation. As soon as inflation rose and policy tightened, large budget deficits appeared.
3. An offsetting increase of $2 to $3 billion in other taxes.
4. An increase in the rate of inflation of 1 percent per year.

The financial markets, after some initial misgivings when the plan was originally announced, accepted the eventual Kennedy-Johnson tax plan wholeheartedly. It was known by February 1964 that such a tax cut would be passed;* the stock market, which had already shown good strength in the latter half of 1963 except for the temporary setback caused by the Kennedy assassination, rose steadily from early 1964 through mid-1965, with the Dow Jones Industrial Average increasing from almost 750 to 950 during this span.

This record stands in stark contrast to the panic of the financial markets in the aftermath of the Reagan bill in August 1981. As soon as the markets had absorbed the major changes that occurred in the last minute jockeying to produce a majority for the bill, interest rates suddenly jumped an additional 2 percent and the stock market collapsed almost 20 percent. Three major differences alarmed the financial markets in August 1981, whereas they had not in March 1964.

1. The economic environment. As already mentioned, the federal budget was virtually in balance in 1963, the year before the major portion of the Ken-

*The tax cut was actually signed into law February 26, 1964.

nedy-Johnson tax cuts. This is compared with Carter's $60 billion deficit in his final year. Furthermore, inflation during the 1959–63 period was virtually nonexistent. The wholesale price index actually declined over that period, while the consumer price index increased at an average annual rate of only 1.3 percent. The contrast here could not have been sharper. From a 5 percent rate of inflation in 1976, the rate of inflation had increased steadily to 6.5 percent, 7.7 percent, 11.3 percent, and 13.4 percent. Not a very enviable record for Carter, and clearly one of the reasons why he was not re-elected.

2. The "Christmas tree ornaments." The Kennedy-Johnson tax cut did reduce personal income tax rates by 20 percent across the board; but contained no other personal tax cuts and tightened up on some other sections of the tax code, particularly the rescinding of the 4 percent tax credit for dividend income. A number of other minor changes were also implemented, including speeding up payments for payroll and corporate income taxes. The Reagan plan, by comparison, included a whole host of additional add-ons, the most important of which were the reduction in the marriage penalty, the so-called All Savers certificates, more lenient treatment of foreign earnings, reduction in estate and gift taxes, and expansion of Individual Retirement Accounts. Although many of these were equitable and some contributed to the stated aim of increasing saving, together they added up to additional tax losses estimated at $25 billion per year.

Much the same could be said for the corporate income tax cuts. Whereas the Kennedy-Johnson tax cuts were well-defined, the Reagan plan was muddied by the inclusion of a provision for the selling of investment tax credits by firms with little or no profits to more profitable firms, generally known as Safe Harbor Leasing. The original intent of such legislation was to help the beleaguered "smokestack industries" and the auto industry, but the net effect was to spawn another huge area of tax shelters. It not only had the effect of subsidizing the losers at the expense of the winners but put an additional $6 billion annual dent in Treasury revenues, and for those reasons was later repealed; of course financial markets could not know that in 1981.

3. Indexation in 1985 and later years. Indexation refers to the downward adjustment of tax brackets to offset the effect of inflation. For example, suppose Jones earns $30,000 per year and is in the 28 percent marginal tax bracket. Next year, because inflation and his salary both go up 10 percent, he is earning $33,000, which of course is no change at all in real income. However, because his nominal income is higher, he is boosted into the 32 percent tax bracket, so his real income has dropped. Indexation would keep the tax brackets the same for all levels of real (that is, inflation adjusted) income.

The concept of indexation has much to recommend it. Indeed, it would tend to reduce rather than to increase inflation because it would raise labor productivity, increase individual incentive, and moderate wage demands. However, coming on top of the already mammoth tax cuts contained in the rest of the legislation, the financial community viewed it as the final guarantee that the budget would not be balanced for at least the next five years and probably not for the remainder of the decade. It was the inclusion of indexation without any similar adjustment on the spending side which, more than any other plank, sent the financial markets recoiling in horror and bond and stock prices plummeting.

What Did Wall Street Want?

It is clear enough that the financial markets could not brook the Reagan plan to perpetuate large budget deficits indefinitely. Yet they hardly could have been enamored of an ever-increasing public sector and perpetually higher taxes. What did they want?

Clearly their favorite plan would have been that tried and true formula preached by old-line conservative economists and practiced by the Eisenhower administration. It worked like this.

First, cut defense spending. By winding down the Korean War, Eisenhower reduced defense spending by 21 percent during his first two years in office.*

Second, hold the line on other spending programs. Here the gain in 1954 and 1955 was less than a total of $1 billion for both years.* Most economists are realistic enough to know that it is virtually impossible to generate actual cuts in spending, and hence projections of balanced budgets based on this presumption are automatically suspect. Holding the line on existing programs, however, is both an economically admirable and a politically reasonable objective.

Third, wait until the budget is balanced before doing anything about reducing taxes, particularly across-the-board personal income tax cuts. It is clear where Eisenhower stood on this matter:

> In spite of some things that I have seen in the papers over the last 8 or 9 months, I personally have never promised a reduction in taxes. Never.
>
> What I have said is, reduction of taxes is a very necessary objective of government—that if our form of economy is to endure, we must not forget private incentives and initiative and the production that comes from it. Therefore, the objective

*These figures refer to 1954 and 1955, since the 1953 budget was fixed before Eisenhower assumed office.

of tax reduction is an absolutely essential one, and must be attained in its proper order.

But I believe, and I think this can be demonstrated as fact by economists, both on the basis of history and on their theoretical and abstract reasoning, that until the deficit is eliminated from our budget, there is no hope of keeping our money stable. It is bound to continue to be cheapened, and if it is cheapened, then the necessary expenses of government each year cost more because the money is worth less. Therefore, there is no end to the inflation; there is finally no end to taxation; and the eventual result would, of course, be catastrophe.

So, whether we are ready to face the job this minute or any other time, the fact is there must be balanced budgets before we are again on a safe and sound system in our economy. That means, to my mind, that we cannot afford to reduce taxes, reduce income, until we have in sight a program of expenditures that shows that the factors of income and of outgo will be balanced. Now that is just to my mind sheer necessity.[6]

Twenty-eight years later Wall Street still believed every word of this.

Unlike so many political speeches, this one was not just words. Eisenhower stood firm in his assessment against deficit spending and still adamantly opposed any tax cut when the economy nose-dived into the 1958 recession (the first severe setback in twenty years), even though this cost his party its occupancy of the White House.

Fourth, continue to hold out the enticement of major tax reductions in the unlikely event that surpluses do develop. This will assure the populace that these additional revenues will not automatically be transformed into additional spending programs, for these programs often have a camel's-nose-under-the-tent-door property which results in great proliferation of expenditures in later years. So much the worse if the budget never quite makes it back to balance, but that precludes having to cut taxes while all the time promising the public that taxes will indeed be reduced just as soon as fiscal prudence permits.

As a matter of fact, this plan was not so good for the economy. It produced three recessions in eight years, a record in negative growthmanship until it was tied by the three recessions in the 1974–82 period, two of which occurred in that period's last two years. Furthermore, the unemployment rate rose from 3 percent the day Eisenhower took office to over 6 percent the day he left. But Wall Street loved it! The Dow Jones Industrial Average rose from 250 when Eisenhower was elected to over 600 by the time he stepped down—an average annual gain of almost 12 percent, which is phenomenal when compared to an underlying inflation rate of 1.4 percent. Only the Roaring Twenties have so far matched this virtuoso stock market performance.

In order for Reagan to come even close to emulating the Eisenhower fiscal policies, it was clear that Reagan would have to cut defense spending, cut social programs through the reworking of indexation and entitlements, or raise taxes. Wall Street has never been lacking in the ability to work out the numbers, and never for a minute did it believe that Reagan could make significant inroads into reducing the deficit without hammering away at these three areas.

Thus the Reagan hope that interest rates would decline upon the announcement of his revolutionary program to balance the budget by cutting taxes was stillborn before it ever came to pass. The financial community never accepted the spurious assumptions on which these projections were based, and as a result interest rates rose almost steadily from the time of the Reagan election until the beginning of the 1981–82 recession. While that was not the only flaw in the Reagan program, this one was easily defeated in the opening round.

CHAPTER 3

Myth 2: Tight Money and Fiscal Ease Can Generate Balanced, Non-inflationary Growth

The Mundell Theory of Separable Policy Levers

The first great myth of supply-side economics was thus demolished with ridiculous ease. Interest rates rose even before Reagan assumed office and continued to escalate as soon as the budget plan was unveiled. The stock market peaked in December 1980 and did not stage another significant rally until August 1982.

However, many of the hard-core supply siders were unrepentant. The reason interest rates went up, they claimed, was that money supply was growing too fast, thereby worsening inflationary expectations. In order for the tax cuts to work, they had to be combined with a tight monetary policy. Thus the second great myth of supply-side economics was launched—that an easy fiscal policy could be used to stimulate the economy, while inflation could be constrained through tight money.

Unlike the first myth, this one is not so easily destroyed, for it contains some germ of truth and is based on some of the fundamental constructs of supply-side economics. Ultimately, of course, it too failed, as tight money was unable to avert—some would say, was responsible for—the severe 1981–82 recession. Yet this combination of policies could have worked under more propitious circumstances. To understand why, it is useful to review the background of this concept and to explore the conditions under which tight money could lead to lower interest rates and thus eventually to higher growth.

Every postwar business cycle upturn before 1980 was always accompanied by an accommodative monetary policy, by which is meant that money supply growth accelerated and interest rates did not rise very much if at all. However, the long-term effects of this policy were not nearly as positive. Once the recoveries were well underway, inflation usually reaccelerated about two years later resulting in an increase in interest rates, credit tightening, and another recession a year or two after that. Thus short-term gains were often eroded by long-term losses; and after it was all over, the stimulative fiscal policy had unfortunately accomplished nothing, for both unemployment and inflation had risen.

Thus, much of the cyclical behavior of the postwar U.S. economy has been abetted by stimulative fiscal and monetary policy initially combining to create an expansion, only to be eventually stalled by contractionary policies three or four years later. What would happen if, instead of both kinds of policies being used to stimulate the economy, the expansionary aspects of fiscal policy were tempered with less accommodating monetary policies right from the outset? That is the basic idea which, as will be seen in this chapter, has provided much of the underpinnings of modern supply-side theory.

Throughout the years, this idea has been far outside the mainstream of economic thought. Orthodox economists have always assumed, albeit without much discussion, that monetary and fiscal policies should both move in the same direction. When the economy has unused resources, government spending should be expanded, taxes reduced, and the money supply increased more rapidly. When it is approaching full capacity, all these factors should be reversed.

It might at first appear counterproductive, if not absurd, for fiscal and monetary policies to contradict each other. It does not seem sensible to have the government providing stimulus in the form of increased spending if the monetary authorities will not provide the necessary credit for the larger quantity of goods and services. In that case, nothing would be accomplished except larger budget deficits.

This conventional wisdom was challenged by Robert Mundell—considered by many the intellectual father of supply-side economics—as early as 1961,[1] although his views were not generally circulated and publicized until about ten years later.[2] He argued that the optimal blend of government policies to fight recessions would be easy fiscal policies, by which he actually meant tax cuts rather than increased spending, while keeping money supply growth tight. According to Mundell's logic, tax cuts would expand both aggregate demand and supply—thus lessening bottlenecks and shortages as the economy grew more rapidly—whereas tight money policies would keep speculative inflation under control. In other words, both aggregate demand and supply would grow at the same expanded rate, while moderate growth in the money supply would assure that excess demand would not widen the spread between prices and costs.

The Mundell arguments on the benefits of tax cuts were thus an early precursor to supply-side economics. Tax cuts *diminish* inflation, he argued, because they increase the supply of available goods and services. Higher unemployment is actually inflationary because it reduces the supply of goods and services, and if supply is reduced, prices must eventually rise.

Mundell first proposed his theories as a cure for the 1960–61 recession, but was virtually ignored. The Kennedy-Johnson tax cut was the quintessential supply-side tax-cut program, but it was indeed accompanied by easy monetary policies, as has been seen, and the name Mundell was never mentioned. When he proposed his views again as a cure for the 1970 recession, his voice was still not heard in Washington; but this time his ideas were for the most part accepted by leading academic economists, and the presentation of his ideas at a number of conferences received high marks. Indeed, Lord Lionel Robbins, chairman of the Court of Governors of the London School of Economics, remarked in 1971, "Bob—here I lay down a sociological law—is seldom wrong. And even when you disagree with him, you must disagree with your hat in the hand."[3]

By the time the 1974–75 recession was upon us, Mundell's views were beginning to receive much more widespread acceptance. In "It's Time to Cut Taxes," Jude Wanniski espoused the essence of the Mundell argument and quoted his views at length.

> Professor Mundell departs from the traditional belief that monetary and fiscal policies should always be working in the same direction. He believes that inflation and unemployment are separable problems and that to combat them distinct policy instruments are required. He believes that tight money should be used to combat the inflation, while expansive fiscal policies—preferably through lower taxes—can be used to combat the recession in a way that also works against inflation.[4]

In one sense the Mundell prescription was not quite as radical as Wanniski suggested. Editorializing the day after the Kennedy-Johnson tax cut was based, the *Wall Street Journal* opined:

Myth 2: Tight Money and Fiscal Ease

> For the tax cut to prove beneficial rather than harmful or downright dangerous, the Government must make other changes. It is spending too much, it is still running heavy deficits, and it continues to try to keep money artificially easy. . . . It is said that the tax-cut stimulus would be diluted if the Government were to make substantial reductions in expenditures and permit money to tighten somewhat. But not only are these measures necessary to check the inflationary potential; they would also contribute to sound economic growth.[5]

Yet it is fair to say that the Mundell prescription to reduce inflation was unusual in that it did focus on increasing supply rather than restricting aggregate demand.

Finally, on November 29, 1979, Robert L. Bartley, by then the editor of the *Wall Street Journal,* gave his official blessings to the procedure by stating, "I thought it bizarre when I first heard Columbia University economist Bob Mundell propose tight money and big tax cuts, but I no longer think this. I now see more wisdom in a remark he keeps repeating; that for every policy goal you need a policy lever. He means monetary policy for one half of stagflation, fiscal policy for the other half." After that, the Mundell viewpoint was a frequent visitor on the editorial pages of the *Wall Street Journal.* In fact, as late as August 1981, Bartley wrote, "Fighting recession is a job for fiscal policy . . . recession threat or not, the Fed ought to keep monetary policy focused on the job of fighting inflation."[6]

One of the reasons the Mundell theory was so enthusiastically accepted by many supply-side economists as the true doctrine was that it appeared to cut the Gordian knot of the Phillips curve*—the claim that the economy could reduce inflation only by suffering more unemployment. For if Mundell were correct, the economy could enjoy more growth and less unemployment through expansionary fiscal policy while at the same time generating less inflation through a tight monetary policy. It sounded too good to be true—and it was.

For the Mundell theory ended up on the scrap heap by the end of 1981 as the economy crashed into recession while interest rates remained high. Yet in many respects it received an undeserved burial, since it contains many nuggets that are more realistic than the standard Keynesian demand theories. It is indeed the case that an increase in supply does reduce inflationary pressures, and that a reduction in demand that lowers investment and productivity eventually raises those pressures. In that sense tax cuts—especially those which stimulate saving, investment, and productivity—are not inflationary.

It will come as cold comfort to those who lost their jobs, businesses, or fortunes in the 1981–82 recession to learn that the Mundell theory probably

---

*The Phillips curve, discussed in more detail in chapter 11, posits a trade-off between the rate of inflation and the rate of unemployment.

51

would have been the correct strategy, had it been applied, to fight the 1970 and 1974–75 recessions. Mundell himself is very careful to spell out the circumstances under which his policies work and those under which they do not, although most of his followers and popularizers ignored these fine distinctions. However, by the time they were tried in 1981, circumstances had switched so much that his plan was doomed to failure; expectations about future growth in the money supply and the size of the budget deficits had changed dramatically from 1970 and 1975 to 1981. But that is getting just a bit ahead of our story. First it is in order to analyze how the Mundell program works under what would be optimal conditions.

The basic constructs of the Mundell theory can be stated very simply. As already mentioned, by an easy fiscal policy Mundell really means tax cuts; increases in government spending are not an acceptable substitute. For tax cuts increase productivity and reduce inflation by lowering costs; this is one of the fundamental pillars of supply-side economics. Second, by tight money he means no additional accommodation for the extra growth that would otherwise occur when the tax cut spurs economic activity; he does not mean less monetary growth than would have occurred in the absence of the tax cut. Mundell acknowledges that this will indeed raise interest rates, but that, he says, is quite all right. In particular, he claims:

> The correct policy mix is based on fiscal ease to get more production out of the economy, in combination with monetary restraint to stop inflation. The increased momentum of the economy provided by the stimulus of a tax cut will cause a sufficient demand for credit to permit real monetary expansion *at higher interest rates* (emphasis added).[7]

As far as the commonplace fears that tax cuts will fuel inflation, Mundell explains:

> Tax reduction however is expansionary, not inflationary, when there is substantial underutilized capacity, as we have stressed enough. The distinction revolves around the effect on supply. Whether tax reductions raises or lowers price depends on how aggregate supply responds to aggregate demand, and on the impact of tax reduction on costs. Prices will rise only if the increase in aggregate demand exceeds the increase in aggregate supply and if any excess of the demand price over the supply price of aggregate output is not offset by a reduction in wage (cum tax) and other costs.[8]

The thrust of the last sentence is that even if demand forces would push prices up somewhat, the increase will be offset by more moderate wage gains and higher productivity. At least in this author's opinion, this is the very essence of supply-side economics.

To be sure, a tax cut means an increase in the deficit. That worried Mundell not at all, for it will be paid for by the increase in private sector savings which are generated by the tax cut. Indeed, Mundell seems to take almost a cavalier attitude over the fact that the deficit will rise. In answer to one of his detractors, Mundell replied:

> Suppose it does mean a budget deficit in the United States—who cares? . . . I'm frankly not worried about this problem at all. I think it's a mirage, and I think it's shocking that, thirty-five years after the Keynesian revolution, we should be squabbling about an issue that should have long been laid to rest.[9]

Unfortunately, by the time triple-digit deficits had rolled around in 1982, the answer to Mundell's question of "who cares" was: the entire Federal Reserve Board, the president of the United States, most of the members of Congress, and the entire financial community. And, in a nutshell, *that* has turned out to be the fatal flaw in Mundell's theory.

Can Tight Money Lower Inflation Without Causing a Recession?

Mundell's theory can be questioned on two other important grounds as well. The first is whether a decrease in the money supply can actually reduce prices without going through the route of diminishing output. The second, which is even more critical—and controversial—is whether tighter money lowers or raises interest rates. Let us turn to each of these issues.

As is shown in figure 3.1, changes in the money supply clearly lead to changes in the rate of inflation with a lag of approximately two years. It is, however, quite another issue to decide whether the change in prices occurs because of a change in output, or whether changes in money supply impact inflation directly. For if a decline in money supply growth can lower inflation without causing a recession, then the Mundell theory may be right most, if not all, of the time. If, on the other hand, lower inflation occurs only because of depressed economic activity, no new breakthrough has occurred. For the trade-off between inflation and unemployment has been in force for years; the challenge of supply-side economics is to negate this trade-off, creating instead a set of policies which will generate faster growth without higher inflation.

The Quantity Theory monetarists champion the viewpoint that money supply can affect prices without first changing output by their claim that when

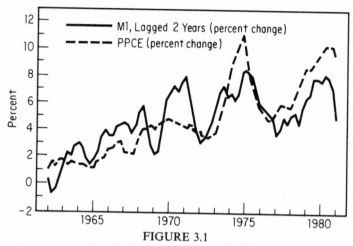

FIGURE 3.1

Money Supply Growth and Inflation

SOURCE: Prepared by Evans Economics, Inc.

money supply declines, velocity and output do not change, but prices do fall. If fiscal policy can then be used to stimulate investment, output can rise at the same time that inflation is declining by using the combination of tight money and easy fiscal policy.

To see whether a decline in the money supply can lead to lower prices only without lowering output, consider the following identity, one which is just as tautological as the Quantity Theory and is in fact the basis of national income accounting, but is not as often quoted. It states that:

Wage Income + Gross Capital Income* + Excise Taxes = Prices × Output

This can be rewritten as:

Prices = Unit Labor Costs + Unit Capital Costs (including profits) + Excise Tax Rates

Assuming that excise tax rates do not change—although this is in fact another way to change prices—it logically follows that prices cannot diminish unless either unit labor costs or profit margins decrease.

It surely comes as no surprise that profit margins diminish during a recession, and if the recession lasts long enough wage demands also moderate, as happened in 1982. However, we are trying to verify the quantity theorist argument that prices can decline *without any reduction in real GNP*. Based on the above identity, this could occur if a decline in the money supply would cause

*This includes all returns to capital: profits, depreciation, interest, and rents and royalties.

wage rates to rise less rapidly, productivity to improve, or interest rates to decline. The latter reduces prices through lowering unit capital costs.

The direct links between money supply growth and wage rates are tenuous at best, once the effect the change in the money supply has on the unemployment rate is excluded. Certainly workers would not be expected to alter their stance at the bargaining table based on recent trends in money supply growth. Employers might be more likely to offer large wage increases if they thought the forthcoming price gains would be validated in the marketplace by faster growth in the money supply, and conversely to be more stingy if they were reasonably sure higher prices could not be passed on. However, that would depend on the business community having a reasonably accurate estimate of what the Fed will do in the future; a pastime which so far has eluded absolutely everyone else. We have estimated the effect of changes in the money supply on the real wage by using various different estimates of expected future changes but have always come up empty-handed. This appears to be a decidedly unpromising line of approach.

Similarly, changes in the money supply have very little independent effect on productivity other than through changes in investment, which means that aggregate demand and output are affected directly. Productivity growth has declined from over 3 percent per year for the first twenty years of the postwar period to approximately $-\frac{1}{2}$ percent per year for the past five years as a result of lower saving and investment, higher marginal tax rates, a sharp rise in the amount of government regulation, a change in the demographic mix of the labor supply, and the decline of the work ethic—but not fluctuations in the money supply. If anything, faster growth in the real money supply usually leads to faster productivity growth, although much of that is simply due to cyclical factors.

The evidence would thus appear to be incontrovertible—although it is obvious that some old-line monetarists will never give up—that (a) changes in the money supply definitely influence inflation with about a two-year lag; and (b) this causality occurs only through changes in the level of output and employment.

Indeed, only twice in the entire postwar period has the rate of inflation declined without a corresponding dip in output; and these were exactly the times when Presidents Truman and Nixon imposed price controls. In the first case, the higher inflation was due to the speculative outburst following the Korean War and probably would have waned in any case; but for good measure taxes were raised to pay for the war, credit controls were tightened, and production diverted from consumer to defense needs. The release of controls coincided with the onset of a recession, so that whatever pent-up price pressures remained were transferred to the next boom. In the case of Nixon, of course, the economy was gunned unmercifully under the protective cover of the controls and the end result was double-digit inflation.

Except for these two instances, which fortify rather than detract from our logic, inflation has never declined in the postwar period except during or shortly after a recession. Furthermore, the onset of a recession has always reduced the rate of inflation, at least temporarily.

Yet the fact that the economy is batting 0 for 7 on fighting inflation without recession does not necessarily mean that the subject is entirely closed, for there is one final escape route, as it were—the relationship between money supply and interest rates. For if it could be demonstrated that tight money leads to lower interest rates, it could then be argued that these lower interest rates would stimulate the economy without raising inflation; for most of the growth would come in the area of higher investment, which would increase productivity and hence reduce unit labor costs.

Mundell is not prepared to go quite this far, for, as has been discussed, he explicitly claims that his theory is based on a combination of easy fiscal and tight monetary policies raising interest rates, although not enough to choke off the recovery. However, it is a matter of degree. If the tight money/easy fiscal policy combination were to raise interest rates only slightly, the net effect would be one of stimulus; if it actually lowers rather than raises interest rates, that improves the efficacy of the program even more.

Does Tight Money Raise or Lower Interest Rates?

The question of whether an increase in the money supply raises or lowers interest rates has become one of paramount interest and importance to the Reagan administration, since if in the longer run tight money will bring interest rates down, then Paul Volcker is essentially on the right track, although it is taking a painfully long time to accomplish his stated goals; but if he is on the wrong track, the economy is headed for another time like in the 1930s, at least until someone pulls the switches and reroutes the train.

The situation has been further confused because, under the unprecedented volatility in the money supply under the Volcker regime, critics have had plenty of ammunition in both directions. From June through December 1980 the basic money supply (M1) grew at an annual rate of almost 16 percent—more than double the maximum Fed target of 6 percent. This was accompanied by almost a 10 percent rise in short-term rates and about a 2½ percent rise in long-term rates. After a mixed pattern, M1 then actually declined by \$2.5 billion from April to August 1981. However, interest rates—particularly long-term rates—continued to rise.

Thus on one hand, the monetarists pointed to the relationship during late 1980 as proof that rapid growth in the money supply would lead to higher interest rates because of expectations that this rapid growth would eventually be inflationary. Keynesians, on the other hand, pointed to the experience from April to August 1981 as proof that a decline in the money supply led to an increase in interest rates because it restricted credit and hence caused borrowers to bid up interest rates. Obviously more is at work here than a simple bivariate relationship between money supply and interest rates, and a much fuller explanation of the determinants of interest rates is required.

Although Mundell would argue that his preferred policy mix would raise rather than lower interest rates, his list of the determinants is a useful point of departure.

Interest rates rise when there is (1) an increase in shortage of capital, (2) a strengthening of the domestic economy, (3) expectations of accelerated monetary expansion and inflation, and (4) monetary restriction caused by open-market sales of securities with unchanged expectations.[10]

Turning to the first point, the economy has undergone a marked decline in each key sector of the total saving ratio since 1976, as has been illustrated in chapter 2. It is these declines in saving that have been instrumental in keeping interest rates high even while inflation fell by 4 percent during the first year of the Reagan administration.

Mundell is correct when he argues that easy money cannot really cure the shortage of capital. Although loosening the purse strings on the money supply will initially provide more funds, it cannot induce either individuals, corporations, or governments to save more. Indeed, inasmuch as it has any effect at all, easy money is likely to diminish personal saving, since the decline in interest rates will be translated into a lower rate of return on saving. As is shown in some detail in chapter 6, the personal saving rate is significantly affected by the after-tax real rate of return on saving.

A rise in the rate of inflation sometimes appears to create an increase in the corporate and government saving rates, but this is only illusory. At the corporate level, higher prices are initially translated into higher profits, as fixed costs by definition lag behind the rise in prices. However, these increases in profits are actually phony ones, since the assets representing these fixed costs will eventually have to be replaced at higher prices. As firms replace assets at their new, inflated values, they end up borrowing more than before.

A similar sleight of hand occurs in the government sector accounting. As a general rule, the budget deficit initially shrinks during periods when inflation increases. Once again there is a very simple reason for this. As a first order of approximation, tax receipts are based on this year's rate of inflation, whereas most expenditures are based on last year's inflation because of the lag in indexing. Furthermore, bracket creep causes taxes to rise more rapidly the higher the rate of inflation is. These gains are phony because higher government spending eventually closes the gap. Thus, while easy money apparently leads to an increase in reported saving because it raises inflation, it actually causes a decline in real saving.

The second factor cited by Mundell, namely that interest rates will rise with an increase in economic activity, requires little comment except to note that it holds only with other factors remaining constant. Thus, for example, if economic activity increased but *ex ante* saving rose faster than investment, interest rates might remain constant or could even decline, as they did during much of 1976. However, any decline in interest rates during an upturn is more likely to occur because the monetary authorities accommodate this increase by permitting or encouraging the money supply to grow more rapidly, hence offsetting the rise in rates that would otherwise take place. After a while, further increases in the money supply usually lead financial markets to expect that these increases will be inflationary, and hence rates then *rise* on the news of further growth in the money supply. Thus, the relationship between money supply and interest rates really is essentially a question of expectations—as Mundell stresses in his third and fourth points.

These two latter points may be reinforcing or contradictory. For example, if the Fed tightens and the marketplace sees this as a sign that money supply growth and inflation will henceforth diminish, this will probably lead to a decline in rates, particularly if that tightening is accompanied by a recession. On the other hand, if the Fed tightens but financial markets do not see this move as affecting underlying trends—that is, expectations are not changed—interest rates will rise.

Even though expectations about what will happen in financial markets cannot be reduced to a specific list, they are largely based on the following three variables: (1) fiscal policy of the current administration, especially the size of the budget deficit; (2) underlying trends of inflation, as indicated primarily by unit labor costs; and (3) credibility of the Fed itself.

In a nutshell, in 1981 and 1982 the financial community was worried that the combination of triple-digit deficits and a prolonged recession would eventually induce the Fed to monetize the deficit through increased monetary expansion, thereby laying the groundwork for the return to double-digit inflation. Whereas Volcker himself might stand fast against such shenanigans, it

Myth 2: Tight Money and Fiscal Ease

was conceded, his term does expire in August 1983, and perhaps one of his successors might turn out to be more pliable. In order to understand how this deep distrust of the Fed evolved, we review briefly the history of the Fed's attempts to exercise independent control over monetary policy.

The Role of the Federal Reserve System in Determining Expectations

Before the existence of the Federal Reserve System, the country went through periodic spasms involving spectacular financial crashes and wholesale destruction of the money supply through failure of commercial banks. It was the Crash of 1907 which finally convinced legislators that something had to be done to control the institutions of money and banking in the United States, and six years later the Federal Reserve System was born.

The Fed didn't do very much at first. World War I provided prosperity for almost everyone; and the reversion to a peacetime economy, while it did include a severe recession—some say a depression—in 1920–21,* quickly emerged into the prosperity of the 1920s during which growth and stable prices co-existed with a minimum of competition. Two mild recessions occurring in 1924 and 1927 did little to mar the overall pattern of growth during the decade.

In 1928 the Fed began to become alarmed about the speculative activity on the stock market and attempted to take steps to curb this activity. Unfortunately at the time it did not possess the necessary tools such as margin requirements, and in fact it was more or less limited to raising interest rates. Even doing this, however, had a noticeable effect, and many commentators of the times, including John Maynard Keynes—not usually classified among the monetarists—claimed that the clash between the Fed and Wall Street was one of the major factors leading to the stock market collapse.

The Fed hardly could be blamed for trying to bring speculation under control, but after the initial stock market crash virtually every policy step that was undertaken amplified the damage. Congress passed the Hawley-Smoot Tariff Act in 1930, which essentially cut off our imports from Europe, driving that continent into a depression which was intensified when the Creditanstalt in Vienna failed in 1931. Of course monetary policy could not be blamed for

---

*The unemployment rate averaged 11.9 percent in 1921 and the index of industrial production declined some 23 percent. By our standards we would call this a depression, although not a major one.

this, but in addition the Fed, instead of reducing interest rates in the face of a declining economy and deflation, raised them even further. Finally, as was mentioned in chapter 1, in 1932 Congress quadrupled the lowest tax bracket and raised the top bracket from 25 percent to 63 percent; even worse, it made the tax increase retroactive to the first of the year even though Hoover did not sign the legislation until June 6. Those who think we ought to raise taxes in the middle of a recession should look back at 1932, a year in which real GNP fell 15 percent and total corporate profits were −$3 billion—a figure that at today's level of GNP would correspond to −$150 billion! Taxpayers had to withdraw their funds from the banks to meet these extra assessments on or before March 15, 1933, and the banking system virtually collapsed. The Fed was absolutely no help at all; the economy would have been better off had it not existed.

For this uniquely incompetent performance the Fed was "grounded" for the next twenty years. Roosevelt of course had no use for high interest rates during the midst of a depression, and the Fed kept interest rates so low that the rate on Treasury bills was occasionally negative during the late 1930s. When World War II arrived and the demand for funds increased, the Fed was drafted, so to speak, like everyone else. It was told to keep interest rates low so the government could borrow whatever it needed at a cost of about 2½ percent. During a period of total mobilization when the very existence of the country was at stake, few could complain about this method of financing.

After the war ended, however, President Truman faced a much different set of alternatives. He could either keep interest rates at their low wartime level, which meant convincing the Fed to continue buying bonds in the open market whenever someone wanted to sell them, or to permit rates to rise and bond prices to sink, hence keeping money supply and inflation under control.

Truman had absolutely no trouble making that decision. He recalled only too vividly how his own little haberdasher's shop had gone bankrupt in the 1920–21 recession because high interest rates caused massive foreclosures and caused a sharp decline in purchasing power. He was not going to let the small businessman be hurt again in the aftermath of World War II. Consequently, the Fed was instructed to keep interest rates down to about 2½ percent, which is precisely what it did. For the almost eight years that Truman was president, long-term interest rates (Aaa corporate bond yield) fluctuated in an extremely narrow range of between 2½ percent and 3 percent even though inflation zoomed as high as 14.4 percent in 1947.

The stability of interest rates could not have been accomplished without Fed accommodation; yet on the other hand that could not possibly have been the only reason for the remarkable negative spread between interest rates and inflation. In today's environment, for example, it would be literally impossible for the Fed to maneuver long-term bond rates down to 3 percent, no matter what it did to the money supply.

One major difference between then and now was that the federal government ran significant budget surpluses. The average surplus during the first five years of the postwar period averaged about $6½ billion, equivalent to 2.6 percent of GNP, or a surplus of about $80 billion at 1982 levels. The immediate postwar period was also characterized by surprisingly modest growth in the money supply. Indeed, from 1945 to 1952, the basic money supply increased at an average rate of only 1.8 percent per year,* compared to an average annual growth rate in nominal GNP of 7.2 percent.

Most important, expectations were oriented primarily toward deflation rather than inflation. Although the consumer price index (CPI) rose an average of 5.7 percent annually during this period, most people still vividly remembered the Great Depression and its bias toward deflation. Indeed, a majority of prominent economists predicted that once World War II ended the economy would fall back into depression and prices would start declining again. In other words, long-term bondholders acted as if the underlying rate of inflation were zero.

While it is not worth exhuming early postwar history in great detail, it is instructive to point out that inflation and interest rates are not always closely correlated. As long as people believe that the current level of inflation is only temporary, they will not require that interest rates reflect the current bulge in prices. The widespread belief that prices would soon stabilize, coupled with those large budget surpluses, kept interest rates at what now seem like exceptionally low levels. In the same vein, it is currently taking investors years to get over the high rates of inflation of the late 1970s even though inflation declined to 5 percent in 1982.

Still, when Eisenhower became president, he did not care for pegging interest rates, so he arranged what became known as the "accord" between the Treasury and the Federal Reserve, which meant that the Fed no longer had to buy the Treasury debt or keep rates pegged at their previous low levels. The Fed was now free, within some limits, to permit interest rates to rise and fall with market conditions. Thus liberated, interest rates rose somewhat, but only increased about 50 basis points before the post-Korean War recession pulled them back to previous levels.

William McChesney Martin, who had also been chairman of the Fed during Truman's later days, worked very well within the scope of Eisenhower's economic policies; he raised interest rates to 4 percent when inflation intensified in 1956 and 1957, lowered them again during the 1958 recession, and then increased them when inflation appeared to be a recurring problem in 1959.

*The figure excluding government demand deposits was a still modest 3.4 percent.

This was a period of rather sluggish growth—a 2.3 percent annual rate from 1956 through 1960—but it did reduce the underlying rate of inflation. In any case, the budget remained virtually in balance during the Eisenhower years, inflation averaged 2 percent, and the Fed made it clear that it would act to tighten the money supply any time inflation threatened to get out of hand.

In the meantime, however, the perceived equilibrium rate of inflation moved up from 0 percent to about 1½ percent, which means that the long-term bond yields moved up from 3 percent to 4½ percent. This bothered some people—a favorite phrase of certain otherwise stuffy bankers being "a little inflation is like being a little bit pregnant"—but in general the economy seemed to work well under 1½ percent inflation and those who groused about economic performance were usually worried about sluggish growth and high unemployment rather than too much inflation. McChesney Martin was generally given high marks all around.

Martin also managed to work very well with Kennedy and his Treasury Secretary, Douglas Dillon, during the key transition period of the 1964 tax cut. In particular, Martin permitted the money supply to expand fast enough that real growth could zoom to 6 percent in both 1965 and early 1966 without raising interest rates because inflation seemed under control and the budget remained in balance.

This twenty-year symbiotic relationship started to deteriorate in late 1966; when the wage-price guidelines broke down, the economy overheated under the twin burdens of the Vietnam War and the Great Society, and inflation moved into the 4 percent range. Martin, according to accounts at the time, raised the discount rate to 4.5 percent in opposition to Johnson's orders. In this author's opinion, however, nothing of the sort happened. After he retired, Martin admitted that he never disobeyed an explicit "suggestion" from any of the five presidents under whom he served. Johnson at that time was at the height of his Imperial Presidency frame of mind, and in keeping with other orders he gave his lieutenants, and the problems that he was having enforcing the wage-price guidelines, it is my belief that he told Martin it was quite all right to raise the discount rate and show those bastards that they could not get away with violating the guidelines. For Martin, of course, it was a good chance to show his "independence."

In any case, money supply was tightened, the commercial paper rate jumped from 4½ percent to 6 percent, and the first credit crunch appeared as housing starts declined from 1.38 million in April to 0.85 million in October 1966. The entire episode ended very quickly: by mid-1967 the commercial paper rate receded to 4½ percent, the inflation rate declined to 2 percent; and yet the economy avoided a recession. Unemployment rose only from 3.5 percent to 4.0 percent, and while real growth slowed from its superheated 6 percent annual gain in 1965 and 1966, it still rose 2.7 percent in 1967. After all, not even the cockeyed optimists expected 6 percent real growth as a steady diet.

It is important to note that *tight* money led to a substantial *decline* in interest rates and inflation within a year; while growth slowed somewhat, unemployment hardly rose at all so the cost was fairly minimal. The majority of people still believed that money supply, inflation, and the budget would remain under control. Thus, whereas the initial result of tighter money was to raise interest rates, the financial markets soon believed that would mean less growth and inflation soon afterward. Hence the decline in the money supply which began in July 1966 caused interest rates to start to fall by December.

More and more people began to wonder, however, whether the overly stimulative fiscal policy of Johnson would not cause the economy to bolt from the equilibrium path it had followed for the past twenty years. Thus the next time the economy overheated, Johnson and Martin were not so fortunate. Real growth climbed to 4.6 percent in 1968 and inflation now exceeded the 4 percent mark, so the Fed tightened for the second time in three years. This time, however, the result backfired. Instead of dropping quickly, the prime rate rose from 6.0 percent to 8.5 percent. Inflation increased from 3.0 percent in 1967 to 4.7 percent in 1968 and 6.1 percent in 1969 as the first signs of the buy-now-because-it-will-cost-more-later syndrome surfaced. The saving rate dropped precipitously because of the surcharge, a point covered in detail in chapter 6. Unlike 1967, a full-fledged recession developed, while at the same time inflation continued to mount. Clearly some of the assurance that tight monetary policies and a balanced budget would always come to the rescue was rapidly being eroded.

Eventually the decline in economic activity and the increase in the personal saving rate due to the termination of the income tax surcharge brought interest rates down by the end of 1970. They then fell further when Nixon announced the wage-and-price freeze, which represented a sudden and clearcut case of changed expectations. During 1972, however, Nixon and Arthur Burns, by then chairman of the Fed, combined to raise money supply by a record 9.3 percent, a rate not matched even during the later 1970s when inflation was much higher. Yet interest rates did not increase very much during the year, even though the saving rate declined and real GNP rose a buoyant 5.7 percent. Again Mundell explains why, in an explanation written well *before* the freeze occurred:

Monetary policy can promote real expansion if *it bites on some rigidities in the economy.* If wage rates are fixed while prices go on rising, real wages would fall relative to productivity and that would stimulate more employment. Another route is through interest rates. Monetary expansion can lower interest rates if expectations about future prices do not adjust, and lower interest rates stimulate spending on durable goods . . . in the early stages of inflation monetary policy can stimulate expansion by increasing aggregate demand in an economy with unsophisticated expectations. An important route is through a reduction in interest rates, which may fall with monetary acceleration if the public is not aware of the link between monetary policy and inflation.[11]

What happened in 1972 was quite clear. Financial markets naïvely believed that the wage-and-price controls could somehow permanently suppress inflation in spite of highly expansionary fiscal and monetary policies. Thus the markets were willing to accept unrealistically low rates of interest as long as this myth persisted.

Once Nixon moved to his Phase III of the controls, inflation took off with a vengeance. Interest rates started to climb steadily, with the federal funds rate rising from 5.3 percent at the beginning of 1973 to 10.8 percent by September. However, since the interest rates still remained below the rate of inflation, the Fed did not appear to be serious about fighting inflation, even though growth in the money supply was cut to 5.5 percent. Thus the Fed was facing the worst of both worlds as far as expectations were concerned. On the one hand, markets now expected accelerated monetary expansion to continue to validate the increased inflation, as witnessed by the fact that Nixon through Burns insisted on keeping interest rates below inflation. To compound the felony, Burns, operating under what appeared to be a convoluted version of interest rate controls, threw oil on the fire by forcing the prime rate under the cost of borrowed funds in 1973. This invited businesses to borrow at what were actually negative spreads—that is, the customer could borrow at 10 percent and reinvest the proceeds in the market at 11 percent. On the other hand, the monetary restriction that did occur did not change expectations, thereby driving rates even higher by shutting off the flow of credit.

Finally in mid-1974, Burns got desperate. He first tried calling all the big banks in the country and telling them to cut back on their loans, which had just about the effect you might expect. Then with Nixon on the way out, Burns suddenly remembered his economics. He raised the federal funds rate to 13 percent, which was above the rate of inflation. Suddenly inflationary expectations snapped; the economy headed into the most severe recession of the postwar period, and unemployment soared to a peak of 9 percent. Monetary policy continued to be tight for a while, but by this time the back of inflationary expectations had been broken and interest rates, aided by the sharp recession, plummeted 8 percent in a period of only eight months.

It is hard not to agree that the Fed also failed this major test miserably. It gunned the economy far more than was justified under any rational economic assumptions during the election year of 1972 by hiding under the cloak of suppressed inflation in the guise of wage and price controls. It then failed to raise interest rates high enough when inflation did start to take off, and finally it plunged the economy into a recession—when belatedly it did take action. The Fed's credibility had lost another giant notch.

With Gerald Ford taking over the presidency, hard-line conservative Alan Greenspan installed as chairman of the Council, and Arthur Burns putting his "Prosperity without Inflation" hat back on, markets calmed down for the next two years and expectations returned to normal; that is to say, the average economist and financial analyst viewed the 4.8 percent rate of inflation in 1976 as sustainable if not improvable. The Ford-Greenspan-Burns triumvirate looked set for a while, and expectations headed for lower, rather than higher, inflation.

The only problem with this game plan was that the economy was not responding very well. With unemployment remaining around 8 percent, the voters opted for Carter. He, in turn, finding Burns too inflexible, discarded him at the earliest possible moment,* and installed G. William Miller, a man of his own choice without any background in either financial or political circles. Miller decided that independence of the Fed was something to describe in textbooks but had no meaning in the real world. As a tool of the Carter administration, he continued to balloon the money supply, in general by keeping interest rates below the rate of inflation; and when the economy temporarily declined in the second quarter of 1979, he candidly admitted pumping up the money supply in order to keep the economy out of recession in the coming election year.

Whereas Miller was perhaps more blatant about his intentions than other chairmen of the Fed, the fact is that ever since the Eisenhower-Martin days the Fed had always been rather prone to monetary ease when expansionary fiscal policy was desired by the president. Thus Martin supported both the Kennedy-Johnson tax cut and the initial phases of the Great Society and Vietnam War expansions; the first credit crunch in 1966 was an attempt to scare people back into observing the wage and price guidelines. Martin also provided an overly healthy dollop of monetary growth during 1968, allegedly to offset the surcharge that went into effect in the middle of the year. And Burns, as has been seen, exhibited profligacy in permitting the money supply to increase 9.3 percent during the 1972 election year.

Miller's actions did manage to hold interest rates constant for several more months, but inflation continued to accelerate and the slippage of the dollar began to turn into a rout. Carter, whose knowledge of financial affairs might

---

*Burns's term expired January 31, 1978. Carter asked him to stay on as a member of the Federal Reserve Board of Governors, but not as chairman, a highly insulting move Carter knew would be rejected. The way was then clear for Miller to take over.

be judged from the fact that his first choice for chairman of the Fed was allegedly Bert Lance, became quite alarmed. Moving Miller over to the Treasury, he appointed no-nonsense Paul Volcker as chairman of the Fed. Volcker had been ostentatiously passed over a year earlier when Miller had been selected and thus was widely thought to owe no allegiance to Carter. Here was a man who would tighten money supply even at the temporary discomfort of higher interest rates even in an election year.

For a while it looked like Volcker might be able to make the difference. Within two months of his becoming chairman of the Fed, he pushed the federal funds rate up to 15 percent and, when that failed to slow down inflation, he instituted credit controls and pushed the rate up to a peak of over 17 percent. This combination brought about the sharpest one-quarter decline in the entire postwar period, with real GNP falling at an annual rate of 10 percent during the second quarter of 1980.

The money supply (M1) fell an unprecedented $6 billion in April 1980, to about $390 billion, and remained at that level during May, and rates also slid by record amounts, with the federal funds rate plunging from a peak of over 19 percent to 9 percent in the matter of just eight weeks. To a large extent that decline was due to the recession and the increase in the saving rate, but it was also due to changed expectations about money supply growth and inflation. In particular, many financial market participants stated that they thought inflation could be reduced to 3 percent in the near future. It seems fair to say that, at least temporarily, expectations were significantly changed. Maybe the tough-talking Volcker would be able to do the trick after all.

Unfortunately, Volcker was unable to carry out his mandate successfully. As would be expected, the economy started to rebound from the recession as soon as interest rates declined and the credit controls were lifted. Real GNP increased at an annual rate of 4.6 percent during the next three quarters, which was generally in line, although somewhat below, the average rebound during the first year of previous recoveries. However, money supply went berserk, rising at an annual rate of 16 percent from June to December. Interest rates not only recovered from their troughs but rose to new peaks, with the prime rate hitting 21.5 percent late in December. Never before had the financial sector reacted this way to an increase in the money supply.

The Overadjustment of Expectations

The latter half of 1980 was the first time such large upward movements in both money supply and interest rates had ever occurred at the same time. Previously, there had always been some lag; large increases in the money supply were at least initially accompanied by declines in interest rates. This episode completely destroyed whatever faith financial markets had left in the Fed's ability to control the money supply. Mr. Volcker had strode into office telling everyone to "keep your eye on the money supply ball" and yet it was bouncing up and down faster than ever before in the history of the Federal Reserve. As Mundell said back in 1971:

> If interest rates *overadjust* to the inflation, *monetary acceleration can reduce real demand, because interest rates rise by more than the actual inflation rate.* Expectations themselves become conditioned by the expected monetary policy and make their adjustments accordingly. The effect of monetary acceleration on real demand depends on whether expectations are underadjusted or overadjusted.[12] (emphasis added)

Under previous historical relationships, an increase in the money supply at an annual rate of 16 percent during the second half of 1980 would have produced a tremendous boom about six months later. Yet real GNP started to decline in January 1981, and six months after that another severe recession started. Clearly expectations had finally started to overadjust.

With this latest development, the Fed found itself in a virtually impossible situation. For a given level of economic activity and saving, *easy* money would *raise* interest rates because of expectations that this would lead to higher inflation ahead. On the other hand, *tight* money would *also raise* interest rates because it would withdraw funds from the banking system without changing expectations. In other words, easy money would raise interest rates because it was expected to be permanent, while tight money would raise interest rates because it was expected to be temporary. The loss of confidence in the Fed was complete.

Thus, interest rates were basically doomed to go higher and higher until (a) expectations were reversed, (b) total saving increased, or (c) a recession occurred. Without more favorable circumstances, it was impossible for the Mundell prescription to work, for tight money would raise interest rates enough to choke off any recovery.

Causing a recession was clearly viewed as a suboptimal way to lower interest rates, although that is in fact what happened, as individual saving responded very slowly to higher real rates of interest. Yet cutting government spending should have remained a viable option. Indeed, President Reagan's first estimate of the FY 1982 budget called for the ratio of government spending to GNP to decline from 23.3 percent to 21.8 percent which clearly would have been a giant step in the right direction. By the time the first year had passed, however, the February 1982 estimates showed that this ratio had crept up to 24.2 percent, an all-time postwar record.

This new budget estimate was the second jolt that the financial markets had received in six months. Market expectations had already deteriorated noticeably when the tax cut was passed in August 1981 and was found to contain about $25 billion more per year in tax cuts than previously anticipated. The second negative jolt occurred when the budget document released in February 1982 showed that Reagan had no plan to balance the budget even by 1987—in spite of some exceedingly optimistic estimates of real growth starting in 1983. This caused expectations about inflation to worsen and interest rates to rise further, even though the Fed did not take any overt action nor did the economic situation materially change.

By mid-1980 it had become clear that the market was now overadjusting to increases in the money supply, imputing to them inflationary attributes they did not possess. These fears worsened in 1981 and 1982, fueled by the monotonically increasing estimates of the budget deficit, and by the claims of Volcker and others that the decline in inflation that had occurred—CPI growth declined from over 10 percent during the first three quarters of 1981 to 4 percent for the next two quarters—was ephemeral due to exogenous factors like bountiful harvests and oil gluts, and would probably be reversed in the near future.

In an attempt to avert criticism of the Fed, particularly in the aftermath of the mammoth rise in the money supply in the second half of 1980, the Federal Open Market Committee (FOMC) consistently voted to keep interest rates high well into 1981 even though economic activity once again started to deteriorate. It was generally expected that once the underlying rate of inflation started to decline, FOMC members would permit rates to drop to a lower level. Yet they demurred throughout 1981 on the grounds that the signs of lower inflation were not yet clear enough and that they were worried about the size of the budget deficit. As Henry Wallich once remarked to this author, "Tell us again, Mike, how larger budget deficits help fight inflation." Thus tight monetary policies clearly were unable to rescue the economy from another recession in late 1981.

We now return to the supply-side myth which is the subject of this chapter, namely that the economy could enjoy rapid growth and lower inflation by using a combination of easy fiscal and tight monetary policies. Nobody could say that the Mundell prescription was not tried. We certainly had easy fiscal policies—a 4 percent increase in government spending in real terms, massive tax cuts, and triple-digit deficits. We certainly had tight monetary policies—5 percent or less growth in the money supply and rates of interest as much as 10 percent above the inflation rate. But the result was almost a total disappointment. While the rate of inflation did decline dramatically, the economy entered a recession the very month the Reagan tax package was signed, with the unem-

Myth 2: Tight Money and Fiscal Ease

ployment rate eventually rising above the 10 percent level. The size of the budget deficit, which Mundell had earlier designated as unimportant, twisted expectations so much that markets viewed every move of the Fed to increase the money supply as potentially inflationary.

In addition, the Mundell formula can be successful only if the *ex ante* decline in economic activity due to the increase in interest rates is less than the stimulus provided by the tax cuts. If the rise in interest rates more than offsets the beneficial effects of lower tax rates, the economy will flounder and growth will be reduced at the same time that inflation is declining. In the worst possible case, real growth will falter and actual inflation will diminish, but expectations about future inflation will worsen because of the increase in the budget deficit, thus pushing rates even higher and overwhelming the beneficial effects of the tax cut. This is in fact what happened in 1981 and 1982.

The Mundell philosophy might have worked in 1970 or even in 1974–75, when expectations about inflation were much more benign and worries of the deficits far more subdued. By 1981, however, the combined beliefs that (a) the Fed would not or could not stick to its announced goals, (b) inflation was endemic and embedded in society on almost a permanent basis, and (c) the budget deficit could not be brought under control in the indefinite future, kept interest rates at record high levels that dropped only briefly during periods of outright recession. The negative expectations about the budget deficit thus swamped the positive expectations which should have come from tighter money, and hence tight money led to higher rather than lower interest rates. Whereas consumption was affected to a certain degree, it was primarily investment that suffered the most from the rise in interest rates, as will now be discussed in chapter 4.

CHAPTER 4

Myth 3: Business Tax Cuts Would

Increase Investment Immediately

The Bipartisan Support for Business Tax Cuts

The third great myth promulgated by the supply-side community was the belief that investment would increase well ahead of the benefits eventually conferred by the new supply-side program. Even if interest rates were to remain high, demand sluggish, and capacity utilization low, capital spending would pick up as soon as the tax cuts were implemented—if not before—for did not the Reagan plan "guarantee" three years of uninterrupted expansion?

Before dispelling this myth, we should point out that the response of investment to changes in the tax rates is one of the few areas where supply-side and Keynesian economists generally tend to agree. As early as 1967 the Brookings Institution, clearly not sympathetic to supply-side economics then or now, sponsored a conference entitled "Tax Incentives and Capital Spending." Virtually all the participants agreed that the corporate income tax changes instituted by Kennedy had some significant positive effect on investment, and Dale Jorgenson, then at Berkeley and now at Harvard, concluded:

> The investment tax credit has had a greater impact than any of the other changes in tax policy during the postwar period . . . [T]he shortening of lifetimes used in calculating depreciation have been very important determinants of levels of invest-

ment expenditures since 1954. Suspension of the investment tax credit and accelerated depreciation from late 1966 to early 1967 had an important restraining effect on the level of investment.[1]

More recently, Charles Schultze, as chairman of the Council of Economic Advisors, was moved to write in the *1981 Economic Report of the President:*

> It seems unwise to assume that the average productivity of the labor force will be improved by a personal tax cut . . . [M]ost empirical studies have concluded that changes in personal income tax rates would have only a small effect on personal saving . . . [S]pecific investment-oriented tax reductions for business are likely to increase saving, investment, and productivity by a much more significant degree than cuts in personal income taxes.[2]

Walter Heller, testifying on the Reagan tax cut proposals, was even more direct. In his usual blunt and forceful manner, he claimed:

> Business tax cuts of $21 billion out of $136 billion by 1983 doesn't sound, to me, like a balanced tax cut. Strangely enough, this reverses the approach taken by the Kennedy administration, which Mr. Kemp and the other supply-siders say they are emulating . . . [I]t seems to me that if the current tax cutters want to draw the right lesson from the Kennedy tax cut experience it would be this: utilize the existing margin for tax cuts first and foremost for the carefully crafted and sharply focused incentives to capital formation [and] restructure the 1981 tax cut to put much more emphasis on incentives for investment.[3]

Heller then concluded, "Heavier emphasis on accelerated depreciation and more liberal investment tax credits—both with a proven tax record—should be the first order of tax business."[4]

With this kind of bipartisan support—the supply siders were of course delighted to agree with the need for business tax cuts—that section of the Reagan tax bill was assured an easy victory. Both policy makers and forecasters expected a strong boost in capital spending in 1982 which would serve as the backbone for the first stage of the Reagan economic recovery.

Indeed, forecasters were quite misled by some positive statistics during the early months of the Reagan administration. From the trough of the recession in June 1980 until August 1981, new orders for non-defense capital spending rose 10 percent in real terms. Although this was not quite up to par for robust recoveries, it still represented a significant increase in the face of ragged economic conditions, and hence it was not unreasonable to expect investment to mount a sustained drive once the tax cut had received the official blessing of the president's signature.

For during the five quarters of recovery in 1980 and 1981, which were sandwiched between the two recessions, the increase in capital spending actually outperformed the rest of the economy, an event that had never previously occurred in the beginning stages of any postwar recovery. This fact was featured prominently in forecasts made by this author in August 1981, while the editorial page of the *Wall Street Journal* also trumpeted this fact as a sign that capital spending was likely to propel the economy back into the orbit of rapid growth during 1982. "The surprising durability in the real economy," it said in August 1981, "is hard to understand except as a reaction to the new incentives on the horizon as a result of the Reagan tax policies."[5]

The events of August and September thus caught the entire economic forecasting profession by surprise. It was not merely a question of the business community being unimpressed with the tax cuts; they retreated and ran for cover. In the first two months after the tax cut was passed, new orders for non-defense capital goods plummeted *the full 10 percent* they had risen during the entire previous year. The economy was back to square one.

The degree to which this was unexpected can be gauged by considering the change in the consensus forecast during the latter half of 1981. As measured by Eggert Economic Enterprises, the predicted growth in real GNP for 1982 declined from 3.2 percent in July to 0.5 percent in December.[6] Bob Eggert, who has been compiling the consensus forecast for the past twenty years, conceded that never before in his experience had it changed so violently in a six-month period. Yet all this occurred even though the final form of the 1981 tax bill, with the very lucrative investment tax swapping and leaseback provisions, contained much larger incentives for capital formation than had been expected even a few weeks earlier.

Admittedly some sections of supply-side economics are still quite controversial. For example, the evidence that a reduction in tax rates will moderate wage demands and increase work incentives, which is presented in chapters 9 and 11, is still not accepted by a majority of economists even though the supporting evidence at the micro level is abundant. The idea that large deficits can stimulate the economy without increasing inflation as long as the total national saving rate rises is also not generally accepted. However, the one link in supply-side economics to which virtually all stripes of economists subscribe is that raising the rate of return on investment through tax advantages will stimulate capital spending. It was this noncontroversial theory that was used to support the reduction in the effective corporate tax rate in 1954, 1962, 1965, 1971, 1975, and 1979; these are discussed in greater detail in chapter 7.

Yet the business community appeared to have developed almost an allergic reaction to the 1981 tax cut as capital spending in constant dollars declined 8.2 percent during the next five quarters. If we are ever to solve the puzzle of why the Reagan attempt at supply-side economics failed, it is incumbent to understand why this supposedly strongest link failed to hold.

Myth 3: Investment Up

The hypothesis that businessmen did not approve of the president's general program is quickly dismissed. The Eggert consensus survey showed that as late as February 1982, long after the depth and severity of the recession had become apparent, economists rated the business tax cuts as 8 on a scale of 10, virtually unchanged from 8.1 six months earlier.[7] The *Industry Week* poll of chief executives taken in the fall of 1981 was even more definitive, revealing:

An overwhelming 90% of the survey respondents believe that the policies of the Reagan Administration "have a good chance of permanently changing the economic direction of the country". Among their encouraging conclusions:

83% believe inflation will be lower by 1984.
81% believe real economic growth will be higher.
68% say productivity will be enhanced.
62% say capital spending will increase significantly.
66% think overall corporate profitability will improve in the next year.
76% think the stock market will show better growth.[8]

Why the 1981 Business Tax Cuts Failed

In spite of this enthusiasm for Reaganomics in general and business tax cuts in particular, the business community was virtually unanimous in identifying late 1981 as a time for retrenchment, not expansion. In taking a cold, hard look at the events of 1981 without being burdened by the excess baggage of Reagan euphoria, the decline in investment perhaps should not have come as such a shock to the forecasting community. For previous experience of the postwar period had always indicated the following about investment behavior.

1. In the short run, changes in output will overwhelm financial variables. The economy was starting to move into another recession because of high interest rates even before the tax cut was ever signed by Reagan. Indeed, the National Bureau of Economic Research, the official arbiter in such matters, has since dated the peak of the cycle as July 1981.

2. Changes in either output or financial variables will have a proportionately much larger effect on investment when capacity utilization is high rather than when it is low; when the economy is in a boom rather than a recession.

3. Financial effects are asymmetrical. A sudden reduction in the rate of return will cause cancellations to occur much more quickly than an increase in this rate would cause capital spending to improve.

4. The increase in interest rates that had occurred during the previous two years—the Aaa corporate bond rate rose from 9.3 percent in 1979.3 to 14.9 percent in 1981.3—dwarfed the advantages of the business tax cuts.

5. Investment decisions take time to implement and are based on what happened last year, not what is currently happening and certainly not what is expected next year. It was this relationship that the Reagan people thought they had repealed, only to find it still held with as much force as ever.

The remainder of this chapter is basically an examination of these five points.

Let us first turn to the relationship between investment, output, and the rate of return. In the long run, a 1 percent change in output results in a 1 percent change in investment. Besides appearing to make common sense, the output/capital ratio has remained virtually constant over the entire postwar period, compared to a doubling of the output/labor ratio. In the long run, a 1 percent change in the rate of return also results in a 1 percent change in investment. While no long-term economic ratios exist to support this statement, it logically follows from the theory of profit maximization and also has been supported by a large body of empirical work, most notably by Dale Jorgenson.

The short-term results are much different, however, as the effects of changes in output are much larger and of the rate of return much smaller. The disproportionately large short-term effect of output can be easily explained by what economists call the accelerator principle. For those not familiar with the concept or who dozed through it in economics class, the underlying idea is quite straightforward. Assume that it takes ten machines to manufacture fifty xygots (the space-age equivalent of widgets). The demand for xygots now rises 10 percent this year, so that eleven machines are now needed. We also assume that two of the ten machines are replaced every year. This year, however, the firm buys three machines—two as replacements and one new—so that investment has risen by 50 percent even though demand has risen by only 10 percent. If demand stays at fifty-five xygots the firm will only need two machines the next year, so that investment declines one third in the following year even though sales have not fallen.

In real life changes are not this abrupt, because the increase in income and employment caused by producing an extra machine raises the demand for xygots even further. This process continues indefinitely if the demand for goods and society's ability to produce them grows apace. More often, the demand for xygot-producing machines outstrips the available supply, shortages and bottlenecks begin to develop, inflation rises, fiscal and monetary policy are tightened, and eventually another recession develops. However, investment initially responds more than proportionately to an increase in output and also falls more than output declines, as firms choose not to replace capital goods on the regular cycle. A 10 percent decline in output, in this example, would result in the decision not to replace one of the machines, in which case investment would decline by 50 percent.

Let us now consider an increase in the rate of return, either through a decline in interest rates or a tax cut. In either case, assume that the cost of funds to the firm for this particular investment declines from 10 percent to 5 percent.

Several positive results may occur because of this decline in costs. The firm may decide to replace its capital stock more quickly since newer capital goods are generally more productive. It may also decide, when replacing old equipment, to purchase a new machine with greater capacity, since the cost of capital per unit of output has declined. But both of these changes involve waiting for the replacement cycle. It is very unlikely that the firm will increase capacity if the economy is not expanding, for it might not be able to sell all of its additional output without cutting prices, thereby wiping out any gain in profit margins from lower capital costs. Hence a reduction in the cost of capital will not raise investment during periods of low capacity utilization.

As the replacement cycle eventually works its way through the entire stock of capital goods, the full effect of the lower cost of funds will be felt. Initially, however, the effect is much slimmer. This point will become obvious after the empirical evidence is presented on the differential effects of business tax cuts over the past twenty years during periods of high and low capacity utilization.

While both trend ratios and theoretical economics tell us that the long-run elasticities of investment with respect to output and the rate of return should both be unity, they tell us nothing about the short-run elasticities. The body of received empirical doctrine, however, indicates that in the first two years following an initial stimulus, a 1 percent increase in output raises investment by about 2 percent, while a 1 percent increase in the rate of return only raises investment by about ½ percent. Hence a 1 percent change in output would initially result in *four times* as great an impact on investment as would a 1 percent change in the rate of return.

Now suppose that the government undertakes a particular fiscal policy that causes people to save more and spend less. If this change were to result in equal percentage changes in output and interest rates, the initial effect would be to *depress* investment. Even if the interest rate effect were twice as large as the output effect, investment would still decline during the first two years after this policy were undertaken.

Thus even under the best of circumstances, a change in fiscal policy that increased personal saving by lowering consumption would initially have a negative effect on GNP. By the third year, the interest rate effect would start to match the output effect and would eventually outweigh it as the effect of the accelerator diminished. Furthermore, the other advantages of the tax cut, namely lower inflation and higher productivity, would also affect the economy favorably. Yet the first year weights are definitely tilted in favor of the negative effect of lower output. Furthermore, August 1981 was hardly the most favorable climate for investment in view of the ensuing recession and near-record high interest rates.

The economy had already suffered a severe shock in the second quarter of 1980 when the combination of high interest rates and the imposition of credit controls had caused real GNP to plummet at a record 10 percent annual rate. However, interest rates declined as much as 9 percent during that quarter, with the Treasury bill rate at one point falling all the way to 6½ percent. The federal funds rate declined from a 17.2 percent average in March to 9.0 percent in July, while the prime rate fell from 20 percent to 11 percent. For one fleeting instant—July 1980—inflation seemed to be licked, with the consumer price index registering a gain of only 0.1 percent (the initial release actually showed no change at all).

As a result of this temporary improvement in interest and inflation rates, the economy began to rebound quite rapidly, with real GNP increasing at a 4.6 percent annual rate during the three quarters from the third quarter of 1980 to the first quarter of 1981. This led many forecasters, who just a few months earlier had been predicting a prolonged recession and sluggish upturn, to write off the dip in the spring of 1980 as a temporary fluke brought on by credit controls and to predict that the economy was set for the type of vigorous upturn that usually occurs in the first year or two of recovery. If this traditional pattern had been repeated, capital spending would have started to increase sharply in the second half of 1981. It was this normal recovery pattern, rather than anticipation of the Reagan tax cuts, that actually accounted for the surge in new orders in early 1981.

As the spring of 1981 wore on, however, it became more and more apparent that this recovery would not follow the usual pattern, for real GNP declined 1.5 percent in the second quarter. In retrospect, this was caused by the record high interest rates in the fourth quarter of 1981 reacting with the usual two-quarter lag. Whether the cause was recognized at the time or not, businessmen could not ignore the fact that their sales were diminishing, which interjected a new note of caution in their planning by June or July.

Furthermore, even though the aggregate capital spending numbers had posted acceptable if not superlative gains over the past two years, much of the strength was concentrated in energy and telecommunications. The industrial heartland of the U.S. economy never recovered from the slump that started in the second quarter of 1979. By mid-1981 production in the key sectors of automobiles, metals, and construction was about 20 percent below the peak values of late 1978 or early 1979. With so much excess capacity, the demand for expansion and even modernization of capital goods in these industries paled. General Motors, which had earlier announced an extremely ambitious $40 billion capital goods program over the next five years, began to cut back just as the tax cuts were activated.

The decline in capacity utilization in these key industrial sectors carried with it a marked decline in corporate profits. Squeezed by high interest rates, rapidly rising wage rates, declining productivity, and the strength of the dollar—which diluted foreign earnings and made it more difficult to sell American goods abroad—profit margins* declined from 4.8 percent of GNP in 1978 to 3.7 percent in mid-1981, on their way down to a more than forty-year low of 3.5 percent in the first quarter of 1982. Indeed, the brunt of the declining rate of inflation was initially borne by shrinking profit margins, for productivity continued to stagnate and wage demands had not yet started to abate.

Hence the economic conditions of the time certainly were not ripe for a major investment boom. As is shown next, the slack economy essentially deadened much of the stimulus that would otherwise have stemmed from the business tax reductions.

Business Tax Cuts Work Better in Booms than Recessions

The lack of effectiveness of business tax cuts on investment during periods of slack demand or unfavorable financial conditions can best be illustrated by what happened in 1962. In that year President Kennedy proposed an 8 percent, and Congress passed a 7 percent, investment tax credit. In addition, depreciation lives were reduced by an average of 30 percent to 40 percent. As already mentioned in chapter 2, these tax cuts amounted to $2.4 billion, which at the time represented about 5 percent of total capital spending—that is, equivalent to about an $18 billion tax cut at 1982 levels of investment. This was a substantial breakthrough for the business community, especially coming from a Democratic president, House, and Senate.

Yet the response by the business community in 1962 and 1963 was hardly what could be termed encouraging. During the next four quarters, capital spending increased only 2.6 percent in real terms, compared with the 8.9 percent increase that had occurred in the four quarters *before* the tax cut went into effect. The two major reasons for this negative response were (a) the sluggish behavior of the economy, with the unemployment rate stuck at 5½ per-

*These are after-tax profits adjusted for the effects of inflation on inventories and capital assets.

cent (then considered unacceptably high) and capacity utilization rates around 80 percent, and (b) the collapse of the stock market culminating in May 1962, which was caused in its later stages by the angry confrontation between Kennedy and the steel industry.

The lackluster response of the business community to the 1962 tax reductions can be compared to the reaction to the reduction in the corporate income tax rate from 52 percent to 48 percent in 1964. This was followed by an 18 percent increase in real capital spending in 1965—a one-year record that still stands. The reasons, of course, were that the underlying economic situation was just the opposite of 1962. The economy was growing rapidly, unemployment was declining, and capacity utilization rates were improving. In the financial sector, interest rates had stabilized and the stock market was booming.

Another conclusion that might be drawn from the 1962–65 developments is that the corporate income tax cut is a much more powerful weapon for stimulating investment than is a change in the investment tax credit or depreciation lives. This is not an entirely hollow argument, since a reduction in corporate income tax rates is a more efficient tax cut; it does not incorporate any distortions that might favor one type of investment over another. For example, the investment tax credit applies only to equipment and not to plant and is not fully applicable for assets with shorter lives. Reductions in depreciation lives, while quite welcome, still do not fully compensate for the fact that depreciation allowances are inadequate during periods of severe inflation because they are based on historical rather than replacement cost. In fact, we have calculated that for every dollar of tax reduction, the investment response to changes in the investment tax credit or depreciation lives is only about 75 percent as great as that due to a reduction in corporate income taxes.

However, these essentially second-order effects are swamped by changes in output and interest rates. For example, the 1970s experience of the relative efficacy of the investment tax credit and depreciation vis-à-vis the corporate tax rate was diametrically opposite the experience of the early 1960s.

One of the first things Nixon did when he took office was to undo much of Kennedy's good work in the area of investment incentives by suspending the investment tax credit. This was billed at the time as an anti-inflationary device; later when the credit was reinstated, it was also billed as an anti-inflationary move because it improved productivity. The combination of 1969 suspension, the income tax surcharge, higher interest rates, and the winding down of the Vietnam War was enough to generate the first recession in almost ten years. The recovery that began in early 1971 was unexpectedly sluggish; and Nixon, beginning to panic from the polls that showed him trailing Edmund Muskie, decided to goad the economy with a number of stimulative programs. The main ones were a reinstatement of the 7 percent investment tax credit and a further 20 percent reduction in depreciation lives, which was done without the consent of Congress and thus later challenged in the courts but found to be valid. Unlike the 1962 experience, however, investment responded very handsomely, rising 8 percent and 15 percent in real terms in 1972 and 1973, respectively.

Even the naïve would not attribute all of this rise to the change in the investment laws themselves. Both years were marked by very strong growth, due to the artificial stimulation provided by the wage and price controls and the resulting reduction in interest rates. The country paid the price for this in 1974 and 1975 by suffering what at that time was the most severe recession of the postwar period. However, initially capital spending responded enthusiastically to the very changes in the tax laws that were so unimpressive in 1962 and 1963.

Conversely, the reduction in the corporate income tax rate from 48 percent to 46 percent in 1979 appeared to have no effect on capital spending at all, which actually declined 3 percent in real terms in 1980. Once again this was due to the recession and high interest rates, but if the tax cut had any positive effect on investment, it was well hidden.

It has thus been shown that one of the major reasons the business tax cuts did not work in 1981 was that the economy was entering another recession. Now let us consider how lowering the rate of return will cause investment to decline quickly, but increasing the rate of return will raise investment only with a substantial lag.

The best examples of this asymmetry occur in 1966 and 1969, when the investment tax credit was temporarily suspended. More recently politicians have realized that the tax credit is of maximum value as a long-term incentive to capital spending rather than a short-term control variable, but in the 1960s it was widely viewed along the lines of experiments tried in the Swedish economy, where tax incentives and penalties are routinely used to try to smooth cyclical fluctuations.

In any case, Johnson suspended the investment tax credit on October 10, 1966; for good measure he also reduced accelerated depreciation for structures. The effect on investment was almost immediate. Whereas capital spending had taken approximately two years to respond favorably to the investment tax credit, it started declining the very next quarter and continued to drop throughout 1967. Capital spending similarly plunged when the investment credit tax was suspended on April 18, 1969, although in this case an actual reduction did not set in until the fourth quarter. However, when the credit was reinstated in August 1971 and again when it was raised to 10 percent in March 1975, plant and equipment spending did not respond until almost a year later.

The reasons for this asymmetry are not hard to find. The decision to modernize or expand requires, at least in large bureaucratic corporations, several levels of planning and decision making. However, the decision to cancel—or at least to postpone—can be made almost immediately. For once the new capital goods have been received, they can in general be resold only at a very substantial discount; the risk/reward ratio is heavily skewed in the direction of not increasing capital stock during unfavorable economic conditions.

Cancellations of tax benefits are not the only type of change that can convince firms to act quickly. An even sharper method for reducing investment is to restrict credit, thereby forcing some firms out of the credit markets entirely. If the capital good is already ordered but the financing is suddenly withdrawn, or becomes so expensive that the profitability of the new investment would be lost, the decision to cancel can be made virtually overnight. The offer of expanded financing at a lower rate, on the other hand, simply does not carry the same message of urgency.

Thus another proximate cause of the decline in new orders, just as the Reagan tax bill was being signed, was the sharp rise in long-term interest rates; the Aaa corporate rate had risen from 12.8 percent in January to 14.9 percent in August of 1981. Even though the rate of inflation had started to diminish and money supply growth had been contained well within the Federal Reserve Board's target range, long-term interest rates continued to climb until the onset of the recession in October of that year reduced all rates. Here again the asymmetry worked against the Reagan administration; the fast-acting increase in interest rates overwhelmed the slow-acting benefits of the tax cut.

The increase in interest rates during 1981 was especially painful because of the declining movements in other economic factors. During periods of increasing inflation, one could at least argue that some of the sting of higher interest rates would be offset by the fact that the money would be paid back in depreciated dollars—although even this argument does not hold fully, since depreciation allowances are valued in historical instead of replacement costs, and thus the firm must eventually replace its capital stock in inflated dollars. However, during 1981 the underlying rate of inflation was gradually declining, thus boosting the real rate of interest from close to zero in late 1980 to over 5 percent by mid-1981. Similarly, a rise in interest rates when the demand for funds was surging could be explained, but an increase during a slackening of economic activity had not happened since the early 1930s.

With short-term rates approaching 20 percent during the summer of 1981, many firms realized that their highest rate of return could be earned by investing the funds in essentially riskless assets instead of purchasing new plant and equipment. This trade-off has always been present, but previously the gap between internal rates of return and market interest rates had been so great that even substantial changes in the latter did not cause the two rates to intersect.

Myth 3: Investment Up

Firms usually try to earn a rate of return on invested capital of 20 percent to 25 percent, although even this had recently slipped, as the rate of return on stockholders' equity for all manufacturing corporations during the previous four quarters (the second quarter of 1980 through the first quarter of 1981) had fallen to only 15 percent. Thus if market rates were to move from 5 percent to 8 percent, the gap would still be too large to influence most investment decisions. As market rates themselves approach the 20 percent level, however, the two rates began to coincide. By the summer of 1981 many firms had chosen the passive, safer investments.

In summary to this point, the business tax cuts contained in the Reagan 1981 tax package initially had little effect on investment because (a) the economy was headed into another recession at the time; (b) tax reductions have historically had very little effect on stimulating investment during periods of economic slack; (c) long-term interest rates had risen almost steadily during the past two years and were now approaching all-time peaks in both nominal and real terms; and (d) the actual benefits conferred on businesses by the tax cuts were far smaller than the penalties imposed by higher interest rates. Even if none of these had been true, however, the tax benefits still would not have stimulated investment immediately because of the simple fact that investment decisions take time to implement. Except for cancellations, changes in the principle variables that influence investment have never generated an immediate reaction.

Capital Spending Has Always Been a Lagging Indicator

Our general knowledge of how the economy responds to various stimuli, particularly with respect to the leads and lags involved, is pitifully small after almost thirty years of econometric experimentation. However, if there is one factor that has been consistently documented, it is that investment is a lagging indicator. Decisions made by committees involving hundreds of millions, if not billions, of dollars are not made overnight. Even after the orders are placed, a further substantial lag exists before the goods are actually delivered or the construction takes place. In the case of equipment, lags of six to twelve months are commonplace, whereas in the case of construction, the building must be designed, necessary permits obtained, and so forth before any work actually commences. For all these reasons, the record is clear—capital spending always lags, never leads, the recovery, as is shown in table 4.1. Except for 1955, it has always taken a full year before the upturn in investment has taken hold.

Capital spending has never increased in anticipation of good times ahead—and the 1981 tax cut was to be no exception. As mentioned earlier, the increase in new orders in early 1981 was not so much in anticipation of the new Reagan tax cut as it was the normal reaction to the beginning of what appeared to be a vigorous recovery starting in mid-1980.

None of this should be taken to imply that tax cuts that reduce the effective corporate income tax rate will never stimulate investment. In explaining why the August 1981 tax cuts were followed by a decline in capital spending in 1982, it must be remembered that under ordinary circumstances a reduction in tax rates will indeed produce an investment boom the next year.

However, it should have been perfectly clear that the behavior of the economy in 1981 did not even approximate normal behavior. Although the year got off to a promising start, real GNP declined in the second quarter and yet

TABLE 4.1

Relationship of GNP and Capital Spending During Early Stages of Recovery

Year of Recession	% Change in Real GNP[a]	% Change in Investment[b]
1954		
1st 4Q[c]	7.4	7.2
2nd 4Q[d]	2.6	12.7
1958		
1st 4Q	6.9	−1.9
2nd 4Q	4.1	9.4
1960		
1st 4Q	6.4	2.7
2nd 4Q	3.7	5.0
1970		
1st 4Q	4.7	−0.3
2nd 4Q	7.0	12.1
1975		
1st 4Q	6.7	−0.6
2nd 4Q	4.2	8.9

SOURCE: Calculated by Evans Economics, Inc.
NOTES:
[a]Percentage change in total GNP in constant dollars.
[b]Percentage change in capital spending excluding automobile purchases counted as investment, in constant dollars.
[c]1st 4Q refers to first four quarters of the recovery.
[d]2nd 4Q refers to second four quarters of the recovery.

Myth 3: Investment Up

interest rates took another giant step up. Profit margins declined sharply as real GNP dipped for the third time in three years. When it turned out that the increase in interest rates was far more powerful than the tax benefits, the game was over. The business community, while wholeheartedly applauding the thrust of Reaganomics, did nothing tangible to back up its enthusiasm with increased investment. The lack of capital spending virtually guaranteed that the economy would enter its second recession in two years, leading to a sudden and sharp escalation of federal budget deficit estimates to over $100 billion per year indefinitely. It was the belief that these huge deficits could be avoided which is the last great myth of supply-side economics, which we will now discuss in chapter 5.

CHAPTER 5

Myth 4: The Reagan Economic

Program Would Balance the Budget

by 1984

How Higher Growth Would Have Reduced the Deficit

Of all the promises issued by Reagan as a candidate, probably the one most cherished by the average American was the return to a balanced budget. While not affecting the average citizen directly, the budget deficit represented a deep-seated belief that runaway government spending has been largely responsible for the long-term secular increase in inflation and decline in productivity that has ravaged the economy since 1965. Thus while few demanded or expected an immediate turnaround, it was generally thought that with the proper fiscal discipline the budget could be balanced in two or three years. As already mentioned in chapter 1, two thirds of the economics forecast profession predicted in March 1981 that this goal could be accomplished by 1984. Thus it came as a distinct shock when, only six months later, the same economists were predicting not only that the budget could not be balanced by 1984 but that the deficits would increase steadily, and for the four-year Reagan term the cumulative total might even reach the staggering sum of $500 billion.

Myth 4: Balanced Budget by 1984

The Reagan team, of course, hastened to point out that the deficits were primarily a result of unexpectedly sluggish real growth, surprisingly low inflation rates, and unprecedented high real interest rates. Once again, none of these arguments is faulty. Taken together, however, they fall far short of explaining the gap between the original Reagan estimate of a balanced budget by 1984, his estimate one year later of a $90 billion deficit for that year, and the views of many private economists that the deficit would exceed $200 billion by FY 1984. The myth of how the budget could be balanced overwhelmed the reality—the fourth great myth of supply-side economics.

The balanced-budget myth actually incorporated two separate legends. First, and more straightforward, Reagan evidently believed that he could convince Congress to cut spending by the full amount originally proposed. The second part, which is slightly more complicated, revolves around the concept of reflows. Basically, the Reagan projections initially showed that much of the tax cut would be recouped by higher revenues stemming from the faster growth rates; this was based on a misunderstanding of what happened following the Kennedy-Johnson tax cut. Later these estimates were revised, but by then the political damage and loss of credibility were accomplished facts.

Yet before being too harsh on the Reagan forecasters, it should be pointed out that the general framework of reducing deficits through higher growth had previously been well established by previous Democratic administrations. In fact, Walter Heller had felt emboldened enough by the success of the Kennedy-Johnson tax cuts to popularize the concepts of fiscal drag and fiscal dividend. Federal government expenditures tended to grow at the same rate as GNP, he argued, while taxes grew faster because of the progressive nature of our income tax schedule. Thus if the government failed to keep spending more on new programs, it would run increasingly large *surpluses,* which would serve as a fiscal drag on the economy. This dilemma could be solved in one of two ways: either cut taxes further, or increase government spending at a faster rate. As Heller explained in 1966:

An average advance in GNP of just over 4 percent in real terms . . . will leave something over $7 billion of new revenue each year—a rise of nearly $40 billion between 1966 and 1971—to rear its ugly head as fiscal drag or, properly managed, its lovely head in the form of recurring fiscal dividends. The remarkable power of our Federal Revenue system is such that, if defense spending were to level off at the rate programmed in the fiscal 1967 budget, a potential fiscal drag would reach nearly $20 billion by fiscal 1970. . . . We would still be fighting a war overseas, and yet have to take deliberately expansionary fiscal steps to maintain the health of the economy at home. If we did not, we could find ourselves risking both war and recession in 1968.[1]

Heller went to some pains to point out that tax cuts were not always the proper remedy; at other times, increased spending for social welfare purposes might be a much higher priority. He specifically stated:

> I would hope that the tax cut lesson of the past few years has been learned wisely, but not *too* well. The on-target success of the 1964 tax cut should not blind us to the special circumstances that made massive tax cuts the clear choice over more rapid expenditure increases at that time—circumstances that may not repeat themselves in the near future.[2]

It is hard to believe in this day and age of triple-digit deficits that the question of how to spend those extra surpluses was ever a problem, yet the Heller logic remains sound under certain well defined circumstances. Specifically, at 1982 levels of GNP, the relationship between government spending, taxes, and deficits is as follows:

1. If real GNP increases 4 percent per year, if the rate of inflation remains unchanged, if government spending grows at the same rate as GNP, and if tax rates remain unchanged, then the deficit will shrink about $15 billion per year.
2. If government spending is held constant in real terms and the above economic assumptions continue to hold, then taxes could be cut by 4 percent per year and the deficit would still diminish by $15 billion per year. Assuming a two-thirds to one-third split between personal and business taxes, which is in line with the Kennedy-Johnson tax reductions (see chapter 2), this would imply about a 7 percent annual reduction in personal income tax rates.

However, if Reagan wanted to cut taxes more than that, either government spending would have to be reduced in real terms or the deficit would decline by less than $15 billion per year. Furthermore, if he wanted to increase defense spending 10 percent per year in real terms, as originally announced, then for the deficit to shrink $15 billion per year all other government spending would have to be cut 3 percent per year in real terms, since defense spending is slightly less than one fourth of the budget.

The $15 billion per year figure has been used as a benchmark because Carter bequeathed the legacy of a $60 billion budget deficit. Hence if Reagan were to dispose of it in equal annual installments by 1984, the required reduction each year would be $15 billion.

As is quite obvious in hindsight, virtually everything went wrong with the Reagan projections. Far from improving to 4 percent growth, the economy promptly went into another tailspin late in 1981 which lasted throughout 1982. Inflation declined sharply; and whereas most would count this as a plus, it had a material effect on ballooning the deficit, as is discussed in some detail later in this chapter. Interest rates, reflecting worsened expectations and the shortage of saving, moved higher even as inflation was diminishing.

But the economy alone cannot be blamed for the "unexpected" Reagan deficits. The above calculations clearly point out that even if the economy had performed precisely as expected, it would have taken a superhuman effort by Reagan and the Congress to have balanced the budget by 1984. The fact that personal income tax rates were cut 10 percent for three years in a row instead of 7 percent for four years in a row was only a minor part of the problem. More importantly, the 3 percent annual cuts in real terms for non-defense spending are pure surrealism. Never has any administration come close to matching these kinds of decreases; even Eisenhower could not manage to cut non-defense spending in real terms. Thus the two fatal flaws in the Reagan plan were (a) the amount that government spending could realistically be cut, and (b) the degree to which the economy would respond and the resulting revenue reflows that would result. When the carefully structured Reagan tax package turned into a free-for-all in the last-minute rush and all the sweeteners were thrown in (as discussed in detail later in this chapter), the entire concept of a balanced budget was blown sky-high—and the financial markets reacted accordingly. Yet the Reagan program was in serious trouble long before that ever occurred. The rest of this chapter explores in detail the plethora of errors in the original Reagan plan to balance the budget by 1984.

How—and How Not—to Pay for Higher Defense Spending

The federal government budget for FY 1982 was $725 billion. Of this sum, approximately $300 billion represented retirement benefits and Medicare, $200 billion represented defense expenditures, and $100 billion represented interest on the public debt, leaving only about $125 billion for all other categories of spending. One does not have to be a Ph.D. economist to realize that if the administration was serious about cutting spending, it had to attack the Big Three. Even cutting all other programs in half would not satisfy the requirements of a balanced budget under the assumptions of a 10 percent annual increase in real defense spending and no changes in retirement benefits, Medicare, or interest payments.

Of all the functions performed by government, both liberals and conservatives alike would agree that defending the country against enemy attack is at the top of the list. The proof of this, if one is needed, is that virtually no incumbent government has survived the loss of a war; in most cases, not only the political party but the form of government actually changes. Thus national defense spending is not something to be raised or lowered as a method of controlling the economy or balancing the budget.

Ever since the end of World War II, the nationalistic stance of the Soviet Union has required that the U.S. devote a relatively large proportion of its resources to defense expenditures. The USSR did not become any more peacelike during the 1970s, in spite of several alleged strategic arms limitations agreements, and the United States' decline in defense expenditures during the previous decade—they actually fell from $102 billion in 1969 to $65 billion in 1978 in constant dollars—certainly did not discourage the Russians from attacking Afghanistan and Poland.

The general tendency is to blame Carter for the decline in defense spending, but as is shown in figure 5.1, the decline actually occurred under Nixon and Ford; defense spending in real terms rose under Carter. The initial winding down of the defense budget was a reaction to Vietnam, a self-flagellation that this country was unworthy of its illustrious history and should not maintain the capability to wage major warfare. After 1972, however, this extreme viewpoint subsided and the main reason for cutting defense spending was much more pragmatic: it was very expensive, the budget was chronically in deficit, and pressing social programs seemed to use up an increasing share of the government tax revenues. In other words, the easiest way out of the budget dilemma was simply to let defense spending slide further. By 1978 the defense budget in constant dollars was actually $10 billion less than it had been in 1955.

This euphoria was rudely shattered by the Soviet incursion into Afghanistan. Jimmy Carter admitted that he had been badly fooled; and the rebuilding of our defense capability, which most Republicans had been pushing all along, received bipartisan support. As a result, a strong majority initially supported the Reagan aim to rebuild the defense establishment, even if it meant increasing real defense spending by 10 percent per year for the next five years. The aim was not really questioned; the real issue was simply how to pay for it. The cost would be roughly equivalent to the cost of another Vietnam; it would raise defense spending from 5.2 percent to 7.0 percent of GNP, just as this ratio had increased from 7.1 percent to 8.9 percent in the late 1960s. In absolute dollar terms, the amount spent would rise from $153 billion in 1981 to $363 billion per year in 1986, assuming an annual inflation rate of 8 percent. This buildup would still leave the ratio of defense spending/GNP below what it was *before* Vietnam, but it did represent a significant increase from current levels. Besides, most people still do have some money illusion, and $363 billion per year sounds like a lot to spend on defense.

Myth 4: Balanced Budget by 1984

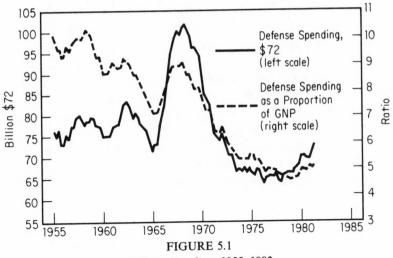

FIGURE 5.1

Defense Spending, 1955–1982

SOURCE: Prepared by Evans Economics, Inc.

Politically, the situation was unique in the sense that all other major military buildups have been in response to actual armed conflicts, whereas this one was aimed at regaining parity with the Soviets and hopefully forestalling any further armed conflict. From the economic point of view, the two situations were much the same except for one important difference—time was not that much of the essence, so the buildup could proceed at a more measured pace. This presumably would put less strain on the economy and result in less inefficiency and waste. But the basic question remained: how were we going to pay for it?

A review of all the other major military buildups—World War I, World War II, Korea, and Vietnam—reveal recurring patterns, although of course of much different magnitudes: higher taxes, some kind of credit restriction on consumption and, except for the Korean War, deficit spending. Non-defense programs generally were not cut back at all to pay for these wars, although until Vietnam they were a much smaller proportion of GNP. In 1955 non-defense federal government expenditures were 7 percent of GNP; and even in 1965 they were only 10 percent, compared to 18 percent in 1982.

The most frequent way to pay for wars always has been to raise taxes, a concept that goes back long before functional finance or any Keynesian ideas came into fashion. The Vietnam War was partially financed by a surcharge, and tax increases also have occurred during all other major wars. Because these seldom covered the full costs of the war, other methods have been used to restrain consumer buying, variously taking the forms of lessened availability of durables, credit controls or restrictions, or patriotic appeals to buy war bonds. But in any case consumer spending, particularly for durables, diminished. During the Vietnam War this decline was accomplished by two credit crunches that took the place of more formal controls.

But Reagan clearly did not wish to follow any of these avenues. Instead of tax increases, the whole thrust of his economic program was built around tax reductions. Credit controls, just tried the previous year, were found to be an unmitigated disaster and were in any case anathema to Reagan's concept of free market economics. This apparently left deficit spending, but that was also counter to the pledge to balance the budget by 1984. Having eschewed all the usual ways of paying for a war, Reagan was left with one, and only one, option—to diminish government spending in other areas.

Taking Dead Aim at the Entitlements Programs

Even this option could have been accomplished providing that Reagan had mounted a concerted effort to reduce the growth in Social Security payments and other entitlement programs. But both these had to be cut significantly for, as has been already shown, the other programs simply were not large enough for their reductions to pay for the increases in defense spending.

From an economic point of view, nothing about the currently structured Social Security system makes very much sense. First, the American public generally is now aware that it is not a trust fund at all but simply a scheme of transfer payments between generations. Indeed, a recent poll of Americans under forty-five years old showed that two out of three did not expect their Social Security benefits still to be available by the time they retired.[3] Second, there is nothing mandatory about sixty-five being the retirement age. If one simply updates the actuarial tables from 1935, when Social Security was originally introduced, the comparable age today would be seventy-two. Third, during the past decade Social Security recipients have benefited at the expense of almost every other sector of society. During 1972–81 the implicit GNP deflator increased 88 percent, the consumer price index—which overstates the true rate of inflation, particularly for the elderly—increased 106 percent, whereas per capita Social Security benefits increased by a whopping 187 percent, as is shown in table 5.1. Fourth, there is no reason why add-ons to Social Security benefits—disability, health, death benefits, aid to college youth, and so on—need to expand at the same explosive rate as the basic retirement program.

TABLE 5.1
Overindexation of Social Security

| | Social Security Payments | | Increase in CPI, Previous year % change[a] | Increase in Population Over 65 % change[a] | Implicit GNP Deflator[a], % change | Increase in Average Hourly Earnings[a], % change | Overindexed Additional Benefits Based on CPI, % change |
	Dollars (Billions)	% change					
FY 1972	38.0		3.3	2.2	4.2	6.2	16.4
FY 1973	46.6	22.6	6.2	2.3	5.7	6.2	5.1
FY 1974	53.2	14.2	11.0	2.7	8.7	8.0	1.4
FY 1975	61.5	15.6	9.1	2.4	9.3	8.4	2.3
FY 1976	70.3	14.3	7.3	3.0	6.5	9.6	4.4
FY 1977[b]	81.1	15.4	6.5	2.4	5.8	7.6	1.0
FY 1978	89.3	10.1	7.7	2.4	7.3	8.1	1.0
FY 1979	99.4	11.3	10.6	2.4	8.3	8.0	1.0
FY 1980	113.7	14.4	14.0	2.4	9.9	9.0	1.0
FY 1981	134.1	17.9					
Percent Increase 1972–81	252.9		106.1	23.1	88.3	98.1	39.1

SOURCE: Calculated by Evans Economics, Inc.
[a]Calculated as the percentage of change during the previous fiscal year adjusted for the reporting lag used for the CPI calculation (that is, 1972–76 calendar year; 1977–81 1st quarter over 1st quarter).
[b]Five-quarter increase because of transitional quarter, but $81.1 billion figure does not include transitional quarter payment.

In order to see how these programs have proliferated, let us go back to 1955, the last year when Social Security benefits simply represented old-age pension payments. In 1982 total Social Security benefits including Medicare (the figures in table 5.1 exclude Medicare) totaled $203.3 billion. In 1955, by comparison, they totaled only $4.9 billion. Even if these benefits had been fully indexed, using the biased CPI, and taking into account the fact that the number of elderly people grew at a 2.3 percent annual rate over the 1955–81 period compared to 1.2 percent for the population at large, the total benefits in 1982 still would have been only $31 billion if the basic program had remained unchanged. The additional $172 billion represents the expansion in the various Social Security programs and the effects of overindexing.

The first major boost in Social Security benefits occurred in 1956, when then Majority Leader Lyndon Johnson, preparing his thirteen-point program for a drive he hoped would eventually lead him to the presidency, proposed adding disability insurance to Social Security benefits. The program was bitterly opposed by President Eisenhower, but since he had lost his clout with Johnson by vetoing the natural gas deregulation bill, disability insurance passed by a narrow margin. Note the damage this incurred—it distorted our energy policies for the next thirty years *and* started transfer payments on a growth pattern that has never been reversed.

The second change in the Social Security program occurred in 1966, when President Johnson pushed through Medicare, this time without substantial opposition since the Republicans had publicly immolated themselves with the

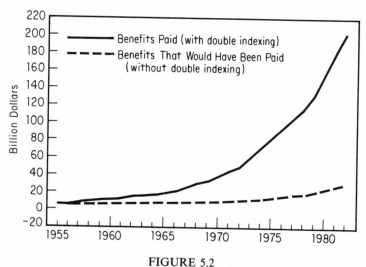

FIGURE 5.2

Social Security Benefits, 1955–1982

SOURCE: Prepared by Evans Economics, Inc.

nomination of Barry Goldwater. The third occurred in 1972 when Nixon pushed Social Security benefits up 20 percent, goaded perhaps in part by a Hubert Humphrey campaign speech to Florida retirees stating that benefits should be raised 25 percent. It was this flagrant politicking that caused Congress to decide that any latitude for election-year raises must be removed. Discretionary increases were out, and Congress passed legislation to confine any future increase in benefits to the growth in inflation.

However, Congress made a serious methodological error, with the result that benefits were indexed to *both* prices and wages. In other words, benefits only rose with inflation but also increased proportionately with the average gain in wage rates. This resulted in a 13.8 percent average in benefits for the 1974–77 period in addition to the 22.6 percent largesse passed in 1972, as is shown in table 5.1. Not until 1977 did Congress decide to curb this profligacy and bring benefits back in line with inflation. The 1 percent gain per year since 1977 in excess of inflation and the number of elderly, as is indicated in table 5.1, represents expanded coverage through increases in benefits to college students, earlier retirement patterns, and other smaller changes in the programs.

Thus Social Security benefits have outpaced even the overstated rate of inflation as measured by the CPI by almost 40 percent over the past decade. If the rise in per capita benefits is compared to the increase in the implicit GNP deflator, the gap is an even larger 52 percent; and they have risen 45 percent faster than average hourly earnings, the factor that is ultimately the tax base for supporting these payments.

In light of these economic facts, a number of alternative proposals have been suggested. Realizing that it is both politically and morally repugnant to terminate benefits for those already receiving them, this author favors a plan of a gradual increase in the retirement age from 65 to 70 for those who have not yet retired. With the improvements in health-care levels in general and geriatric medicine in particular, there is no good reason why 65 should still be the retirement age. We propose increasing that age to 70 in small steps—six months per calendar year, for example, so that the retirement age would rise to 65½ in 1983, 66 in 1984, and so forth. Once again, this would not prejudice the benefits of anyone currently retired or disabled, and it would permit those approaching retirement age to plan their careers and lives accordingly.

Such a program could be easily explained to working-aged people on the grounds that whereas their benefits would be reduced, the solvency of the system would thus be guaranteed. We think such a plan would be applauded, not defeated. People are finally beginning to realize that benefits cannot continue to increase forever, and the time to act is right now—before the deficit and the bankruptcy of the Social Security system get completely out of hand.

In addition, a more realistic indexation scheme is clearly indicated for those actually receiving the benefits. This easily could be done by having the Bureau of Labor Statistics prepare an index of the costs of living for the elderly. Presumably it would have a much lower weight for new houses, since few over sixty-five buy new houses, and for medical care, since most of these expenses are covered under Medicare and Medicaid. In addition, we would propose that the 40 percent overstatement in the indexation formula over the past decade be gradually phased out by 1992.

The savings to such a plan are enormous. At current levels of inflation and the number of elderly, each year that the retirement age is raised saves about $11 billion in benefits. Hence, increasing the age to seventy would save about $50 billion per year at 1982 levels—the curve is not quite linear. By 1992 the saving would rise to $130 billion per year. Removing the 40 percent premium included in existing payments would save an additional $120 billion per year by 1992. As a result, Social Security payments and Medicare would increase only from $203 billion in 1982 to $276 billion in 1992 instead of ballooning to $526 billion per year, which will indeed occur if inflation rises 7 percent per year over the next decade and no changes are made in the existing laws. Thus our reforms would save a whopping *$250 billion per year* by 1992.

However, the sad fact of the matter is that no meaningful cuts in Social Security or Medicare were ever seriously considered by either the Reagan administration or Congress. Reagan did try to lop a few of the extraneous programs off Social Security, but these met with such furious opposition that the attempt to implement even minor changes was finally discarded.

Reagan has been more insistent about pushing for budget cuts in the remaining 20 percent of the budget, and a few reductions in welfare, job training programs, and grants to state and local governments were passed by Congress in 1981. When these failed to make an observable dent in the size of the budget deficit—after all, they amounted to less than 2 percent of the total budget—Reagan then appealed to Congress to make these cuts deeper. This time, however, the horror stories mounted about how the indigent were suffering and how the cuts had a perverse effect; slashing of benefits now meant that poor people were better off going on welfare than trying to earn part of their income. Thus Congress balked in 1982 and refused to pass any further meaningful reductions in income security programs.

With no major spending cuts in sight, the entire hope of the Reagan administration for a balanced budget with higher defense spending then hinged on some miracle that tax receipts would somehow bridge the gap. Some of the true believers still held tight. Ignoring the fact that the budget had returned to balance the year after the Kennedy-Johnson tax cut precisely because government spending did not increase, they clung to the scant hope of the Immaculate Reflows.

Can Tax Cuts Pay for Themselves?

The idea that tax cuts would pay for themselves—that a reduction in tax rates would raise tax receipts—strikes many people as akin to the alchemist's pledge to turn lead into gold, and not without good reason. Before dismissing this idea as a complete piece of sophistry, however, those circumstances where tax rates and tax receipts do move in the opposite direction should be noted.

To do this it is necessary to consider the concept of elasticities. Tax rates and tax receipts will move in the same direction if the income or sales elasticity—the percentage change in income or sales divided by the percentage change in tax receipts—is less than unity. If, for example, tax rates increase 10 percent, tax receipts would go up as long as sales declined by less than 10 percent.

It is a general rule that the size of the elasticity is directly related to the degree to which close substitutes are available. If a very close substitute exists, the elasticity is likely to be quite large. For example, a tax on beer cans but not beer bottles would result in most people switching to bottles. A tax on beer but not wine would induce more people to drink wine. A tax on all alcoholic beverages would have a much smaller effect, the only alternatives being a reduction in alcohol consumption or a move to the bootleg variety. Whereas both of these are theoretically possible, increases in excise taxes on alcoholic beverages generally have only a minuscule effect on consumption; the elasticities are usually 0.1 or less, which means that a 1 percent increase in the tax rate results in a decline of 0.1 percent or less in the quantity purchased.

In the vast majority of cases, the change in income or sales is quite modest relative to the change in tax rates, partly because governing authorities try to raise taxes on those items when the elasticity is very small. Sometimes, however, they miscalculate. If the gasoline tax goes up 6 cents a gallon, people grumble about it a lot but their consumption of gasoline hardly changes. If, however, the D.C. government raises taxes 6 cents a gallon but Maryland and Virginia do nothing, it is a completely different story. Motorists head for the nearest suburban gasoline pump, D.C. revenues actually fall, and eventually the District government has to rescind the increase.

Another example of high tax rates being counterproductive is the 23 cent per pack tax on cigarettes in New York City, which encourages smuggling from North Carolina where the state tax is only 2 cents a pack. No exact estimates of the amount of cigarettes smuggled into New York City are available, for obvious reasons, but informed estimates put the figure at least at one half and possibly as high as two thirds of total consumption. If New York City would cut its tax rate in half, revenues would probably increase. It is not clear why the city refuses to do this, except that might expose the amount of corruption which actually does exist and thus embarass all concerned.

These changes in excise tax rates, however, are used only for illustrative purposes and do not really relate to the question at hand, which is whether broad-based reductions in personal income tax rates would cause a significant increase in the amount of taxable income. With the framework developed above, it would at first seem that the elasticity would be very small. For the taxpayers are apparently faced with a very meager choice of substitutes: not working as hard, not declaring the income at all, or avoiding taxes by sheltering income.

The first possibility, that tax rate cuts will pay for themselves because people will work harder and longer, is an illusion that fades quickly when the empirical results are examined. This is not to say that these effects do not exist at all; that claim is just as foolish as automatically assuming a zero effect. However, they are not very large. The body of empirical evidence discussed in chapter 9 indicates that the elasticity is about 0.2, meaning that a 1 percent reduction in tax rates would cause about a 0.2 percent increase in work effort, which would raise revenues by less than 0.1 percent. Although this is not negligible, it turns out to be the least important of the various reasons why tax revenues increase when rates are cut.

The second possibility, that people will declare more of their incomes at lower tax rates, has some empirical foundation but similarly falls far short of generating the needed revenue for tax cuts to pay for themselves. No formal estimates of elasticities are available, but based on IRS and other data, they are also believed to be less than 0.1 percent. A more detailed discussion of this point is given in chapter 9.

The third possibility is that at higher tax rates people do shelter their income and would utilize these shelters less intensively at lower tax rates. This makes much more sense from an economic viewpoint because here, unlike in the first two cases, very good substitutes are plentiful. To pick just one example, anyone can invest his funds in an altogether legal tax-free municipal bond and not pay any federal income taxes at all on the interest received. The rate of interest is usually 75 percent to 80 percent of a comparable federal government or corporate bond yield, which means that anyone in the 20 percent to 25 percent or higher tax bracket is obviously better off with a municipal bond. Indeed, the 1981 tax reduction act provided so many loopholes for tax reduction that shortly after its passage the rate on munis briefly soared over 90 percent of the yield on comparable government bonds.

Similarly, the investor can choose assets where the return is earned through capital gains rather than through interest or dividend payments. Growth stocks, real estate, gold and silver, objets d'art, and so forth are the preferred type of investment in this situation. Yet another possibility is investing earnings abroad, where they are subject to much lower tax rates. The last is also perfectly legal, providing that the taxpayer declares the funds anytime he moves $5,000 or more out of the country. This last restriction is particularly ludicrous; almost anyone can find a Swiss company to send him an invoice for $100,000, for example, for services rendered. As the result of these alternatives, virtually no one pays a marginal tax rate of more than 35 percent, even though until October 1981 the stated top rate was 70 percent.

In other words, as long as lowering tax rates results in (a) switching investment income from tax-free into taxable sources, (b) reducing dependence on tax shelters, (c) switching assets from nonproductive into productive assets (that is, from gold or silver into bonds or stocks), or (d) reclassifying income from capital gains to wages, evidence of the backward-bending tax curve for upper income tax rates is likely to be found.

Thus unlike broad-based tax cuts, reducing upper-income tax rates does increase tax receipts, precisely because of the availability of close substitutes. Upper-income tax rate cuts are thus a win-win situation: people pay less tax, the Treasury gets more revenues, incentives are strengthened, and capital flows are improved. This important link of supply-side economics is discussed in greater detail in chapter 9, where it is shown that the reduction of the top marginal rate from 70 percent to 50 percent generates an extra $3 billion per year in tax revenues for the Treasury. Furthermore, results presented there indicate that the top marginal tax rate that would maximize revenues is between 25 percent and 35 percent; below that, a decline in personal income tax rates would result in a loss in revenues.

Thus the idea that taxing the rich less would produce more revenue is true, but the reverie ends there. For the Reagan administration tax cut was of course a broad-based tax cut, with most of the actual reductions below the 25 percent marginal rate. Hence, the gains in upper-income tax cuts were only a ripple in the $120 billion pond of general tax reduction. Furthermore, special upper-income tax cuts were not part of the original game plan, as the idea to cut the top rate from 70 percent to 50 percent all in the first year was added only at the last minute.

No serious economist really believes that across-the-board tax rate cuts will pay for themselves through an increase in reported, taxable income. By comparison, the general idea of reflows—that at least a good part of the tax cut can be recouped because of the higher level of economic activity—is still popular in many circles. This argument is not just the province of doctrinaire supply-side ideologues but has its roots in the Democratic mainstream. We next consider the situations under which reflows are, and are not, significant.

Reflows from Cutting Taxes

The general idea of reflows is that cutting taxes stimulates the economy through higher spending, thus creating more output, employment, and personal and corporate income. A certain proportion of that income gets paid back in taxes, so that the actual increase in the deficit is significantly less than the original cut in taxes.

The importance of these reflows can be gauged by first considering some simple numerical examples. Federal tax receipts are currently close to 20 percent of GNP. Assume that GNP is $1,000 so that taxes are $200. Now suppose tax rates are cut by 10 percent; on an *ex ante* basis that would reduce taxes to $180. Furthermore assume that the multiplier effect is 2, which means that every $1 of tax reduction raises GNP by $2. This is also a fairly common estimate. In this case, GNP rises $40, and since taxes are 20 percent of GNP, tax receipts rise $8. Since $8 is two fifths of the original $20 tax cut, the reflows in this case are 40 percent.

It should be obvious that the higher the tax burden the more likely it is that the reflows will pay for themselves. In the previous example, if taxes had been 30 percent, the reflows would have been 60 percent. A country where taxes are more than 50 percent of GNP, such as Sweden, probably would increase revenues by cutting tax rates. If, on the other hand, tax rates were cut to zero, it is clear that tax receipts would also fall to zero no matter how beneficial were the other aspects of tax reduction. Thus proximity to the backward-bending part of the tax curve is very much a function of the current level of the overall tax burden.

In terms of the real world, the multiplier over a one to two year period is usually estimated to be about 2, although it does depend on what causes the initial stimulus and the reaction of the monetary authorities. However, it is seldom higher than 2. A multiplier of 5 would be necessary for a tax cut to pay for itself in the current U.S. economy, since taxes are about 20 percent of GNP, and such a value is clearly outside the range of reasonableness.

While the preceding simple example is a useful pedagogical device, it contains one major flaw, namely that prices are assumed to remain unchanged. For the stimulus caused by a tax cut might well raise prices, particularly if it were a demand-side tax cut. A reasonable estimate is that the 4 percent increase in GNP in the previous example would raise prices by 1 percent in the absence of supply-side effects. If that occurred, tax receipts would rise by an additional $2 because of higher inflation and bracket creep. In this case the reflows would be 50 percent rather than 40 percent.

Myth 4: Balanced Budget by 1984

So far it has been assumed that taxes and income rise proportionately. As a matter of fact, taxes are likely to rise faster than income in a growing economy for two reasons. First, the United States has a progressive tax system, which means that the tax rate rises as income increases. This system was originally designed under the notion of equity: the rich should pay a larger proportion of their income in taxes, although some would question the equity involved in any case. However, the progressive system works just as well if inflation pushes the taxpayer into a higher bracket; the tax table does not know whether the increase in income is due to more purchasing power or simply higher inflation. Second, as prices increase, book profits rise more than proportionately, although this too is eventually a sham transaction because the gain in profits comes from increasingly undervalued fixed costs that must eventually rise with inflation. Since the marginal corporate profit tax rate is 46 percent compared to the marginal personal income tax rate of about 30 percent, tax receipts initially go up when income is redistributed from labor to capital.

The generally accepted estimate of the progressive tax structure shift for the U.S. economy is an elasticity of about 1.5, which means every 1 percent increase in nominal income caused by higher inflation raises federal tax receipts by 1.5 percent. If higher prices are accompanied by a major shift to profits, which would occur if the economy is growing rapidly, the total elasticity can rise to 2 for a year or two. With inflation rising 1 percent because of the tax cut stimulus, taxes could thus increase up to twice as fast, or 2 percent. That would push reflows from 40 percent of the tax cut up to 60 percent.

Some supply siders claimed that the reflows with the Reagan tax cuts would be even greater than 60 percent. Jude Wanniski, for example, approvingly quotes "the Kemp assumptions that the lower tax rates would expand the private sector fast enough to bring about an actual increase in revenues."[4] The Wanniski-Kemp reasoning was as follows. Whereas ordinary tax cuts simply increase GNP by a multiplier of 2 through higher spending, the Reagan tax cuts should have a much larger multiplier for two reasons. First, output and employment would increase from the work incentive effects as well as the demand effects. Second, the three-year tax cut horizon would signal more permanence in fiscal policy, and hence individuals and businessmen would be able to plan ahead with greater assurance than would be the case under a one-time tax cut. With these assumptions, perhaps the multiplier would be as large as 3. Kemp and the others did not think prices would rise; but they did apply the 1.5 elasticity to the gains in real income, which is a debatable but not necessarily erroneous assumption. Under these conditions, the reflows could reach 90 percent, virtually close enough to unity to say that the tax cut paid for itself.

The reflow calculations are not particularly unreasonable. Reflows are one of the ingredients that balanced the budget the year after the Kennedy-Johnson tax cuts, although the spending pause was more important. But they did not work for the Reagan program for two reasons. The expansionary effects of the tax cuts were overridden by tight monetary policies, as has been already indicated. And the tax cuts were accompanied by a sharp decline in inflation. This turns out to make a crucial difference, as will be discussed next.

How Lower Inflation Raises the Deficit

For a constant level of government spending, a decline in the rate of inflation initially leads to bigger rather than smaller deficits. This turns out to be a matter of simple arithmetic and is a case of reverse bracket creep, as illustrated in the following example.

Jones has an income of $30,000. He pays $6,000 in federal income taxes and his top marginal bracket is 30 percent. Now let us assume that prices decline by 10 percent and so does Jones's nominal income. He is actually better off, because he drops back to the 25 percent marginal tax bracket and his average tax rate declines to 18 percent, or $4,860. While his after-tax nominal income has declined from $24,000 to $22,140, with prices down 10 percent the purchasing power of that income has risen to $24,600, a 2.5 percent increase. The federal government collects $1,140 less in taxes, so the budget deficit widens. It would be fatuous to say that the resulting larger deficit is inflationary.

Of course prices still continued to rise under Reaganomics, but at a much slower rate. Inflation declined from 13.5 percent in 1980 to 6.2 percent in 1982, so the analogy is appropriate.

Thus what has happened under Reagan is that even if the economy had responded handsomely to the tax cuts—if monetary policy had not interfered and the multiplier of 2 had held—the reduction in inflation was so dramatic that both personal and corporate income taxes were much lower than they would have been had double-digit inflation remained intact. Indeed, corporate profits taxes have declined sharply in absolute as well as relative terms in 1981 and 1982.

Thus the reduction in inflation—one of the most important benefits of the Reagan administration—created the side effect of enlarging budget deficits; this did not have so harmful an economic impact but carried a devastating psychological impact, particularly since the country was originally promised a balanced budget by 1984.

Let us now return to our numerical example, where the tax cut multiplier is 2 and tax receipts are 20 percent of GNP. This time, however, instead of prices increasing as a result of the tax cut, let us assume that they decline 4 percent, which is indeed what happened to the rate of inflation in 1981. Thus nominal GNP, instead of rising from $1,000 to $1,040 because of the tax cut, remains at $1,000. However, because of the tax cut, tax receipts have fallen from $200 to $180. The *ex post* deficit is just as large as the original cut; *the reflows have completely disappeared.*

That example is based on a strong positive response in real GNP. In the case of the 1981–82 Reagan tax cuts, the economy hardly grew at all, with corporate profits taking a nose dive. Worse yet, interest rates continued to rise even as inflation abated. The Treasury got lower tax receipts from declining inflation but no payoff from higher income because tight monetary policy choked off the expansion. When these other negative factors are included, it is small wonder that the deficit widened steadily.

One major reason the budget deficit ballooned from $60 billion in FY 1981 to over $180 billion in FY 1983 was that Congress was much more enthusiastic about cutting taxes than reducing government spending. However, the budget deficit will always bulge when inflation starts to decline, no matter how well fiscal policy is organized. We have already indicated how reverse bracket creep will widen the deficit. In addition, during a period of declining inflation, the cutbacks in government spending lag behind the reduction in tax receipts, for the latter are based on the current level of income and prices, while most spending programs are based on last year's level of prices. The method of indexing Social Security is a perfect example. During the four quarters from 1981.3 through 1982.2, when inflation averaged 6.8 percent, benefits were based on the rate of inflation from 1980.2 through 1981.1, which was 11.2 percent, thus creating almost a 4½ percent gap between the rise in spending and receipts. Similarly, interest rates, especially long-term rates, follow the rate of inflation over the past three years and thus invariably lag behind declines in inflation even in the absence of large budget deficits. Thus during the transition period from higher to lower inflation rates, the bulge in the budget deficit appears even worse than would be indicated by the underlying economic conditions.

Overdosing on Tax Reductions

Although the 1981 tax reduction bill contained many beneficial aspects, it was far from the optional size or shape. For in the last-minute dealings to get his tax-cut bill passed, Reagan agreed to an additional $25 billion worth of tax cuts that accomplished very little in terms of saving or incentives. The major offenders can be categorized as follows:

Marriage-penalty relief, 10 percent exclusion up to $3,000
All Savers certificates
Windfall-profits tax credit up to 2 barrels/day
25 percent tax credit for research and development
Swapping and leaseback of investment tax credits to firms otherwise unable to utilize these credits

The marriage-tax penalty cannot be solved equitably as long as there is a progressive income tax system, for the following dilemma will always exist. Consider three employees and taxpayers A, B, and C, each of whom is paid $30,000 per year for doing the identical job. One day B and C decide to get married. Should their tax burden increase?

Before jumping to the conclusion that the answer should be "definitely not," let us point out that if their tax burden does not rise, this implies that the remaining single, A, must pay a much higher marginal tax rate for any given level of income than the married couple B and C. Before 1977 that is exactly the situation that existed, a situation that led to the outcry that tax policy was discriminatory against single people. The resulting change provided an economic disincentive for marriage. However, relief from the marriage-tax penalty pushes the pendulum in the other direction.

The problem, it turns out, can never be resolved to everyone's satisfaction unless we move to a proportional income tax system. However, removing this penalty up to $3,000 per couple costs the Treasury about $8 billion per year.

The All Savers certificates introduced in October 1981 turned out to help neither the thrift institutions nor the housing industry, nor did they raise personal saving. They did, however, result in a $5 billion raid on the federal Treasury. Seldom has such a bill cost so much yet benefited so few.

The 25 percent tax credit on Research & Development (R&D) spending is another one of those ideas that sounds terrific in principle. After all, the relative decline in R&D spending is one of the main reasons for lower productivity growth over the past fifteen years. However, this credit makes no distinction between R&D for logical circuitry and R&D for new toothpaste. The only area in which it discriminates at all is that the R&D cannot be undertaken for projects in the humanities or social sciences, which was clearly a slap at the liberal-tinged think tanks and research institutes of the 1970s.

This credit may spur some increase in R&D but has primarily turned into just one more tax shelter. Admittedly, the R&D tax shelter has been around for years and has been used for (among other things) motion pictures, books, records, computer programs for options trading, a new version of the Learjet, and the ill-fated DeLorean sports car. But more innovative and extensive uses sprang up after the passage of the 1981 tax bill, with a resulting revenue loss to the Treasury expected to reach $5 billion per year.

The transferable investment tax credit, more commonly known as safe harbor leasing, is just a resuscitated version of the refundable investment tax credit, a Carter idea originally hooted down by the Republicans. It is primarily intended to benefit the losers—those firms that do not make enough profits to utilize the tax credits. If tax refund dollars are scarce resources, as they certainly turned out to be, it would seem more logical to spend these tax dollars to benefit firms making money instead of those that are losing it. This tax break was essentially gutted by the 1982 tax-increase bill, but it cost the Treasury about $6 billion the one year it was in existence.

In conclusion, the grand Reagan scheme to balance the budget unraveled skein by skein. First, the President refused to consider any substantive change in Social Security or other retirement benefits and was unable to get Congress to agree to any other meaningful spending cuts. Second, he tacitly encouraged the Fed to tighten up on interest rates, thereby raising government spending and depressing the economy. Third, he permitted approximately $25 billion per year of additional tax relief to creep into the bill under the guise of last-minute bargaining for votes. When it turned out that the bill also contained a commitment to indexation beyond 1984, the markets reeled in despair, and the next recession was on its way—thereby further depressing government receipts and augmenting expenditures.

In trying to sell his FY 1982 budget, Reagan made one last pitch to the voting electorate, namely that cutting taxes would in the long run cut spending because Congress could not spend the revenues it did not have. While this claim has a certain rhetorical charm, it is unfortunately at odds with the facts. Congress has been perfectly adept at spending revenues it has not had—from 1970 to 1981, the budget deficit averaged 9.1 percent of federal spending through good and bad years alike. Furthermore, the huge Reagan deficits seemed almost to have a perverse effect on many members of Congress. Whereas elected representatives might well cut spending by the last $10 billion in order to balance the budget, they would be unwilling to risk voter resentment by canceling popular programs if the resulting cuts would still leave the deficit at $90 rather than $100 billion.

Thus the last great myth of Reaganomics was exposed. With massive tax cuts, higher defense spending, and tight monetary policy, the budget clearly could not be balanced by 1984. Yet whereas the original promise to balance the budget was a crowd pleaser, it was not an economic requirement. For although budget deficits caused by profligate government spending are clearly inflationary, those caused by a reduction in the rate of inflation, a slowdown in the economy, and tax cuts that stimulate saving and investment are not at all inflationary. Hence once the redundant restraint of the balanced budget is removed, a set of policies begins to emerge which, although it still functions under the rubric of supply-side economics, begins to make some economic sense. The third part of this book turns to the realities of supply-side economics and shows how, given the proper amount of time to nurture, they can still be salvaged to generate long-term balanced non-inflationary growth for the U.S. economy.

CHAPTER 6

Higher Rates of Return

Will Raise Personal Saving

Overview

The Reagan economic plan turned out to be such a disappointment that many economists, Republicans as well as Democrats, were soon ready to give up on supply-side economics altogether. To do so, however, would have been an even worse mistake than to accept the Reagan programs that were implemented. It is all too easy to forget how close the economy was to collapse at the start of the Reagan administration; how the flight of money from productive investments into fixed-supply assets—which allegedly would always outperform inflation—would have robbed the country of what remaining economic vitality it still possessed.

Supply-side economics is a rich and complex discipline, involving the interaction of virtually *all* facets of the economy as they affect productivity, inflation, and real growth. Besides the critical decisions about saving and investment, supply-side economics also concerns itself with work effort, incentives, and labor productivity; the size and scope of the government sector; the regulation and efficacy of markets; and the interaction of the international as well as the domestic sphere.

However, for most people, supply-side economics is identified with the tax cuts promulgated by the Reagan administration especially that 30 percent

—later reduced to 25 percent—across-the-board reduction in personal income tax rates. Whereas this is not the only element of supply-side economics, it would be foolish to deny that this tax cut is the cornerstone of the entire program. And though the success of the tax cut does not by itself guarantee that the economy would be able to generate faster growth with lower inflation, it is true that if the tax cut does not work as claimed, this goal will not be attainable.

It is also the tax cut that has been most scorned and ridiculed both among economists and by the press. Few have gone so far as Vice-President Bush, who called the program "voodoo economics" and claimed that it would raise the inflation rate to 30 percent. But many mainstream economists have contended that far from moderating the rate of price increase, the tax cut would be inflationary.

For example, Otto Eckstein testified early in 1981 that "business tax cuts stimulate capital formation and reduce . . . the underlying rate of inflation. Tax cuts to individuals increase disposable income and stimulate consumption. Personal tax cuts will tend to be inflationary."[1] *Business Week,* far more acerbic about the whole idea, called it "moonshine."[2] And Walter Heller, actually somewhat more cautious, conceded that the first year of the tax cut would not raise inflation, but said that "my real concerns about the inflationary impact of taxes come in the second and third stages of the Kemp-Roth rocket."[3]

The tax cut was always opposed by liberals on the grounds that it would accrue mainly to the rich, but for a time many of them held their fire to see whether "trickle-down" would work and all of society would be better off. When it became clear that the economy was mired in a severe recession and the unemployment rate was headed toward 10 percent, liberals reacted heatedly, with many of them disparaging the "moral bankruptcy" of the Reagan program.[4] Repeal of at least the third year of the tax cut was actively discussed as the benefits of a multiyear planning horizon, supposed to be one of the major benefits of the Reagan plan, were pulverized on the rocks of uncertainty.

The Reagan tax cut was also hampered by its association with the so-called Laffer curve, which apparently violated the first maxim of economics, namely that there is no free lunch. It was not enough to argue that the tax cut would stimulate the economy, reduce unemployment, and raise productivity. The Laffer curve stated baldly that in addition the budget could be balanced by cutting taxes, a point dismissed in chapter 5.

Yet an across-the-board tax rate reduction will generate important and lasting benefits to the economy, for it will:

1. Raise the personal saving rate, thus providing more funds for investment and eventually raising productivity and the standard of living.

2. Raise labor force participation, improve the willingness to work of those already in the labor force, and increase the quality of work by providing greater incentives.

3. Reduce the gain in wage rates on the grounds that giving workers a *de facto* raise through lower taxes will moderate their demands for higher wages at the bargaining table.

4. Up to a point, raise tax receipts through expanded economic growth, an increase in labor income, and less tax avoidance through tax shelters and evasion. Even if receipts do decline, the shortfall would be far less than indicated by static analysis. However, this latter point should not be overstated and these conclusions do not rest on it.

The biggest drawback to a large reduction in income taxes is the likelihood that it would be inflationary. Clearly this would be the case under certain circumstances; if not, simply reduce all tax rates to zero and watch the economy move back to full employment as the inflation rate declines. The viewpoint that cutting tax rates without offsetting declines in government spending or monetary restraint will reduce inflation belongs back in the myth section of this book. As mentioned in the introduction, the correct, balanced approach depends on utilizing all three legs of the stool—personal tax cuts, business tax cuts, and government spending cuts. Unless all three are enacted, optimal economic behavior will not be realized. If the other legs of the stool are in place, however, a broad-based reduction in personal income tax rates will indeed diminish inflation because it will raise the saving rate, improve labor productivity, and moderate wage demands. The rest of this chapter examines the links between tax rates and personal saving; the importance of lower taxes on productivity and wage rates are covered in chapters 9 and 11, respectively.

The Rate of Return Effect

One of the major claims of supply-side economists is that most of an across-the-board tax cut will be saved, at least in the first year. The first-year argument is particularly important, for even if most of the additional income is spent later on, the initial savings will presumably have been utilized to generate the additional capacity necessary to provide more goods and services.

The claim that most of the tax cut will be saved rests on three principal assumptions. First, a reduction in tax rates will increase the rate of return on saving and thus raise the proportion of income that is saved. Second, most of any across-the-board tax cut will be received by those above the median income, who do virtually all of the saving in this economy. Third, consumers base their spending patterns on income averaged over several years; hence a tax cut will initially have very little effect on consumption.

It is the first argument that has received the heaviest broadside from the conventional Keynesians. Their distinction between investment and saving in this regard is particularly puzzling. Virtually all economists agree that investment depends significantly on the rate of return. Few people would be so foolish as to invest their money in a project if they think they could earn more by investing it elsewhere. If buying a machine or constructing a building is likely to generate only a 10 percent rate of return at a time when government bonds will yield 15 percent, private investment will suffer. Furthermore, if -2 percent or -3 percent looks like the best rate of return that can be earned after taxes and inflation, the would-be investor may decide to go to Las Vegas for the weekend and at least get some enjoyment out of spending his money. More likely he will use the funds to buy real estate, gold or silver, or other collectibles expected to appreciate in real as well as nominal terms.

Yet for some reason the idea that the rate of return also influences personal saving does not enjoy similar acceptance, even though in many cases the individuals making the saving and investment decisions are identical. It is claimed that people save because they are taught that thrift is a good idea; or they save for college educations for their children, to buy a new house, or to have something for the retirement years. Based on this logic, thrift is a state of mind that affects some more than others but is not related to the rate of return.

To be sure, people do save for all the reasons listed above, and for many others besides. But this approach to personal saving has no connection with economic logic. True, some people would save if the rate of return were zero or even negative—the Christmas Clubs are testimony to that. On the margin, however, most people will relate their decision to save to the rate of return they expect to earn on their savings.

As the countdown for the Reagan tax-cut bill of 1981 approached, the last desperate ploy of the old-guard liberals who opposed the personal tax cut was their argument that it would decrease saving, and thereby reduce investment and productivity, raise inflation, and generally harm the economy.

Supply-side economists may be permitted a wry smile at this turn of events. For years Keynesian economists had argued that fiscal policy should be directed at increasing consumption as the proven way to better economic performance and full employment. Tax cuts that merely went into saving were "wasted." Now many of these same economists mounted a rearguard attack by claiming that broad-based personal income tax cuts are counterproductive because they do not generate enough saving. Thus, it is argued, the scope and size of personal cuts over the next three years should be restricted until those elusive spending cuts are passed by Congress—which they correctly believed would never happen.

The new battle line of the liberal attack surfaced in response to Treasury Secretary Regan's testimony about the effect of the across-the-board rate cut on the personal saving rate. Regan claimed that one half to two thirds of the across-the-board tax cut would be saved, since most of it would be received by upper-income brackets.[5] Unsympathetic journalists claimed Regan offered "no support" for his statement and said "almost every economist agrees that only a small proportion would be saved,"[6] and Walter Heller went so far as to label this result "crap."[7]

Yet far from overstating the case, all the empirical evidence I has been able to muster suggests that Regan's estimates were essentially correct, based on what occurred in previous years when personal income tax rates were changed. The data show that without exception, personal saving has responded significantly to changes in both the rate of taxation and the rate of interest.

In order to determine the relationship between saving and the rate of return, it is necessary to adjust the latter for taxes and inflation. After all, if the rate of inflation were to rise to 100 percent per year, an increase in the interest rate to 50 percent would hardly attract any savers; the only interested parties would all be borrowers. Similarly, if the marginal tax rate on income from saving was raised to almost 100 percent, reported saving would disappear as well. Under the worst possible combination of high tax rates and high inflation, saving is doubly penalized, for the individual loses both interest (to taxes) and principal (to inflation). Any savings would take the form of assets that were in fixed supply, and thus whose price increases would be likely to equal or exceed the rate of inflation; or which were lightly taxed, either because of more favorable capital gains treatment or because they were outside the not-so-long long arm of the tax collector altogether. From an economic point of view, however, buying an asset from someone else is not saving at all; whereas the purchaser may think he is saving, the seller is dissaving. Thus saving in the economic sense implies a creation of new assets, not the exchange of existing ones.

Although the concept of the rate of return is clear enough, measuring it is not so straightforward. The rate of interest is usually designated as the yield on high-quality, long-term bonds such as Aaa rated corporate bonds; the government bond yield could be used with essentially the same results. The tax rate is the marginal tax rate on personal saving, which is substantially higher than the average tax rate and has averaged about 50 percent for most of the postwar period. While the expected rate of inflation is in the eyes of the saver, it is usually—although not always—a weighted average of previous inflation rates over the past three to four years.

Once the rate of return is adjusted for inflation and taxes, its relationship with the personal saving rate becomes much more apparent. By correlating these two variables, this author and associates have calculated that a 1 percent change in the rate of return—that is, from 3 percent to 4 percent—would change the personal saving rate by about 1 percent,* or $20 billion at 1982 levels of income. A 1 percent change in the rate of return could occur through a 1 percent change in the inflation rate, a 2 percent change in the interest rate, or approximately a 13 percent cut in tax rates (for example, from 50 percent to 43.5 percent).

This finding may appear unremarkable, yet an entire generation of economists claimed to find no empirical correlation between interest rates and the saving rate,[8] hence providing additional weight to the so-called theoretical argument that saving was a function of upbringing and religion rather than rate of return. It was not until 1978 that Michael Boskin was able to verify this relationship by adjusting the rate of return for inflation and taxes.[9] Even now most large-scale econometric models being used for policy analysis fail to include such a term in their consumption or saving functions.

The performance of the rate of return variable is not very sensitive to which long-term bond rate is used, but it is important that an average of the inflation rate over the past several years be used. This is not surprising because fluctuations in the long-term bond rate itself are tied to changes in inflation over the past three to four years.

The rate of return variable does a reasonable job of tracking the longer cyclical movements in the saving rate. For example, both of these variables were low in the late 1950s and early 1960s, the result of an oppressive tax structure for upper-income brackets and a bout of inflation in 1956 and 1957 not matched by higher interest rates. When the Kennedy-Johnson tax cut was passed in 1964, both the rate of return and the saving rate rose substantially. In the late 1970s, negative real rates of return corresponded fairly closely with the decline of the saving rate to thirty-year lows.

Yet, as shown in figure 6.1, the year-to-year fluctuations in the saving rate are really not very well tracked by the rate of return. Obviously another variable is needed, and that variable turns out to be the change in the tax rate. When changes in the rate of return are combined with changes in the average tax rate, the combination tracks annual changes in the personal saving rate very closely, as is shown in figure 6.2.

The relationship does not appear to work too well in the early years but since then has closely tracked all swings in the saving rate except for the increase in 1967. The regression underlying figure 6.2 indicates that *over 70 percent of any given change in taxes is saved during the first year.*

*For those familiar with statistics, this is a partial correlation estimated as part of a regression relating saving to income and several other variables.

Higher Rates of Return Will Raise Personal Saving

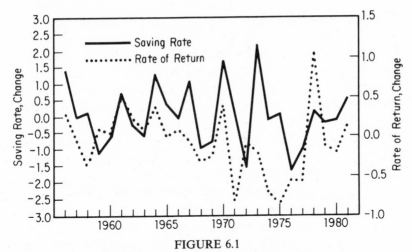

FIGURE 6.1

Changes in the Saving Rate and the Rate of Return

SOURCE: Prepared by Evans Economics, Inc.

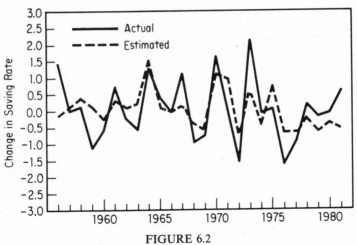

FIGURE 6.2

Estimating Changes in the Saving Rate[a]

SOURCE: Prepared by Evans Economics, Inc.
[a]As a function of rate of return and average tax rate.

The figures given in table 6.1 have been constructed in order to dissect the effects of the previous tax cuts with more precision. For every year we have calculated the "normal" increase in saving, which is simply equal to the change in personal income multiplied by the saving rate of the previous year. "Excess" saving is then defined as the actual change in saving less the normal change.

We have also calculated a "normal" change in personal income taxes, which is simply equal to the change in personal income multiplied by the previous

113

year's tax rate. The change in taxes due to the tax rate is then the actual change in taxes minus the normal change. This method is not perfect because taxes tend to slump during recessions, and it also does not reflect the lack of synchronization between income and tax payments. However, it is a good first approximation to the effect of changes in the tax rate tables.

The results are rather astounding; by comparing the figures in columns 3 and 4 it is evident that virtually all the change in taxes is reflected in saving the first year. In 1964, the year of the Kennedy-Johnson tax cut, tax rates were reduced an average of 15 percent; another 5 percent reduction followed in 1965. Excess savings rose $5.9 billion while the decline in taxes due to the rate cut was $6.0 billion, a ratio of almost 100 percent. Though personal saving presumably increased that year for other reasons as well, such as the above-average growth rate of pre-tax income, the first year increase in saving still appears to have been over two thirds. The Kennedy-Johnson tax cut thereby raised the personal saving rate by about 1½ percent, and it stayed at that higher level until the 1968 surcharge was enacted.

How the 1968 Surtax Reduced Saving

Because Lyndon Johnson had turned the spending tap back on to fight the War on Poverty and the Vietnam War after a one-year pause in government spending, the inflation rate rose from 2 percent to 4 percent; and even the late 1966 pause engineered by Johnson stunned the growth in inflation for only a few months. Thus by 1968 it seemed to most economists that the only alternative left was to propose a 10 percent surcharge on personal and corporate income. This surcharge, it was widely believed at the time, would reduce aggregate demand enough to take the pressure off rising prices, but not enough to kill the boom. Because the extra tax revenues would balance the budget, interest rates would also decline.

Seldom if ever has an economic policy backfired so badly. The rate of inflation, which had averaged 4.1 percent for the preceding four quarters, zoomed even higher to 5.5 percent in the next four quarters. Whereas these numbers may sound positively benign relative to the recent economic climate, the official Johnson target—later adopted by Nixon—was 2 percent inflation. The prime rate soared from 6 percent to 8.5 percent as the budget surplus, far from alleviating credit bottlenecks, was accompanied by the second credit crunch in three years. All this occurred because consumption, rather than declining

TABLE 6.1

Calculating the Marginal Propensity to Save

	Change in Personal Saving	Change in Personal Income Taxes	"Excess" Saving	Change in Taxes Due to Change in Tax Rate
1955	−0.6	2.9	−2.0	0.6
1956	5.0	4.3	3.7	1.7
1957	1.1	2.7	−0.3	0.5
1958	1.2	−0.3	0.5	−1.5
1959	−2.4	3.9	−4.1	0.8
1960	−1.5	4.4	−2.6	2.3
1961	3.4	1.7	2.5	−0.2
1962	0.3	4.7	−1.3	1.5
1963	−1.4	3.5	−2.8	0.6
1964	7.7	−1.7	5.9	−6.0[a]
1965	4.1	6.3	1.3	1.5
1966	2.3	9.6	−0.9	3.9
1967	8.3	7.6	5.4	2.3
1968	−2.3	15.1	−7.2	7.2[a]
1969	−1.4	18.5	−6.0	9.5[a]
1970	15.2	0.1	11.6	−8.5[a]
1971	4.9	0.9	0.3	−7.3[a]
1972	−8.0	24.3	−13.7	13.2
1973	26.3	9.7	18.9	−7.1
1974	6.2	19.5	−2.7	4.9
1975	9.2	−1.3	1.0	−15.4
1976	−11.8	27.9	−22.7	11.0
1977	−4.5	29.7	−14.8	8.7
1978	11.4	32.3	1.0	4.0
1979	7.3	43.2	−6.0	10.4
1980	10.0	26.4	−2.3	4.3
1981	24.0	38.4	9.2	−1.7

SOURCE: Calculated by Evans Economics, Inc.
[a]Years of major changes in tax rates.

in the face of the surcharge, increased by near-record amounts. For the personal saving rate declined dramatically from 7.9 percent to 6.3 percent *the very quarter* the surcharge went into effect. Indeed, consumption in constant dollars rose at an annual rate of 8.1 percent that quarter, almost double the average increase of 4.6 percent during the previous four quarters.

The question of why the surcharge misfired so badly has remained a mystery to many, baffling liberals and conservatives, Democrats and Republicans alike. Even to this day, most Keynesian economists do not understand what transpired in 1968.

The evidence seems incontrovertible that the tax surcharge itself was inflationary, because paradoxically it encouraged spending rather than discouraging it. As I have stressed, an increase in the rate of return will encourage saving and a decrease will discourage it. And clearly the surtax lowered the rate of return significantly.

The increase in inflation diminished the aftertax rate of return even further. To see this, consider the following simple example. In the 1960s the rate of inflation was about 2 percent; the long-term rate of interest was 5 percent, and the marginal tax rate on saving was approximately 50 percent. After taxes savers at this marginal rate earn 2½ percent, but of course the loss in the value of money of 2 percent must be subtracted from that. Thus the after-tax real rate of return is ½ percent, and although that is definitely not splendid, at least it is positive.

Now consider the situation where the rate of inflation moves up to 4 percent, the long-term rate of interest increases pari passu to 7 percent, and the marginal tax rate rises to 55 percent. Using the same calculations as above, the rate of return has now diminished to −0.85 percent. Hence inflation and the higher tax rates have combined to turn a positive real rate of return into a negative one. That is essentially what happened during the 1968–69 period of higher inflation and the tax surcharge. It is small wonder people saved less.

As a result of the tax surcharge and higher inflation, personal and corporate saving diminished so much that the total national saving *declined* in spite of the fact that the federal government ran a substantial *surplus* of $8.4 billion in calendar 1969. This led to another credit crunch and eventually the 1970 recession. Once the recession was certified, off came the surcharge, consumption declined, and the saving rate returned to its previous value.

The surtax was applied in the middle of 1968, in effect for all of 1969, and then dropped in mid-1970. Consequently, the average personal income tax rate rose from 13.0 percent in 1967 to 14.1 percent in 1968 and 15.3 percent in 1969 before falling back to 14.3 percent in 1970 and 13.4 percent in 1971.

The pattern of the personal saving rate during this four-year period is almost a mirror image of the tax rate. The personal saving rate declined from 8.1 percent in 1967 to 7.1 percent and 6.4 percent in 1968 and 1969 before rising to 8.0 percent and 8.1 percent in 1970 and 1971. The 1970 saving rate was biased upward because of the severe GM strike in the fourth quarter of the year. Without any adjustment for the decline in consumption which accompanied that strike, the marginal propensity to save (MPS)* would have been greater than unity for 1970, which is unlikely although there is no theoretical reason why saving could not increase by more than the tax cut if the rate of return rose enough. Making this one adjustment would yield annual MPSs of 0.88,

*The incremental change in saving resulting from a unit change in disposable income.

0.58, 0.78, and 0.85 for 1968 through 1971—again figures that are surprisingly high relative to the conventional wisdom.

Tax Rate and Saving Rate Changes in the 1970s

The personal saving rate thus returned to 8 percent once the surcharge was lifted but then declined sharply during 1972 to 6.5 percent. Two principal factors led to this temporary decline. First, note that table 6.1, in addition to illustrating the 1964 tax cut, the imposition and recision of the surcharge in 1968 and 1970, and the 1975 rebate, also indicates what appears to be a one-year tax increase in 1972, a twist in fiscal policy not previously mentioned. This turns out to be just another economic "dirty trick" of the Nixon administration.

Because Nixon wanted to stimulate the economy but realized that the budget deficit was going to be far larger than publicly advertised, he decided to change the withholding schedules in 1972 so that a larger proportion would be withheld from paychecks. This in essence increased tax collections in 1972 and gave taxpayers big refunds in 1973, which ballooned the budget deficit in the year after election. Hence average tax rates increased in 1972 and decreased in 1973. Most consumers were not fooled by this chicanery, and thus saved less in 1972 and more in 1973.

The second reason was that the average consumer, unlike the average economist or the average presidential advisor, knew that the phony price stability invoked by the controls could not last. Once the controls were lifted, prices would skyrocket unless the underlying causes of inflation were brought under control. Thus consumers hustled to stock up on goods, particularly durables, that would soon accelerate in price.

Further evidence of this theory is provided by the rush to buy consumer durables in the first quarter of 1973, just after the decision to move from Phase II to Phase III of controls had officially been announced. During most of 1972, no one knew how long the controls would remain in effect or what would follow when they were lifted. Near the end of the year Nixon announced that the formal controls would terminate at the end of the year and that Phase III would consist of "guidelines," which many read as tantamount to abandoning ship. Thus in the first quarter of 1973, purchases of consumer durables in constant prices shot up at an annual rate of 26.6 percent from already buoyant 1972 figures, reaching a crest that was not surpassed until 1977. Once this buying orgy had been completed, consumer patterns returned to what was then the normal saving rate. The growth in real GNP declined with amazing suddenness from 11.1 percent in the first quarter to 0.6 percent in the second quarter, with most of the decline due to lower consumption.

The next major change in taxes occurred in 1975 when the average tax rate declined from 14.6 percent to 13.4 percent because of the rebate. The saving rate, however, hardly budged, rising only from 8.5 percent to 8.6 percent, even though taxes were $15.4 billion lower than would have been the case had the tax rate remained constant.* Obviously the difference here is that the rebate was distributed primarily to lower-income groups who do indeed spend most if not all of what they receive—while marginal rates remained untouched.

The saving rate then stayed at above-average levels until 1977, when higher tax brackets caused by bracket creep and the rising rate of inflation once again began to eat away at the rate of return, which by 1980 was severely locked into the negative range. The personal saving rate plunged back to 5.8 percent as inflationary psychology overwhelmed the high nominal rate of interest. The near-record low saving rate correlated closely with the record negative rate of interest after inflation and taxes.

Consumers often react slowly to a change in the real rate of interest because they do not know how inflation will change in the future, but they react much more quickly to a change in the marginal tax rate on saving. Suppose the government announces that effective immediately everyone who saves more than $1,000 per year will receive a 50 percent tax credit on the additional saving. It would not take people three or four years to make up their minds to react to that change. On the other hand, suppose the latest statistics show that the rate of inflation has declined from an annual rate of 12 percent to 6 percent. Bitter experience has taught that the likelihood of such a change being only temporary is quite high; the prudent investor will wait until inflation stays at that level for at least a year or more before he is willing to commit to portfolio changes, and often the reaction time is as long as three to four years.

Establishing a significant relationship between the rate of return on saving and the saving rate itself, while being one of the linchpins of supply-side economics, does not provide a complete answer of how much of an across-the-board tax rate cut would be saved. For the income effect must also be considered; if taxpayers' incomes rise, what percentage of the additional money will be saved, assuming no change in the rate of return? Many of those who opposed the Reagan tax cut argued that if saving averages 7 percent of disposable income, only 7 percent of the extra income would be saved, the ar-

---

*The rebate itself was only about $8 billion: the remainder of the tax reduction was due to the recession-induced decline moving people to lower tax brackets.

gument being that tax reduction dollars carry no identifying label to distinguish them from other increases in income.

Our estimates of the MPS from any across-the-board income tax rate cut are much higher, of course, partly because of the rate-of-return argument but also because of income distribution. Most of any across-the-board tax rate cut goes to those above the median income, since they pay most of the taxes. Since it seems logical to argue that the rich save more than the poor, it might at first be thought that the distribution of the tax cut itself might be enough to carry the argument. However, it turns out the complete answer is much more complicated than that, and that the proportion of income saved depends on the time horizon: the longer the period, the less is saved. However, this conclusion does not necessarily discredit our line of reasoning as long as the personal tax cut is accompanied by business tax cuts and government spending cuts as well.

The Income Distribution Effect: Who Saves?

Any across-the-board tax cut—Mr. Reagan's or anyone else's—means that the rich* get most of the tax reduction, since they pay most of the taxes. Since the rich also do most of the saving, the tax cut will increase the overall personal saving rate. In that sense the argument is very simple.

Estimating how much the rich save, however, is a somewhat more complicated matter. Our estimates rely on Treasury estimates and various surveys; the actual calculations are in the appendix. They can be summarized as: those below the median income (about $20,000 for 1981) on balance save no part of their incomes; those with incomes between $20,000 and $40,000 save about 5 percent; those with incomes ranging from $40,000 to $80,000 save about 15 percent; and those with incomes over $80,000 per year save between 25 percent and 50 percent.

In case readers at this point suddenly feel a sinking feeling that they save much less than the average, let me point out that these figures include pension plans and other forms of contractual saving, and that discretionary cash saving is likely to be well below these numbers. They also include saving from realized

*This term is used in the economic sense: it applies to the upper 1 percent of the income distribution. No connotation about whether someone earning $80,000 a year is rich in the popular sense of the word is indicated.

capital gains, most of which are likely to be saved (and reinvested) at almost all levels of income.

The problem is also more complicated on a theoretical level. If the rich save more, then it would seem that as living standards improve over long periods of time, the personal saving rate would rise. After all, real per capita income is more than four times what it was in the 1920s but the saving rate is just about the same.

This contradiction posed one of the classical paradoxes of economics when aggregate consumption and income figures were first calculated over fifty years ago. When Simon Kuznets put together the original National Income Account statistics, he noted that the personal saving rate tended to remain constant over long periods of time; and though it did fluctuate from year to year, no long-term trend was discernible.[10] This secular constancy of the saving rate has continued for the last fifty years as well. This seems sharply at odds with the finding that the rich save more. For if they do, the overall saving rate should rise as peoples' real income increases over time; yet nothing of the sort is observed.

During the 1930s and the 1940s this dilemma remained unsolved. In fact, the hypothesis that the saving rate increased as income rose was one of the fundamental linchpins of the Keynesian system. Keynes was quite clear on this point. In one of his most often quoted lines, he stated that "men are disposed, as a rule and on the average, to increase their consumption as their income increases, but not by as much as the increase in their income."[11]

Keynes, of course, went on to point out that if saving rose as the economy expanded but private sector investment did not increase to fill the gap, then public sector spending would have to come to the rescue. Government spending thus would continuously increase as a proportion of total demand to keep the economy at full employment.

As a matter of fact, the simplified Keynesian consumption function fell flat on its face in the period immediately following World War II. According to that theory, the withdrawal of huge government defense spending would leave an enormous gap that could not be filled by the private sector, and the economy would return to its state of depression. Dire forecasts of eight million unemployed, which at that time would have been an unemployment rate of about 13 percent, were common.[12] What happened, of course, was that the economy remained at full employment, and high inflation occurred in spite of substantial government budget surpluses.

Once this occurred, economists quickly discarded the oversimplified Keynesian consumption function and started working on more complicated explanations of consumer behavior. One of the most popular at the time was James Duesenberry's relative income hypothesis, which can also be referred to as irreversible standards or "keeping up with the Joneses." Duesenberry stated that it was the relative rather than the absolute level of income that was important in determining patterns of consumption.[13] If a family's real income increased from $10,000 to $20,000 but they stayed at the midpoint of the income distribution, their saving rate would remain unchanged. Furthermore, if their income happened to decline one year for reasons of economic misfortune or extended vacation, consumption would not decline to its previous level because they would try to retain the standards they had previously reached. That, said Duesenberry, explained the negative saving rate during the Great Depression.

The Duesenberry theory was actually rather ingenious and seemed to fit all the facts available at the time. It posited that the saving rate would remain roughly constant except during recessions, when it would decline. That seemed to work well enough in the first postwar recession of 1949 when the saving rate fell to 4.0 percent, and again in 1954 when it again declined from its previous value. Unfortunately the theory fell apart in the first serious postwar recession in 1958 when the saving rate soared to a twelve-year high. It later turned out that the saving rate also rose in the recessions of 1970 and 1975, so this theory was gradually discarded. Furthermore, the Duesenberry theory posited that consumption and income always move in the same direction, which is not at all the case. A more comprehensive theory was needed, one which took into account the difference between short-run and long-run patterns of consumer behavior.

The Timing Effect and the Permanent Income Hypothesis

It fell to Milton Friedman to develop this definitive theory of consumer behavior, in a book which he simply titled *A Theory of the Consumption Function.*[14] Friedman approached the problem by making a sharp distinction between income actually received, which he calls measured income, and the income on which consumers actually base their behavior, which he calls permanent income. A similar distinction is drawn between measured and permanent consumption.

Permanent income is difficult to define exactly, but in a broad sense it represents what the consumer believes to be his average or normal income. More technically it is defined by Friedman as "the amount a consumer unit could consume (or believes that it could) while maintaining its wealth intact."[15]

Friedman believes that the ratio of permanent saving to permanent income, which we might call the permanent saving rate, is not correlated with income. It is the same at low incomes as at high ones.

Not everyone need have the same permanent saving rate. Indeed, Friedman suggests that this ratio may vary depending on the rate of return, the ratio of wealth to income, the variation in actual income, and the age and composition of the consumer or family. However, when consumption and income are measured on a long-term basis, he claims that the saving rate does not rise as income increases.

Thus the theories of the consumption function put forth by Keynes and Friedman represent not only diametrically opposite poles but spawn totally different implications for fiscal policy. If Keynes is right, the government will have to increase its share of GNP over time as income grows in order to avoid depressions, thus providing politicians with a built-in excuse to follow their natural inclinations. If Friedman is right, the share of GNP going to consumption remains the same as income increases, and the share of GNP distributed between consumption and investment depends on the rate of return on saving. Nothing could be more fundamental than this difference.

Friedman's theory attracted attention like a lightening rod because everyday observation tells us that someone with an income of $1,000,000 is much likelier to save most of it than someone with an income of $10,000. Friedman was certainly not going to oppose everyday observation; he was, and in fact, remains, the supreme empiricist. He is always ready, whenever any of his hypotheses is considered biased or incorrect, to be the first to say, "Let's look at the numbers." Yet his basic argument was that measured income is not the correct concept for explaining consumer behavior.

It is more sensible, Friedman claims, to look at normal or permanent income rather than income that happens to fall into some arbitrarily defined time slot. Suppose we slice that time frame down from a year to a week or even a day; then we would expect virtually no correlation between income and consumption or saving. If the time period were to be cut down to one day, someone who gets paid every Friday would have a very high propensity to save on Fridays and a negative propensity the rest of the week. In addition, the propensity to save is different for different types of income. In particular, it is much higher for incomes that are variable in nature, such as business income and income from capital assets that fluctuate widely in price or are converted to cash only infrequently.

Friedman's points are well taken. Relatively few people who find themselves with very high incomes in any given year continue to earn that level of income on a regular basis. The spurts in income may have come from an inheritance, from selling a small business or real estate, from large gains in the stock market, from royalties on a best-selling book or record, or from a relatively short period of being a star performer.

At the other end of the income scale, some people who report below average incomes are permanently poor, but many others are temporarily unemployed, have taken time for an extended vacation, are between jobs, have missed time because of illness, or are retired. In all of these cases it is likely that their rate of saving will be sharply negative. A moment's reflection will reveal that this cannot possibly be a permanent relationship—poor people cannot go through life dissaving on average every year, for most of them have virtually no assets and cannot borrow very much over extended period.

The Friedman hypothesis is a difficult one to test empirically because of the problems of measuring normal or permanent income empirically. A three-year weighted average of income is often used as a measure of permanent income. Sometimes various proxy variables for income such as occupation, level of education, or value of one's principal residence are used.[16] Even these proxies do not cover all contingencies, since one lawyer may have an earnings potential three times another, and for what a garage costs in Beverly Hills one could buy a palace in Cleveland. Yet without the extreme outliers, and given that the income from capital is subject to different savings patterns than income from labor, the permanent income hypothesis does seem to hold in most cases.

While Friedman presumably developed his theory as an antidote to the Keynesian viewpoint that the ratio of government spending to GNP necessarily had to increase over time because consumers would be spending a smaller proportion of their income, it also can be used as an argument against giving the poor more income through tax cuts and transfer payments in order to boost consumption. For if virtually everyone has the same saving rate, then consumption will not be increased by tilting the income distribution scale toward lower income groups.

Yet the latter-day Keynesian apologists very neatly stand this argument on its head and use it against the argument favoring upper-income tax cuts. If the saving rate is invariant to the level of income, argue the suddenly reconstructed Keynesians, then we will not get any more saving by giving the rich another tax break. Indeed, if the rich do not save proportionately more than the poor, then one of the key arguments that across-the-board tax cuts will stimulate saving and investment is invalidated.

The argument to defuse the alleged logic of the latter-day Keynesian position is twofold. First, one of the major points Friedman stresses is that the propensity to save is much greater in the short run than in the long run. A large body of empirical evidence, including the work of Lawrence R. Klein, shows that the first-year marginal propensity to save is four to five times as large as the long-run propensity.[17] Second, the argument that in the long run the rich do not have a higher saving rate does not contradict the finding that someone who suddenly finds himself propelled into the upper-income brackets will save a larger proportion of his income.

For example, a person who usually makes $50,000 a year but finds his income rising to $200,000 for one year, realizing that this is likely to be a once-in-a-lifetime proposition, is more likely to save a large proportion of his income than another person whose annual income is usually $200,000. For it would do the $50,000-per-year person little good to scale up his standard of living if he could not afford it in subsequent years. Of course, some might choose to spend it all on a spectacular vacation or even at the gambling tables, but such cases are a small minority.

Friedman also argues that the marginal propensity to save is higher from incomes that are largely derived from capital. He actually used this argument primarily to distinguish among income received by different types of individuals—wages, dividends, proprietors income, capital gains, and so forth—but it can equally well be used for different types of income received by the same person. Since more income from capital is received by those with above-average incomes, a tax cut in these income brackets will also increase the saving rate.

In addition, the Friedman permanent income hypothesis states that the marginal propensity to save will diminish as the time horizon expands. This means that as the time horizon increases from the date of the original tax cut, the increased spending *will* tend to be inflationary *unless* offset by gains in productivity, which in turn should stem from the higher saving and investment originally engendered by the tax cut.

Thus a large proportion of an across-the-board personal income tax rate cut will be saved for the following reasons:

1. It increases the rate of return on saving.
2. Most of any change in income due to tax cuts is saved in the first year, although this phenomenon disappears in future years.
3. Those with incomes above the median will save more than others. This is fully consistent with the Friedman permanent income hypothesis, which says that the saving rate is invariant with income in the long run. This is reconciled by noting that (a) many of those in the above-average incomes are only temporarily "rich"; (b) those with highly variable incomes have a higher saving rate even in the long run; and (c) the propensity to save income from capital is permanently higher.

Having said all this, an across-the-board tax cut is still not *the* most efficient way to raise personal saving. If the idea of the tax cuts is to raise saving and investment, why not just target tax cuts for these specific purposes and forget about across-the-board tax cuts, which will admittedly result in some increase in consumption? As will be shown in chapters 9 and 11, my answer is that a reduction in tax rates also increases work effort and incentive, raises labor productivity, and moderates wage demands—none of which is accomplished by a tax rate reduction restricted to nonwage income. Still in all, the United States has done much less than virtually any other industrialized country to stimulate saving by individuals, and further moves in this direction would definitely have a beneficial effect on the economy. For this reason, let us now investigate some of the programs currently used in other countries and then briefly discuss some of the programs which could be effectively utilized in the United States.

International Comparisons of Saving Rates

In order to see what is both politically feasible and economically efficient in terms of raising the personal saving rate, we might do a lot worse than examine what has been done in other social democracies. As shown in table 6.2, the United States has the lowest national saving rate and, except for Sweden, the lowest personal saving rate of any industrialized country in the world. It certainly is not because inflation is lower abroad; except for Germany and Japan, the United States inflation record over the past twenty years has been better than other major industrialized countries. It is not that the United States lacks investment opportunities; indeed it offers a much more multifaceted array of investment opportunities that covers virtually the complete spectrum of risk classes and maturities. Apparently these other countries are better at stimulating saving through various clauses in the tax codes.

The schemes adopted by other countries are quite varied and the amounts that benefit from tax preference change at frequent intervals; hence the following list is meant to be illustrative rather than comprehensive. It does, however, indicate the wide-ranging nature of schemes used by other countries to attract the small saver.

In the United Kingdom, for example, anyone can purchase up to £1500 of National Savings Certificates which yield tax-free interest. The government there also offers savings bonds which do have taxable interest but whose holders receive a tax-free bonus if the bonds are held five years to maturity. Another gimmick is the introduction of £1 Premium Savings Bonds, the holders of which are given a chance to win tax-free prizes ranging up to £50,000 in lieu

TABLE 6.2

Average 1960–80
International Comparison of Saving Rates

	Personal Saving Rate	**Total Saving Rate**
United States	6.1	19.2
Canada	7.1	21.6
United Kingdom	9.6	19.8
France	14.3	24.4
Germany	15.6	25.4
Italy	16.6	23.3
Netherlands	13.0	27.1
Belgium	15.0	22.5
Sweden	3.5	23.0
Japan	19.4	34.5

SOURCE: Calculated by Evans Economics, Inc.

of receiving interest. Other schemes include Save As You Earn deposits, under which savings left in Specified Depositories for five years generate a bonus equivalent to fourteen months savings free of tax, and those left for seven years receive a twenty-eight-month, tax-free bonus. Furthermore, tax-free compound interest is paid on deposits withdrawn after the first but before the end of the fifth year.

Germany has a number of measures to promote saving which center around deposits at savings and loan institutions and insurance companies. A certain amount can be deposited tax-free with these institutions; the amount varies depending on marital status and number of children but increases to about $5,000 per year for a married couple with four children. In addition to these tax deductible amounts, savers can also earn premiums of 20 percent to 30 percent up to certain specified maximum deposits at savings banks. In addition, Germany has created another special savings incentive for low-income people known as the "DM 624 Law," which allows them to direct their employers to pay up to DM 624 (about $300) of the employee's salary into a qualified investment plan. The employer is then reimbursed by the tax authorities for the amount of the cash grant.

Germany also has very favorable tax treatment for dividends, even for the largest shareholders. This works primarily through integration of the corporate and personal income tax system, which means in effect that corporate income distributed as dividends is taxed once instead of twice. The corporation pays a marginal rate of 36 percent, and the individual pays an additional marginal rate of 20 percent or less. This can be compared to the United States, where the top marginal tax rate for corporations and individuals is 46 percent and 50 percent, leaving only 27 percent of the income for the stockholder. Before the 1981 Tax Reduction Act, the maximum combined tax rate on dividends was an ever higher 85 percent, and with state and local income taxes it went as high as 90 percent in New York City.

The French system is more personalized, as might be expected in a country where taxes are individually negotiated between the taxpayer and the revenue agent.* The top marginal tax rate on interest income ranges anywhere from 25 percent to 60 percent, based in part on what kind of asset is involved and on whether the tax is withheld at the source. If the taxpayer permits withholding on the interest before it is paid, the rates vary from 25 percent for government bonds to 38 percent on saving deposits and 42 percent for bearer bonds. If the tax is not withheld at the source, the marginal rate increases to 60 percent. Evidently this higher figure includes some estimate of the probability of the French revenue inspector uncovering the interest income if it has not been taxed at the source.

The maximum tax rate on dividend income is 40 percent, with the figure calculated as follows. Suppose, for example, an individual receives $100 of dividend income. A total of $150 is included in taxable income, on which the maximum tax would be $90. From this, the original $50 is subtracted from the maximum tax, resulting in a net tax of $40. This scheme essentially has the result of taxing dividends at very low rates for all income classes except those near the top.

As might be expected, Japan treats interest and dividend income more favorably than virtually any other country. The key program permits each person to receive interest income on ¥14 million (about $60,000) tax-free. This plan is extremely popular for obvious reasons, so much so that even infants in their first year of life manage to have accumulated the requisite ¥14 million. Some might call this tax evasion, but the point is that it does wonders for the saving rate.

The ¥14 million has to be split up a certain way, which does not seem to bother the Japanese at all. ¥3 million must be put in government bond investments, another ¥3 million in post office saving deposits, a third ¥3 million in bank saving deposits, and ¥5 million in savings made through the employer. In a country with only embryonic capital markets, money is not as fungible as in the United States, and these divisions are of somewhat greater importance than they would be in this country.

After that, interest income is taxed at ordinary rates to a maximum of 75 percent, which sounds very high, but any Japanese who chooses may have his

*A standard line in that country is that taxes are determined by an assessment of the worth of the man's house, his car, and his mistress.

dividend and interest income taxed at the source at a maximum rate of 35 percent. A few restrictions apply: the person must not own more than 5 percent of the outstanding shares of any company paying dividends and must not receive more than ¥500,000 of dividend income from any one company per year. However, larger shareholders in general can take their income as capital gains, which are not taxed at all—unless one is a professional trader, in which case the taxes revert to the maximum 75 percent marginal rate.

It may seem odd to include Italy in this discussion, but as is shown in table 6.2, the personal saving rate in Italy ranks fairly high on the overall list. This is no accident since interest income from government bonds is exempt from all income taxes. In addition, the tax rate—once again at the source—is only 10 percent for bonds of Italian resident banks and convertible bonds of companies. It is 20 percent for other corporate bonds and for saving accounts, but for foreign residents this 20 percent figure is reduced to 10 percent. Other interest income is taxed as ordinary income with a maximum rate of 72 percent, but because most of the sources of interest income are taxed at the lower rates, this has almost no effect. Furthermore, interest of up to L4 million (about $3,000) is tax-free if it is paid on agricultural loans or mortgages to Italian residents.

Dividends are not treated as liberally as interest income, with a maximum rate of 47 percent after taking into account the benefits of integration of the tax system. However, dividends from special savings stock are subject to only a 15 percent withholding tax at the source. Hence, Italy turns out to have one of the lowest overall tax rates on interest and dividends, which is why the saving rate remains high in spite of the general disorganization of the economic structure of the country and a higher rate of inflation than any of her major trading partners.

Most other countries do not have massive tax breaks, and in fact the tax on interest and dividend income in Belgium, the Netherlands, and the United Kingdom is somewhat higher than in the United States, although before 1981 the differences were very small. These tax laws are subject to frequent changes, so a comprehensive summary would presumably be somewhat out of date as soon as it was published. However, the overall thrust of these comparisons should be clear. By a combination of tax-exempt interest and dividend income for small savers, integration of the personal and corporate income taxes so that dividends are taxed only once, and an alternative maximum tax in the 35 percent to 40 percent range for large taxpayers, Japan, Germany, France, and Italy have managed to generate a saving rate that is far above the levels reached in the United States. At least until 1981, the United States has used the tax system less to stimulate private sector saving than virtually any other large industrialized nation.

Targeting Personal Saving Directly

While the 1981 Tax Reduction Act cut taxes generally, it still did not do very much for the small saver. The so-called All Savers Bill, which permits purchase of tax-free deposits at commercial banks and savings and loans up to a maximum of $2,000, might at first glance appear to fill the gap, but it was quite unsuccessful. While All Savers certificates totaled about $50 billion, most of the funds were simply transferred from money-market funds or from money-market certificates at the same banking institutions. Indeed, in a bizarre twist, many savers transferred their funds from 5½ percent passbook accounts to the All Savers certificates, thus causing the savings and loans to lose money even on a deal designed especially to benefit them.

The only other boost to saving contained in the 1981 act is the enlargement of Individual Retirement Accounts (IRAs) to make them available to all employees, rather than only to those not covered by any other pension plan. When IRAs were first introduced in 1976, they covered only those who were not otherwise eligible for a pension plan. The 1981 legislation, however, expanded them as follows:

1. IRAs are now available to all employees, not just to those who are not currently covered by a pension plan.
2. The maximum amount of tax-deductible contribution is enlarged from $1,500 to $2,000 per year.
3. Employees are permitted an additional non-deductible contribution of $2,000 per year plus an additional $8,000 over the employee's lifetime.

Approximately 30 million taxpayers were eligible for IRAs under the older regulations; 2.5 million of them took advantage of this part of the tax code. Since the number of employees in the United States—excluding self-employed but including government workers—is approximately 90 million, the number of eligible taxpayers was tripled when IRAs were made available to all employees.

The total increase in saving due to the expansion of the coverage of IRAs, when fully phased in, is estimated to be:

$6.5 billion—making IRAs available to all employees
$3.3 billion—raising the maximum amount deductible from $1,500 to $2,000 per year
$8.5 billion—adding a non-deductible contribution not to exceed $2,000 per year or $10,000 over the employee's lifetime
$18.3 billion—total increase in saving[18]

The revenue loss to the Treasury can be calculated as the $9.8 billion which is deductible times a marginal tax rate of 35 percent or $3.4 billion per year. In addition, the Treasury loses about another $0.8 billion per year because the interest and dividend income generated in the expanded IRAs is tax deferred. The total static revenue loss would be $4.2 billion per year, compared to an $18.3 billion increase in saving.

Thus when the beneficial aspects of the expanded IRAs are fully phased in—a process which we estimate would take about four years—the increase in private sector saving would outweigh the rise in the government deficit by better than a 4:1 margin. Unlike an across-the-board personal income tax rate cut, total net saving in the economy would actually increase as a result of cutting tax rates and raising the *ex ante* budget deficit.

In designing other tax cuts specifically to raise personal saving, the tax breaks should not be given to those who receive income from past saving. Such a plan would not induce any incremental increase in saving unless the tax break started at a level *above* the average amount of interest and dividend income which taxpayers are already earning.

This limit is well above what is ordinarily assumed. Figures given in table 6.3 show that for tax returns that include any interest and dividend income at all, the average amount in 1981 was close to $2,000 per return, even for the lower income levels. They also show that more than half of taxable interest and dividends are earned by tax payers with annual incomes of less than $30,000. Thus it reasonably follows that an increase in the exemption for interest and dividend income from, for example, $200 to $400 would do virtually nothing to spur additional saving on the margin. The exemption would have to be raised to $2,000 per taxpayer; an even better plan would be to have the tax credit start only above the $2,000 level.

No scheme is going to be perfect. Some taxpayers who are already large savers are going to get a free ride on any tax incentive proposal that is submitted. But the main idea is to get the biggest bang for the buck. Besides, people who are already large savers are more likely to be tempted by an increase in the rate of return than those who have never saved a nickel and do not plan to start now. With this basic concept firmly in mind, the following programs have been suggested to raise personal saving:

1. Decoupling the tax table. Under this scheme, the tax table would "start over again" for non-wage sources of income. For example, consider a taxpayer with a $60,000 income of which $50,000 is wages and salaries and $10,000 is interest and dividend income. Under present law, the non-wage income is taxed at high marginal rates. With the decoupling provision, the interest and dividend income would be taxed as if it were the first $10,000 of income, which means at very low marginal tax rates. This sort of scheme would satisfy the equity argument

TABLE 6.3

Average Amounts of Dividend and Interest Income
1981 Levels of Income

Size of Adj. Gross Income	Interest & Dividends per Return averaged over All Returns	Interest & Dividends per Return averaged over Returns with Some Interest & Dividends	% of Total National Interest & Dividends each Income Class or below*
($000)	($)	($)	(%)
All returns, total	1,593	3,080	100.0
$ under 2	370	1,480	**
2– 4	233	728	1.2
4– 6	575	1,587	3.2
6– 8	830	2,254	5.8
8– 10	693	1,982	8.9
10– 12	953	2,202	12.5
12– 14	1,115	2,429	16.2
14– 16	1,017	2,129	20.3
16– 18	1,095	2,156	24.5
18– 20	1,059	1,980	28.9
20– 25	1,291	2,184	40.7
25– 30	1,488	2,161	52.5
30– 50	2,176	2,755	81.0
50– 100	6,817	7,288	93.3
100– 200	23,692	24,080	97.4
200– 500	73,302	74,079	99.0
500– 1,000	262,595	263,736	99.5
1,000+	1,279,389	1,281,338	100.0

SOURCE: Office of the Secretary of the Treasury, Office of Tax Analysis, April 17, 1981.
*For example, returns with less than $16,000 in adjusted gross income received 20.3% of all interest and dividend income.
**Less than 0.05%.

in the sense that someone with $400,000 of interest and dividend income would still be subjected to the highest marginal tax bracket; it would not be a "fat cat" tax cut bill.

2. Raising the exemption for interest and dividend income. For many years taxpayers have been permitted to deduct up to $100 for single and $200 for joint returns. Senator Lloyd Bentsen pushed through an increase to $200 for single and $400 for married taxpayers and broadened it to include interest as well as dividend income, but this provision was terminated in the 1981 Tax Reduction Act to make way for the so-called All Savers bill.

Stephen J. Entin, formerly of Representative Clarence Brown's staff and the minority staff of the Joint Economic Committee and later deputy assistant secretary for economic policy at the Treasury, proposed a 50 percent tax credit on all interest and dividend income without limit; he later revised that proposal to provide a cap at $7,500 in order to meet some of the equity objections that were raised. Brown and Harrison Schmidt later submitted a bill that would provide a 25 percent tax credit with a $12,500 cap. Whereas these bills would certainly increase saving, they could be further modified to create more savings per dollar of tax loss by putting a floor at $2,000. In other words, taxpayers would not receive any credit for interest and dividend income unless it exceeded $2,000 per year. Since that would eliminate most of the revenue loss, the tax credit could be extended to 50 percent or even higher.

The problem with this plan, as Entin would agree, is that it would have virtually no constituency because it would involve such a relatively small proportion of total taxpayers. Furthermore, it would not provide any incentive whatsoever to the small saver in the lower-income brackets, who might actually be persuaded to put away a few hundred dollars under the proper tax scheme, but who could not possibly aspire to save $2,000 per year any time in the foreseeable future. This led to the third plan, which is the most complicated of them all.

3. This version of the Entin plan would provide a 50 percent tax credit only for that saving in excess of the average amount of saving for each particular income class. For example, if taxpayers with an average income of $15,000 per year do not save anything on average, *any* saving undertaken by taxpayers at that income level would be eligible for a tax credit. At $30,000, suppose the average saving rate is 5 percent; in that case, the tax credit would be granted only to those saving more than $1,500 per year. If the average saving rate at $50,000 per year is 10 percent, the credit would not be granted at that income level unless more than $5,000 per year was saved. Note that this applies to *net new saving,* not interest and dividend income on amounts that had previously been saved. The taxpayer would receive no credit unless he saved an additional amount each year.

This plan probably represents the zenith of an economically efficient and equitable bill. No one gets any reduction in taxes unless they save more than the average, but above these levels the change in the rate of return is sufficient to provide substantial incentives. Those who have large interest and dividend incomes because of past thrift, luck, or inheritance receive no tax advantage unless they save a higher-than-average percent of their current income. The tax is also fair to smaller savers, providing them with an incentive that is realistic relative to their fairly meager incomes.

This plan is also so unduly complicated that Entin never really pushed it very hard. The squabbles over measuring what is saving, distinguishing between cash and noncash forms of saving, and determining the average rate of saving for that income level, would be almost insurmountable. Furthermore, considering the amount of trouble that (a) taxpayers have reading their current 1040 forms and (b) the IRS has printing instructions in English, it is not immediately clear how many people would actually be able to take advantage of this tax break even if it were implemented.

Clearly the optimal tax reduction to stimulate personal saving must be reasonably equitable and generate a fair amount of political support as well as being economically efficient. That means in essence that the bill must contain something for the average small saver. Hence from a political point of view, rich individuals will have to be induced to save through low capital gains tax rates and other incentives that attract money into equity financing. Simply cutting the maximum rate enough to stimulate additional saving is not likely to gather many supporters; the tools to be used for the upper-income end of the scale are going to have to be found more in the investment sector.

Thus in view of the political realities, it is still necessary to look at reductions in business tax rates and capital gains tax rates to supply an important proportion, if not an absolute majority, of the stimulus to saving and investment. It is precisely these topics that are discussed in the following two chapters.

Appendix to Chapter 6: Calculating the Marginal Propensity to Save (MPS)

The calculation of the proportion of income saved from any across-the-board tax cut depends on three components: the increase in the rate of return, the income distribution of those receiving the tax cut, and the time horizon. The effects of all three of these factors must be considered in determining how much the Reagan tax cut will raise saving.

The actual rate of return variable which is used in our calculations is:

$$r_{Aaa} (1 - t_{ms}) - PCE_{04}$$

where r_{Aaa} = the corporate bond yield on Aaa rated issues;
t_{ms} = the marginal tax rate on saving, which at present is about 50 percent; and
PCE_{04} = annual rate of change in the implicit consumtion deflator over the past four years.*

For 1981 and 1982 the Aaa corporate bond rate averaged around 14 percent. The marginal tax rate on saving before the tax cut was 52 percent. The 25

*This measure of inflation is similar to the more familiar consumer price index but excludes the distorting affects of housing prices and mortgage rates; it also differs in several more technical aspects.

percent across-the-board tax cut reduced that to 41 percent, which is slightly less than proportional because relatively little interest income was subjected to marginal tax rates above 50 percent in any case.

Hence the rate of return would rise by 0.14×11 percent, or 1.54 percent. It was estimated that a 1 percent change in the rate of return raises the personal saving rate by approximately 1 percent. At 1982 levels, total disposable income was \$2.2 trillion; so when the tax cut was fully phased in, the increase in personal saving due to the rate of return effect would be \$2.2 trillion $\times$ 0.0154, or \$34 billion.

The total three-year tax cut, according to official Treasury estimates, will reduce personal income taxes by \$104 billion when fully implemented. Thus the MPS from the rate of return effect is calculated to be 34/104 or 0.33.

In order to calculate the income distribution effect, a profile of who pays how much in income taxes is necessary. This was provided by the Office of Tax Analysis of the Treasury Department for the original Reagan tax cut proposal in February 1981. These numbers, expanded to include the estimates here of the marginal propensity to save for each income classification, are given in table A.1.

The Treasury tables do not contain figures on the average saving rates at various levels of income, but we do have independent information on that from various consumer surveys. These generally show that consumer spending units (CSUs) with income below the median income do not save, and that in any given year their dissaving rate is about 5 percent. Figures for 1979 and 1980 illustrating this point are given in table A.2. This dissaving occurs for two main reasons: stage of life cycle, and temporary declines in income due to misfortune. Young CSUs just starting their careers and retired people generally dissave. Someone with an average income of \$20,000 per year who has that income cut to \$10,000 through a job layoff, illness, or extended vacation also is likely to dissave in that year.

The figures in table A.1 show that only 20 percent of the tax cut is received by those with income at or below the median. Another 40 percent of the tax cut is received by what could be characterized as middle-income groups: \$20,000 to \$40,000 in 1981 dollars. The final 40 percent of the tax cut is received by those in the upper-income brackets. Thus it is clear that most of the Reagan tax cut is directed at those CSUs who do most of the personal saving in this country.

Table A.1 also shows that 45 percent of the increase in saving due to higher income—that is, excluding for the moment the rate of return calculations—will come from those with incomes over \$100,000 per year, and all but 16 percent of the increase in saving will stem from those with incomes of \$40,000 or more per year. These figures show conclusively that in order to

134

TABLE A.1

Effect of the Administration's Proposed Tax Rate Reductions for 1984,
Distributed by Adjusted Gross Income Class
(1981 Levels of Income)

(1)	(2)	(3)	(4)	(5)	(6)	(7)
		Present Law				Amount Saved from Tax
Adjusted Gross Income Class	Number of Returns	Tax Liability[a]	Change in Tax[b] Amount	Percentage	Long-Term MPS	Reduction Given in Column (4)[c]
($000)	(000s)	(in millions of dollars)	(in millions of dollars)			(7) = −(4)×(6)
Less than 3.0	10,933	−48	−3	n.m.		
3.0– 5.0	7,363	27	−144	−533.3		
5.0– 6.0	3,406	381	−215	−56.4		
6.0– 8.0	6,623	2,073	−814	−39.3		
8.0– 10.0	6,210	3,988	−1,309	−32.8		
10.0– 12.5	7,164	7,425	−2,237	−30.1		
12.5– 15.0	6,303	9,117	−2,648	−29.0		
15.0– 17.5	5,602	10,570	−3,056	−28.9		
17.5– 20.0	5,281	12,610	−3,640	−28.9		
20.0– 25.0	9,377	28,615	−8,122	−28.4	0.02	162
25.0– 30.0	7,683	30,767	−8,563	−27.8	0.04	342
30.0– 35.0	5,592	28,229	−7,826	−27.7	0.06	470
35.0– 40.0	3,772	23,697	−6,551	−27.6	0.08	524
40.0– 50.0	4,185	34,758	−9,524	−27.4	0.11	1,048
50.0– 60.0	1,696	19,426	−5,275	−27.2	0.14	739
60.0– 70.0	813	12,267	−3,320	−27.1	0.17	564
70.0– 80.0	443	8,407	−2,255	−26.8	0.20	451
80.0– 90.0	289	6,735	−1,819	−27.0	0.24	437
90.0–100.0	198	5,333	−1,412	−26.5	0.30	424
100.0–200.0	546	23,765	−5,793	−24.4	0.40	2,317
200 and over	121	18,520	−3,762	−20.3	0.50	1,881
Total	93,599	286,659	−78,285	−27.3		

SOURCE: Office of the Secretary of the Treasury, Office of Tax Analysis, February 13, 1981, with the exception of columns 6 and 7, which were calculated by Evans Economics, Inc.
[a]Includes outlay portion of earned income credit.
[b]Tax rates are reduced approximately 30 percent. To avoid fractional marginal rates, each current law tax rate is not reduced exactly 30 percent under this bill. Also, deviation from a flat 30 percent reduction at all income levels is explained by interaction with the earned income credit and with the current law 50 percent maximum tax on personal service income.
[c]This is the long-run increase in saving due to higher income only. Calculations do *not* include the effect of the higher rate of return. N.B. Details may not add to totals due to rounding.

increase saving, it is necessary to reduce the tax burden of high-income taxpayers.

The long-term propensity to save due to the income distribution effects of the tax cut can be calculated as follows. The total increase in saving due to higher income, taken from column 7 of table A.1, is $9,359 million. The total amount of tax reduction taken from column 4 is $78,285, so the MPS from higher income is 0.12. The long-term MPS without taking into account any changes in rates of return or income distribution is approximately 0.06, so on average people receiving tax cuts from the Reagan across-the-board tax rate reduction are likely to save *twice as much* as the economy-wide average.

The MPS stemming *from income changes alone* is about 0.3 for the first year, 0.15 for the second year, 0.10 for the third year, and 0.06 in the long term excluding any income distribution or rate of return effects; these estimates are the ones commonly found in large-scale Keynesian econometric models. Modifying these figures to take into account the skewed distribution toward upper-income tax cuts yields estimates of 0.4, 0.23, and 0.17 for the MPS over the first three years and 0.12 for the long run. To the 0.12, we now must add the 0.33 MPS that will occur because the after-tax rate of return on saving has risen. Combining all these factors, the calculation of the total marginal propensity to save from an across-the-board tax cut is shown in table A.3.

These calculations can now be related to the three-year Reagan

TABLE A.2

Savings by Income and Education
Net Savings ($MM) by Family Income

	Total	−15,000	$15–25,000	$25,000+
Oct. 1980	427.07	−264.89	38.15	653.81
Jul. 1980	−257.12	−504.41	19.76	227.53
Jun. 1980	713.65	−222.64	188.43	747.86
Mar. 1980	501.16	−187.58	320.39	368.35
Dec. 1979	−56.45	−294.14	−255.92	493.61

Net Savings ($MM) by Education of Head of Household

	Total	Attend Grade	Grad Grade	Attend High	Grad High	Attend College	Grad College	Masters/ Doctors
Oct. 1980	427.06	−0.01	68.55	−33.10	−124.18	226.47	110.48	178.85
Jul. 1980	−257.13	−8.67	−65.76	−104.24	53.23	−72.57	39.62	−98.74
Jun. 1980	713.65	−39.78	−15.69	−52.49	247.98	−54.62	224.29	403.96
Mar. 1980	501.16	7.59	−65.96	−65.20	−1.46	234.23	270.22	121.74
Dec. 1979	−56.47	35.95	−50.57	−138.85	−248.95	33.08	213.57	99.30

SOURCE: Michael K. Evans, "The Source of Personal Saving in the U.S.," *Wall Street Journal,* 23 March 1981. Copyright W. J. Fitzgerald, Inc., 1981. Reprinted by permission.

TABLE A.3

Calculating the MPS from Tax Cuts

Marginal Propensity to Save Due to:	First Year	Second Year	Third Year	Long Term
Higher rate of return	0.33	0.33	0.33	0.33
"Normal" MPS[a]	0.30	0.15	0.10	0.06
Tax cut skewed toward higher income	0.10	0.08	0.07	0.06
Total MPS	0.73	0.56	0.50	0.45

[a]Assuming strictly proportional tax cut with no rate of return effect.

across-the-board tax cut. For ease of exposition let us assume the tax cut was a 30 percent reduction—10 percent per year for three years, with all tax cuts effective at the beginning of the year. Let us also assume the tax cut was $33⅓ billion per year, or a total of $100 billion, although as the economy grows the actual tax reduction is slightly greater in later years.

If taxes were to be reduced in strict proportion to personal income without changing tax rates—a 10 percent rebate, for example—a $100 billion tax cut phased in equally over three years would generate only $18 billion in increased saving the third year and $6 billion in the long term. Because the Reagan tax cut is proportional to taxes paid instead of income received, the increase in saving generated by higher income alone will be $27 billion in the third year and about $12 billion in the long term. Furthermore, the increase in the after-tax real rate of return will raise personal saving an additional $33 billion per year. This will yield a total increase in saving of $60 billion in 1984, as shown in table A.4, when both rate of return and income distribution factors are taken into account. Whereas this figure will decline to $51 billion in 1985, $48 billion in 1986, and $45 billion by 1990, the increase in saving should provide the additional investment and capacity needed to offset the later decline in the saving rate.

TABLE A.4

The Proportion of the Reagan Tax Cut That Would Be Saved

Amounts	First Year	Second Year	Third Year	Long Term
Tax reduction (cumulative)	33 1/3	66 2/3	100	100
Saved from first year tax cut	24	19	17	15
second year tax cut		24	19	15
third year tax cut			24	15
Total increase in saving	24	43	60	45

CHAPTER 7

Lowering Corporate Tax Rates

If Investment Rose, Why Did Productivity Fall?

If there is one area of general agreement among economists about the beneficial aspects of supply-side economics, it is that tax cuts which lower the cost of capital and raise the rate of return on investment stimulate capital spending and productivity. For this reason Congress has taken a bipartisan approach ever since 1954 in promoting the advancement of capital formation. During 1954–81, Congress passed no fewer than seven tax bills designed to lower the effective corporate tax rate; and except for two temporary suspensions of the investment tax credit, none of the reductions were rescinded. This record should stand as an impressive monument in comparison to the stop-go policies that have characterized the remainder of fiscal and monetary policy. On the surface, the results have also been impressive. Before the tax benefits of 1954, the ratio of capital spending to GNP (the "investment ratio") had averaged 9.2 percent for the previous four years. By 1978–81 this ratio had improved to 11.3 percent. This increase represented a gain of $60 billion per year for capital spending at 1981 levels.

But these figures are inconsistent with the improvement in capital stock and productivity. For in the early 1950s when the investment ratio was much lower, capital stock increased more than 5 percent per year—its growth peaked at 5.8 percent per year from 1965 to 1968—and productivity grew at better than 3 percent per year. From 1977 to 1982, capital stock growth diminished to 3 percent per year, whereas the level of productivity actually declined over this five-year period.[1]

To be sure, productivity declined for reasons far removed from the growth in investment or capital—the change in the mix of the labor force, the demise of the work ethic, the increase in government regulation, higher tax rates, disruptions caused by the energy crises, and many other factors. Yet economists are virtually unanimous in agreeing that one of the major ways to spur productivity growth is indeed through greater investment. It does not seem reasonable that these two factors could have moved in diametrically opposite directions.

The paradox is resolved as follows. Although the ratio of total capital spending to GNP has increased over time, investment patterns have undergone a major change in recent years, shifting away from assets with long lives toward assets with short lives. The combination of existing tax breaks, the fact that depreciation allowances are valued in historical instead of replacement costs, and the sharp increase in interest rates and inflation during the 1970s have all worked to shift investment preferences toward assets with shorter lives.

It will come as no surprise that such assets—automobiles and light trucks, aircraft, computers and office machinery, instruments, furniture, and so forth—have been the big gainers, whereas the traditional "heavy investment" goods—industrial construction, machine tools, general industry machinery, electrical transmission and distribution equipment, and utility plant and equipment—have taken a much smaller proportion of the investment dollar.

Two other factors also account for the divergent paths of the investment ratio and productivity. Since 1970 approximately 5 percent of total capital spending has gone for purposes of pollution abatement and control. Whether or not this was the right amount to spend toward cleaner air and water, it is indisputable that these expenditures did not add to productive capital stock; indeed in some cases, such as the scrubbers for electric utilities, they actually decreased output.

The final adjustment factor reflects the fact that capital goods prices have risen somewhat faster than other prices during the postwar period. In particular, construction costs have risen much faster than the cost of manufactured goods because of smaller productivity gains and more rapid wage increases in the construction sector. However, the price of producer durable equipment has also risen faster than for consumer durables, due to some speciality areas such as oil-country goods where prices have increased very rapidly.

When all of these three adjustment factors are taken into account, the investment ratio is thus seen to have declined substantially over the postwar period, as is shown in figure 7.1. The difference is especially noticeable from the high-water mark of the 1965–66 investment boom. Since that time, the unadjusted ratio shows a slight increase of about ½ percent. This increase disappears for the constant-dollar ratio, which shows investment in 1980 and 1981 at virtually the same proportion of GNP as in 1965 and 1966. Pollution control investment subtracts another ½ percent from the ratio for the most recent years.

However, the biggest switch is reflected in the change in assets lives, which has sliced more than 2 percent off the ratio. Seen in this light, the investment ratio since 1975 is near the bottom of the postwar average, not near the top as would be indicated by the unadjusted ratio. Clearly, industrial plant has been neglected at the expense of automobiles and light trucks, furniture, office equipment, and French-fry cookers. It is this trend that is largely responsible for the decline in productivity and the lack of competitiveness with our major foreign trading partners.

Solving this dilemma, however, simply raises another one. If the more or less steady proliferation of tax breaks have not contributed to an increase in productive investment or capacity, why continue to reduce corporate tax rates? This question received added attention when the business tax reductions in the 1981 Reagan tax package were followed by a surprising and demoralizing 8.3 percent decline in real capital spending during the following five quarters.

The answer once again depends on an analysis of the overall economy, not just the specific relationship between investment and tax rates. It will be shown that during periods when the economy was close to equilibrium—with little or no inflation, a balanced budget, and stable interest rates—tax breaks did

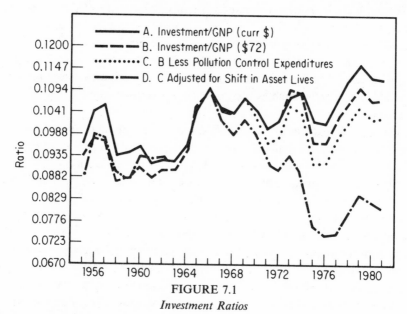

FIGURE 7.1

Investment Ratios

SOURCE: Prepared by Evans Economics, Inc.

indeed raise the investment ratio substantially. During periods of higher inflation, large budget deficits, and rising interest rates, however, the gains in investment evaporated, resulting both in a decline in the overall investment ratio and a shift toward assets with shorter lives. In particular the Reagan business tax cuts of 1981 were overwhelmed by the massive increases in interest rates which occurred in the two preceding years.

Thus once again the evidence is clear-cut that supply-side programs cannot be considered in a vacuum; they must be related to the overall balance between demand and supply, and between the total availability of funds and the demand for these funds. An increase in tax incentives for investment works very well when the additional funds are available at no increase in cost. It does not work at all well when the cost of funds increases so much that the investment would be uneconomic even at a zero tax rate.

The Three Investment Booms of the Postwar Period

Major modifications of the tax code that benefited capital spending occurred in 1954, 1962–64, and 1971. Without exception, each of these changes was followed by an investment boom that began the following year. For many years this history stood as impressive evidence that reductions in the corporate tax rate do indeed stimulate capital formation.

This litany has been challenged by events of the past decade. Since 1973 effective corporate income tax rates have risen, yet investment surged from 1976 to 1979. The 1981 tax cuts, as have been indicated, were followed by almost a free fall in capital spending. Because of these recent experiences, the relationship between the rate of return and capital spending cannot be taken for granted. This section shows why this relationship was so symbiotic during 1955 to 1973; then it evaluates what transpired from 1973 to 1980 and in the aftermath of the Reagan tax cuts.

The first major break for corporate taxpayers occurred in 1954, when for the first time companies were allowed to use accelerated depreciation methods. Before that time, taxpayers had to depreciate capital goods using the straight line (SL) method of depreciation; that is, the amount of depreciation taken each year was constant. The length of depreciable life for each asset had been determined by the Treasury and published in a certain Bulletin F back in 1942.

Whereas two accelerated methods were authorized—sum of the year's digits and double declining balance (DDB)—the latter is slightly more favorable, so that most firms that switched methods at all chose DDB. For those not familiar with the terminology, DDB permits the firm to write off twice as much of the remaining undepreciated balance each year as would be the case under straight line accounting.

For example, suppose a capital good was purchased for $100 and according to Bulletin F had a depreciable life of ten years. Under the old method, the depreciation allowance would be $10 per year. Under DDB, the first year's allowance (providing the good was purchased at the beginning of the year) would be $20, leaving a balance of $80. The second year's depreciation would be 20 percent of $80, or $16, and so on.

A moment's reflection will reveal that under this geometrically declining balance rule, the asset will never be completely depreciated. This problem is handled simply by letting the firm cross over to SL whenever the annual depreciation would otherwise be less under DDB. This occurs at the midpoint of the depreciable life, or five years in this example.

The year 1954 also marked the end of the excess profits tax instituted during the Korean War. In another change that did not directly impact cost of capital to the firm but did affect the rate of return to stockholders, a deduction of $100 per person and a 4 percent tax credit was given for dividend income—the first small, halting step toward tax integration. However, the tax credit was rescinded in the 1964 tax reduction and has never been reinstated.

The 1954 tax reform was not the first time that accelerated depreciation methods had been tried. During the Korean War, firms purchasing capital goods that were allegedly used for war production were allowed to write off the cost of the equipment completely over a five-year period; these write-offs were known as accelerated amortization allowances. However, that was done mainly to counteract the imposition of an excess profits tax which carried a marginal rate as high as 77 percent and hence cannot realistically be considered a spur toward investment. Indeed, because of the reorientation of production toward wartime goods, the investment ratio actually declined during the Korean War years.

The 1954 improvements in the tax laws had a very noticeable effect on capital spending. The investment ratio, which had averaged 9.2 percent in the previous four years, increased to 9.6 percent in 1955 and 10.5 percent in 1956 and 1957. Unfortunately, this investment boom was also accompanied by an increase in inflation from 0 percent to 4 percent. Money supply growth was brought to a halt, interest rates rose, the economy went into its first severe recession in almost 20 years, and the investment ratio fell back to 9.3 percent, which was to be its average for the next six years. This decline caused Kennedy to campaign on his slogan to "get the country moving again" and was instrumental in the massive business as well as personal income tax cuts that occurred from 1962 through 1965.

This period marked the only time in which all three principal instruments of corporate tax reduction were used: cutting the marginal tax rate itself, instituting the investment tax credit, and improving depreciation schedules. The income tax rate fell from 52 percent to 48 percent in two steps, a 7 percent investment tax credit was instituted in 1962, and depreciation lives contained in the Treasury's Bulletin F were reduced 30 to 40 percent. In addition, the number of categories of depreciable assets were streamlined from approximately 5,000 to about 130, thus greatly simplifying accounting procedures.

The idea of an investment tax credit (ITC)—an actual reduction in the tax bill, as opposed to bigger deductions for depreciation—was first introduced by President Kennedy in 1962 at an 8 percent rate. Congress reduced it to 7 percent, but the basic concept remained unchanged. It applies only to equipment, presumably because structures can usually be resold after their tax life has passed, whereas fully depreciated equipment is usually obsolete either in a physical or economic sense. The amount of tax credit was originally deducted from the depreciable base of the asset, so that in effect the firm could depreciate 93 percent instead of 100 percent of the value of the asset; but this was changed in 1964 by the so-called Long Amendment, after which the entire cost could be depreciated. Only one third of the tax credit was originally granted for assets whose tax lives were less than six years, and two thirds of the credit for those with tax lives between six and eight years. The credit for most public utility investment was only 3 percent. The credit was available for only $50,000 of used equipment. Firms could offset their tax liability up to $25,000 and one fourth of the credit above that figure. If firms could not use the tax benefits of the tax credit in the year in which the investment was purchased, they could be carried back three years and forward five years.

The initial response to the investment tax credit was rather sluggish, partly because of the relatively depressed economic conditions of the time and partly because it was viewed by some corporate treasurers as a "gimmick" not important enough to cause them to accept projects that had previously been rejected. However, by the time the corporate tax rate reduction was passed, the economy had improved. Response to the investment incentives was spectacular, both in terms of the increase in capital spending and the change from the economic doldrums of the previous five years, which in 1963 were generally expected to continue indefinitely. William F. Butler, then chief economist of the Chase Manhattan Bank, wrote that "a prediction in 1962 or even early 1963 that business capital investment was about to break out of the pattern of general stagnation which had characterized the previous five years would have been exceedingly useful not only to capital goods producers but also to investors."[2] Indeed, after increasing only 2.1 percent per year for the 1957–63 period, real capital spending then vaulted 12.9 percent per year for the next three years, including an unprecedented 17.8 percent increase in 1965. The investment ratio rose from 9.2 percent in 1961–63 to a peak of 11.0 percent in 1966.

The investment boom came unstuck in 1967 as Johnson unleashed the forces of countercyclicality. He suspended the investment tax credit and reduced accelerated depreciation for five months, and also caused the first credit crunch by pushing the prime rate up to 6 percent. Whereas the investment tax credit had initially received a mixed reaction, its acceptance had gradually become widespread; and both this brief suspension and the 28-month interruption starting in April 1969 caused a noticeable decline in capital spending.

Having momentarily slowed the rate of inflation, Johnson reinstated the tax credit and accelerated depreciation in March 1967, but the investment ratio did not rebound accordingly. Part of the reason for the decline in this ratio was undoubtedly the belief that the investment tax credit would be treated by the government as a yo-yo, disappearing just as firms planned to increase their capital spending. Yet one need not rely on this explanation alone, for most of the other fundamental components of the cost of capital also increased after 1966. Interest rates rose further, with the prime rate reaching 8½ percent in 1969. The corporate surtax clipped profits by an additional 10 percent in 1968 and 1969. And just for good measure, one of Nixon's first fiscal policy moves in 1969 was to suspend the investment tax credit again, which reduced the investment ratio by 0.7 percent over the next two years.

Those who question whether changes in the rate of return affect behavior of capital spending would do well to examine the record from 1963 to 1966 and from 1966 to 1969. Both of these times were basically periods of rapid growth, low unemployment, and high capacity utilization. To be more specific, real GNP excluding capital spending increased at an annual rate of 5.0 percent in the first period and 3.5 percent in the second. During the first period the unemployment rate averaged 5.0 percent; it fell to 3.5 percent during the second. The index of capacity utilization (Commerce Department series) averaged 86 percent during both periods. Yet capital spending in constant dollars grew 12.9 percent per year in the first period when tax incentives were working in favor of higher capital spending, and only 2.6 percent per year in the second when tax rates and interest costs moved higher. Seldom have we seen a more dramatic example of the impact of tax rates on capital spending.

The last major change to the tax code before the 1981 Tax Reduction Act occurred in late 1971 as part of the Nixon New Economic Plan. In addition to restating the investment tax credit, the Treasury adopted the so-called asset depreciation range, which meant in effect that depreciation lives were reduced by 20 percent from the standards promulgated in 1962. The regulations technically state that firms can choose a range of asset lives from 20 percent less to 20 percent more than the 1962 guideline lives, but obviously almost everyone preferred the shorter lives. The investment ratio then rose from 10.0 percent in 1971 to 10.8 percent in 1973 and 10.9 percent in 1974. Since the changes in the tax laws were not as large as in 1954 or 1962–64, the investment boom was correspondingly less impressive.

Throughout this period, reductions in business taxes always resulted in an increase in capital spending relative to GNP, whereas increases in these taxes reduced the investment ratio. However, after 1973 this relationship was to come unstuck, as higher inflation and interest rates distorted decisions affecting capital formation, essentially resulting in purchases of capital goods that were most favorable from a tax rather than an economic point of view.

The 1973–80 Experience: Inflation Erodes Profitability

From 1971 to 1981 little was done to change the tax laws that affected investment. The investment tax credit rose from 7 percent to 10 percent in 1975, and the corporate tax rate was cut from 48 percent to 46 percent in 1979, but these were offset by an increase in the maximum tax rate on long-term capital gains from 25 percent in 1968 to 49.1 percent in 1976, which depressed the stock market and made equity financing much more difficult.

On the surface, investment and profitability did not appear to be hurt during this period. Profit margins, measured as the ratio of aftertax profits to GNP, generally increased during the 1970s; and as already shown in figure 7.1, the investment ratio also trended upward. However, as already mentioned, capital stock growth declined almost by half from 1965–68 to 1977–82. The investment ratio also declined once the trend toward purchasing assets with shorter lives is taken into account. Furthermore, although book profits seemed healthy, economic profits were stagnating badly because of the distorting effects of inflation, which are considered next.

Suppose our xygots firm has sales of $100, variable costs of $70, depreciation of $20, and pre-tax profits of $10. Now assume that prices double. Sales rise to $200 and variable costs increase to $140. Because depreciation allowances are valued in historical instead of replacement terms, they remain at $20. Thus book profits have quadrupled, rising to $40. Assuming a 50 percent marginal tax rate both before and after the price increase, aftertax profits have risen from $5 to $20. So apparently businesses benefit by inflation.

Not really, though. For in fact the firm is not even as well off. Since prices have doubled, it will cost twice as much to replace the machine which produces xygots, and hence depreciation allowances really should have risen $40. If so, that would have reduced pre-tax profits back to $20 and everything would have remained proportional.

Except for taxes. Since nominal profits have quadrupled, so have taxes on these profits, rising from $5 to $20. Hence on an economic basis—that is, correctly valuing depreciation—the firm is left with no profits at all. The effect of inflation has been to raise the tax burden from 50 percent to 100 percent!

The same type of problem arises for the valuation of inventory stocks. Suppose that a certain type of plastics is one of the essential ingredients for manufacturing xygots, and the price level—and value—of the raw material stocks sitting on the shelves doubles—perhaps due to another energy crisis. On the books, the firm has shown a substantial profit. But this is actually no profit at all, for the firm will obviously have to pay the higher price to replace the inventory stock, and the profit will immediately disappear. This is another example of paying real taxes on phony profits.

In the U.S. economy, prices usually do not double from one year to the next, so the simple example is clearly overstated. Yet the general phenomenon is a very real one. Thus, for example, when double-digit inflation surfaced in 1974, the economic tax rate rose from 45 percent to 54 percent even though the accounting tax profit fell from 39 percent to 38 percent.

The increase in the inflation rate has raised the economic tax rate on profits significantly since 1965. As is shown in figure 7.2, the economic and accounting tax rates were virtually the same in that year. From 1965 to 1980, however, the accounting tax rate declined from 0.40 to 0.34, giving rise to the claim that businesses were receiving successively larger tax breaks. Yet the economic tax rate, adjusted for the effect of inflation on inventories and capital stock, rose significantly from 0.39 to 0.45.

Not only has the economic rate of corporate taxation risen since 1965, but the ratio of profits to GNP has fallen sharply. As is shown in figure 7.3, pre-tax profits have declined from 11.2 percent of GNP in 1965 to 9.2 percent in 1980; they subsequently dipped to a postwar low of 5.7 percent in 1982. If pre-tax profits are adjusted for the phony increases due to inflation, there is an even more dramatic decline from 11.6 percent in 1965 to 7.0 percent in 1980, although the reduction in the next two years is then somewhat more modest as much of the reported decline in profits was due to disinflation. Both series,

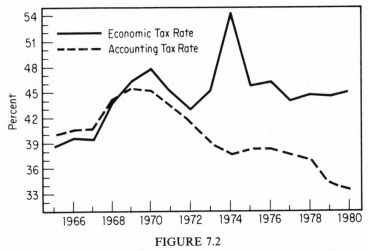

FIGURE 7.2

Tax Rates on Corporate Profits

SOURCE: Prepared by Evans Economics, Inc.

however, point to lower profit margins; and when coupled with higher economic tax rates, they provide the necessary motive for avoiding all but the shortest-lived investments, which until 1981 had the correspondingly largest tax advantages.

An increase in the rate of inflation not only raises the effective tax rate for corporations but also makes it much more expensive to raise debt or equity capital. In the past decade, the rise in inflation has been accompanied by an

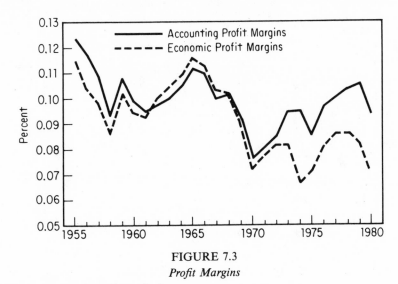

FIGURE 7.3

Profit Margins

SOURCE: Prepared by Evans Economics, Inc.

unprecedented increase in interest rates. A company that floated a bond at 3 percent in 1947 would find essentially that its economic profits had been overstated for many years when it had to refinance the money at 15 percent in 1982. The stock market has also been deeply depressed by the increase in interest rates. The myth that the stock market is a good hedge against inflation has now been entirely debunked by events of the 1970s, since the cost of equity capital also increases as inflation and interest rates rise. With stock prices below book value for many companies, equity financing has been written off for a large proportion of the corporate universe.

Figure 7.4 indicates how far the rate of return on assets and equity have declined both from the postwar peak in 1965 and the secondary peak in 1973. The rate of return on depreciable assets—that is, excluding land and other assets which are not depreciated at all—declined from 14.0 percent in 1965 all the way to an average of 7.6 percent for 1974–81. The rate of return on stockholders' equity has not declined quite as sharply but has diminished from 9.5 percent in 1965 to the 7 percent range in recent years.

Even more damaging is the reduction in the ratio of the value placed on existing plant and equipment by the stock market to the replacement value of these assets. When this ratio exceeds unity, firms are more likely to invest

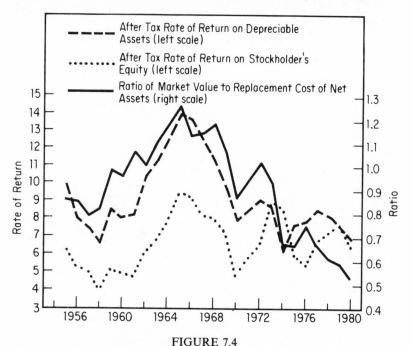

FIGURE 7.4

Determinants of Business Investment

SOURCE: Prepared by Evans Economics, Inc.

in new assets, for purchasing new plant and equipment is cheaper than buying existing companies. When the ratio is less than unity, however, buying existing assets—that is, purchasing existing companies—is less costly than spending the money on new plant and equipment. This ratio has fallen the most sharply of all, declining from 1.3 in 1965 to a meager 0.5 in 1980 and 1981. It is small wonder that merger-and-acquisition activity has reached fever pitch while at the same time purchases of long-lived plant and equipment continues to fall steadily.

Thus on balance the various improvements in the tax code since 1954 have been more than offset by the negative factors of higher inflation, a declining rate of return, and the higher cost of debt and equity financing. The three investment booms that were chronicled in the previous section together accounted for almost a 5 percent increase in the investment ratio. Yet the high ground never seemed to be retained; the ratio always seemed to settle back at a lower level. Over the past twenty-five years the investment ratio has increased only about 1½ percent, and when an adjustment is made for government-mandated investment and change in mix of asset of lives, it has declined almost 2 percent—in spite of the undeniable cyclical stimulus of tax reduction. Clearly a more comprehensive long-term approach was needed.

Thus the economy progressed to the threshold of the 1981 Tax Reduction Act with an apparently high investment ratio but with in reality a slowdown in capital stock growth, neglect of basic industrial facilities, and a serious loss of competitive position in world markets. The reduction in depreciation lives was designed specifically to correct just these problems.

We know that on balance the entire program was a failure—that investment plummeted 5 percent in real terms the next year, productivity showed virtually no gain in 1982, and our foreign trade position deteriorated further. Yet we need to examine whether the Reagan tax cuts were meaningless—or whether they were basically sound but overwhelmed by the combination of unfavorable economic conditions in 1981 and 1982.

The 1981 Tax Reduction Act: Accelerated Cost Recovery and Safe Harbor Leasing

By 1981, economists of virtually all political persuasions agreed that substantial business tax cuts were needed to restructure depreciation allowances and lessen the distorting effects of inflation. A complete overhaul was required that would protect the investor against the inequities caused by inflation. The plan that was chosen, to be described later, is known as Accelerated Cost Recovery System (ACRS).

From an economic point of view, the best choice simply would have been to calculate depreciation allowances in replacement instead of historical cost. Such a method would provide for equitable accounting whether inflation rates were high or low. Furthermore, it would not tip the balance in favor of short-lived assets, which to a certain extent happens under any historical cost method of depreciation.[3]

This plan, however, was received quite unenthusiastically. Many argued that it would be too complicated to compute the rate of inflation for the multitude of different assets. The idea of using one overall index, such as the implicit deflator for capital spending, was rejected on the grounds that some assets, such as computers, actually are declining in price over time and this method would bias investment toward those assets that increased least in price. Although this might be a novel way of keeping down inflation, business lobbyists and Congressmen were generally lukewarm about the concept.

Another possibility briefly considered was the so-called first-year capital recovery system, which had been championed by Berkeley and Harvard economics professor Dale Jorgenson for the past twenty years but until 1981 had received virtually no attention outside economic journals. According to the Jorgenson plan, firms would receive *all* their depreciation during the first year, except that this sum would be discounted over the estimated economic life of the capital good by 4 percent per year, generally estimated to be the rate of return companies earn on their assets after adjusting for inflation. According to Jorgenson, this method would be invariant to the rate of inflation, since inflation and interest rates move together. In other words, if inflation rises, so will interest rates, so that while firms will have to pay more for the capital good when it is replaced, they will have earned more interest by investing the money saved on taxes from their lump-sum depreciation because of higher interest rates. Thus on balance investors will no longer suffer if the rate of inflation increases.

Under the Jorgenson plan, a firm would receive $0.56 for every $1.00 invested for an asset with a ten-year life; for a 20-year life the figure would drop to $0.31 and for a 30-year life to $0.17. Note, however, that firms would receive this sum in the initial year of the investment instead of receiving partial depreciation write-offs each year over the lifetime of the asset.

If the Jorgenson plan had been adopted, it would have turned out to be a bonanza for businesses in 1982, since the real rate of return zoomed from 4 percent to almost 10 percent. The drain on the Treasury would have been correspondingly more severe, but the incentives to investment would have been greater, thus offsetting the painful increase in interest rates on capital spending in general.

In fact, the Jorgenson plan, like replacement cost accounting, is more efficient than ACRS from an economic point of view, for it does not discriminate in favor of assets with shorter tax lives, nor does the relative profitability of investment change as the inflation rate fluctuates. But the Jorgenson plan never had a chance. The concept is somewhat arcane to those schooled to think in terms of yearly depreciation allowances that continue until the tax life of the asset has ended. Furthermore, Jorgenson was not able to carefully explain the nuances of his bill in such a way that the average layman could follow his ideas; he is more used to the atmosphere of academia. His plan was discredited by Charly Walker, whose lobbying skills were finely honed to win the battle of safe harbor leasing, and Jorgenson's plan was dead in the Senate Finance Committee hearing room as soon as Walker testified.[*4]

In any case, ACRS certainly does simplify the tax code. From the 5,000 categories listed in Bulletin F and the 130 categories listed in the 1962 depreciation guidelines, ACRS reduces the tax code to four classifications:

(1) *Three-year lives:* All equipment that previously had a tax life of four years or less, which in practice is automobiles, light trucks, and over-the-road tractor units. Also included in this category are capital goods used for research and experimentation, and—believe it or not—race horses more than two years old and other horses more than twelve years old.

(2) *Five-year lives:* All equipment not covered under categories (1), (3) or (4).

(3) *Ten-year lives:* Most equipment used by public utilities; basically those categories of capital equipment that previously had tax lives of 15 years or more. The major categories in this group are manufactured homes, railroad tank cars, and certain coal utilization property of public utilities.

(4) *Fifteen-year lives:* All construction, plus any public utility equipment that previously had a life of more than twenty-five years.

The net effect of these changes is to reduce depreciation lives by approximately 40 to 50 percent. In the original bill, the reduction was even greater for assets with the longest lives. The bill first proposed by Reagan had only the first three categories—three-, five-, and ten-year lives—but it was thought this would confer too much of a benefit on structures, so the fifteen-year classification was added to the bill in June 1981.

Total capital spending in 1981 was $296 billion. If it is assumed that the average tax life of depreciable assets declined from fifteen to eight years because of ACRS, and that virtually everyone uses the DDB method of deprecia-

---

*Just after Jorgenson finished testifying and walked out of the room, several senators asked Walker if he could explain what Jorgenson was talking about. "No," said Walker, "but I'll tell you what's wrong with it"—and he then launched into a well-rehearsed polemic against "academic tax purists."

tion, then this implies that total depreciation from new investment in 1981 would have risen from $40 to $74 billion in that year. Since the marginal corporate income tax rate is 46 percent, that means an additional tax loss of $16 billion the first year. The tax loss increases rapidly in future years; the loss in 1982, for example, equals the additional first-year depreciation in 1982 plus the second-year depreciation loss from 1981 investment. The number is not quite twice as big since second-year depreciation is somewhat smaller: an asset can be depreciated only once, so larger depreciation allowances early in the life of the good are eventually offset by smaller ones later on. Taking all these factors into account, plus an estimated 10 percent per year growth in investment itself, the tax loss from this bill would have been in excess of $60 billion per year by 1984.

Because this seemed like much too big a tax bite all at once, the administration decided, and Congress agreed, to offset the tax loss from 1981 through 1984 using two methods. The first was to reduce DDB (200 percent) to a 150 percent declining balance. Under the pre-1981 law, first-year depreciation for a $100 capital good with a ten-year tax life would have been $20. With the new depreciation lives and no offset, this would rise to $40 billion. By reintroducing a 150 percent declining balance, the depreciation would be cut to $30.* Thus the additional tax losses would roughly be cut in half. Starting in 1985, by which time the peak tax loss would have passed, the declining balance was to have increased to 175 percent, and then returned to 200 percent in 1986 and later years, but these increases were cancelled in the 1982 tax bill.

The second offset was to cut depreciation allowances in half for the first year, on the grounds that if investment decisions were evenly spaced during the year, the average use of a new capital good during its initial year of purchase would be six months. This would preclude, for example, someone placing a new capital good in service on December 31 and claiming an entire year's depreciation. On the other hand, if a good were placed in service on January 1, the owner still would only be entitled to a half year's depreciation the first year. Thus, for example, capital equipment with a life of five years would now receive annual depreciation of 15 percent the first year, 22 percent the second year, and 21 percent for the remaining three years. The only exception to this rule is construction depreciated over a fifteen-year life, where the initial year's depreciation depends on the month during which the asset is placed in service.

Previously the full investment tax credit was not available for those assets with lives of less than seven years. Since virtually all equipment was reduced to a five-year life, this would have nullified much of the ITC without some

*As an additional bonus to real estate, tax lives were not only to be reduced to fifteen years but the 200 percent declining balance method remained intact throughout.

offsetting changes in the rules. Hence it was decided that all equipment would qualify for the full 10 percent credit except assets with tax lives of three years, where the credit is 6 percent. This essentially restores the range that existed before 1981 and hence should not be thought of as a significant change in the content of the tax laws. However, in 1982 the investment tax credit was cut back from 10 percent to 8 percent.

In order to gauge the importance of ACRS, it is useful to look at the effective tax rates on new depreciable assets for various industries. The importance of ACRS to individual firms and industries clearly depends on how capital intensive they are. In an ordinary year, both capital spending and pre-tax profits are approximately 10 percent of GNP. The combination of ACRS and the investment tax credit reduces taxes by about 20 percent of investment undertaken in any given year. Thus if corporate taxes would ordinarily be about 5 percent of GNP without any tax preferences, they are reduced to 3 percent with the 1981 legislation. In other words, the effect of the tax preferences is to reduce the corporate income tax rate from about 50 percent to about 30 percent on an aggregate basis. Furthermore, the benefits are proportionately larger for those industries where equipment represents a large percentage of total capital spending, since the tax credit applies to equipment but not plant.

Manufacturing is of course much more capital intensive than the trade and service sector of the economy. Many manufacturing industries use twice as much capital per unit of output as the national average but have the same pre-tax profit margins, in which case the combination of ACRS and the investment tax credit would reduce the corporate income tax bill from about 50 percent to 10 percent. In some cases the corporate tax would be *completely eliminated* by these tax breaks.

While this may sound far-fetched, that is exactly what happened as a result of the new tax laws. According to the Office of Tax Analysis, effective tax rates on new investment for the mining, motor vehicles, and transportation services industries did actually become negative in 1982 under the new law. A more comprehensive list of how industries were affected is given in table 7.1.[5]

Since striving to reduce one's tax bill as far as possible is a goal that occupies the minds of the vast majority of the population, one might reasonably expect that those firms and industries that had managed to eliminate their corporate income tax would be ecstatic. However, that is not at all what happened. Far from being delighted, firms and industries that found themselves with no taxes to pay now claimed they would be put at an unfair disadvantage—which led to the other major change in the corporate tax laws in 1981.

Suppose a firm purchases a capital good for $100. Ordinarily it could expect to deduct $10 from its taxes for the ITC and (assuming a 50 percent marginal

TABLE 7.1

Effective Tax Rates on New Depreciable Assets,
Selected Industries, 1982[1]

Industry	Old Law	New Law
Agriculture	32.7	16.6
Mining	28.4	−3.4
Primary metals	34.0	7.5
Machinery and instruments	38.2	18.6
Motor vehicles	25.8	−11.3
Food	44.1	20.8
Pulp and paper	28.5	.9
Chemicals	28.8	8.6
Petroleum refining	35.0	1.1
Transportation services	31.0	−2.9
Utilities	43.2	30.6
Communications	39.8	14.1
Services and trade	53.2	37.1

SOURCE: Department of the Treasury, Office of Tax Analysis.
NOTE: Assumes a 4 percent real after-tax rate of return and 8 percent inflation.
[1]Industries chosen had at least $5 billion in new investment in 1981.

tax rate) another $7.50 for the first year's depreciation, using the half year convention. But suppose the firm has no profits, pays no taxes, and furthermore has losses in so many other years that the carry-back and forward options do not matter either?

Until 1981 the tax credit was unused. The 1981 tax bill, however, contained a provision whereby firms were allowed to sell these tax credits to other firms that did have profits. The idea is actually quite simple. Company A, which is not very capital intensive, has profits of $100 and taxes of $50. Company B, which either is very capital intensive or simply has a loss, just made an investment of $200, which would entitle it to $35 in tax reduction, but it does not have any profits to offset the tax preference. It therefore contacts Company A and offers to sell it the tax benefits. A and B agree to split up the $35 in benefits, and everyone is happy—except, of course, the U.S. Treasury and all the other taxpayers.

Since an outright sale of tax credits was evidently considered a little flagrant even in the 1981 spate of tax cuts, a more dignified strategm was proposed. Company B would not really purchase that capital good for $200. Instead, Company A would purchase it and lease it back to Company B. Company A would take the full $35 tax credit but would adjust the term of the lease so that B actually received whatever proportion of the tax benefits agreed on. Hence the bill was more formally known as the Sale and Leaseback of Tax Credits. Some wag dredged up the name "Safe Harbor Leasing"—presumably on the grounds that the investment was in a safe tax harbor—and that is the name that stuck.

It is not possible to generate precise estimates of how much this tax credit is worth, for that would involve a knowledge of the tax rates of all firms that were both buyers and sellers of the tax credits. Given that many firms had poor years in 1982, however, and that the most capital-intensive sectors of the economy generally have the lowest profit rates in recession years, it is likely that between one third and one half of all capital equipment purchases fell under this plan. Since purchases of producers durable equipment in 1982 were about $200 billion, the value of the investment tax credit for firms engaging in these transactions would be between $6 and $9 billion per year, assuming a 50 percent marginal tax rate for the profitable firms. Furthermore, it affords these firms an unparalleled method of sheltering their profits. In one highly publicized case, General Electric not only paid no taxes in 1981 but filed for a $150 million tax refund for previous years.

Safe harbor leasing was a bad idea from Day One, for it opened the floodgates for much greater corporate and personal tax avoidance. Under ACRS the tax benefits would accrue only to those who increased their capital spending, which was clearly the intent of the bill. However, once safe harbor leasing is added, firms can receive a tax reduction whether or not they increased their capital spending. It is simply a tax avoidance scheme that increases the federal budget deficit without any offsetting benefits to society and abolishes the corporate income tax entirely for many firms. For these reasons Congress voted to rescind these benefits in the 1982 Tax Equity and Fiscal Responsibility Act.

Most economists—not only conservative, free-market economists and business lobbyists but also many noted liberal economists such as Lester Thurow—have long championed abolishing the corporate income tax.[6] In that case, why is abolishing the tax through a combination of ACRS and safe harbor leasing such a bad idea?

First, abolishing the corporate income tax as a specific measure should be accomplished with the framework of total revenue neutrality, which means that the lost tax revenues should be balanced either by increasing taxes elsewhere or reducing government spending. Otherwise the burden of the tax loss is shifted back through high interest rates to the net borrowers in society, who are (a) middle-class homeowners, and (b) corporations that must borrow in order to invest—the latter precisely the same group that the tax benefits are allegedly trying to help.

Second, the use of safe harbor leasing is capricious, rewarding those firms and individuals best able to generate tax savings rather than those contributing the most toward raising the level of investment and productivity. Safe harbor leasing also penalizes small, growing firms without ready access to capital markets and cash flow, which cannot afford to buy the equipment and lease it to some other firm, and which cannot afford to borrow because they have not yet established adequate credit ratings. Indeed, under ACRS and safe harbor leasing, small, dynamic firms would have paid an even greater disproportionate share of the total tax burden.

Third, safe harbor leasing misdirects the flow of capital. In some cases, firms are losing money because of events beyond their control. A sudden switch in markets, a flood of imports, sharp increases in prices of key raw materials, or changes in government regulations may temporarily eliminate their profits. However, it is far more often the case that a company losing money —particularly over a span of several years—is either providing a good or service no longer needed or is guilty of chronic bad management. Should the buggy whip manufacturers be subsidized because a lack of profitability precludes them from investing in more modern equipment to manufacture more buggy whips? Or as a somewhat more up-to-date analogy, should those steel firms that have failed to modernize and update their product lines and those automobile companies that think quality control is un-American be rewarded for their errors in management while profitable firms in the same industries still have to bear the burden of a full tax load?

Fourth, even those who propose elimination of the corporate income tax usually couple this suggestion with what is commonly known as integration of the tax system, that is, combining the personal and corporate income tax so that corporate profits are taxed only once. Under this scheme, the profits of the corporation would flow through to the individual stockholders, who would then be liable for tax on their share of profits whether or not the funds were actually distributed in the form of dividends. This could conceivably put some stockholders in the position of having to pay taxes on money they had never received, so that in practice at least the stockholders' taxes would be distributed. Yet this would avoid the onerous double taxation of dividends, and by lowering the tax burden on the corporation would clearly stimulate capital formation. As was already discussed in chapter 6, direct integration is used in Germany, Italy, and the United Kingdom, and indirect integration—the use of tax credits for dividends—is used in Belgium, Canada, France, and Japan. Obviously the United States is well behind in this area.

Fifth, and most important, abolishing the corporate income tax through the back door, so to speak, rewards the least productive sectors of society and penalizes the most productive. This entire process rewards the stagnant, least efficient sectors of society and starves the most dynamic, fastest growing areas of much-needed capital. Safe harbor leasing essentially reshapes our industrial pattern to be more like Britain and less like Japan—hardly the hope of either the Reagan administration and this or any other Congress.

Why the Reagan Business Tax Cuts Failed
to Stimulate Investment

The introduction of ACRS provided an additional $9 billion to corporations in FY 1982 and would have produced much more than that in the following years: $17 billion in 1983, $28 billion in 1984, $41 billion in 1985, and $62 billion in 1986. In addition, safe harbor leasing, in the brief period before it was repealed, provided an additional $6 billion per year in tax abatements. Thus the Reagan tax package cut corporate taxes by $15 billion for 1982, much of which, it was supposed, would be used to increase capital spending. However, precisely the opposite reaction occurred. Fixed business investment in 1972 dollars declined from $174 billion in the quarter that the tax cut was passed to its trough of $157 billion early in 1983—a $17 billion decline.

To be sure, not all of the reduction in taxes would have been immediately translated into higher investment even under optimal circumstances. Since investment decisions are not made instantaneously, the lagged effect must be taken into account. Furthermore, not all of the tax reduction would be used for higher investment; some would just be used to pay off old debt, for reliquification, and so on. However, the results still should have been substantial. By 1983 we estimate that ACRS should have raised capital spending by about $6 billion, with this figure increasing to $12 billion in 1984, $18 billion in 1985, and so on, as the benefits grew apace. The increased investment stemming from safe harbor leasing is much more difficult to estimate, but a reasonable estimate would be $2 to $3 billion per year. Thus, investment should have risen about $8 to $9 billion per year as the result of the Reagan business tax cuts, providing that none of the other determinants of investment changed.

Obviously this last condition was not satisfied. To be more specific, long-term interest rates, as measured by the Aaa corporate bond yield, rose from an average yield of 9.6 percent in 1979 to an average of 14.7 percent in the first half of 1982—an increase of 5 percent. Such an increase in long-term rates in a two-year period is unprecedented in the entire history of the U.S. economy, going all the way back to 1790.

Table 7.2 shows how investment would be affected by the various factors which comprise the cost of capital—the interest rate, investment tax credit, corporate income tax rate, length of depreciation lives, and accelerated depreciation.

These estimates clearly indicate that a five-percentage-point increase in interest rates overwhelms any changes that would occur from adjusting any of

TABLE 7.2

Change in Capital Spending Due to the Effect of Various Changes in Components of the Cost of Capital

Change in Cost of Capital Component	Change in Investment (billions of 1972 dollars)
Five-percentage-point increase in long-term interest rate[a]	−25.5
Reducing investment tax credit from 10 percent to 5 percent	−8.6
Six-percentage-point decline in corporate income tax rate (46 percent to 40 percent)	6.4
Lowering depreciation lives from fifteen to eight years[b]	9.5
Changing 200 percent (double) declining balance to 150 percent declining balance[b]	−3.9

SOURCE: Calculations by Evans Economics, Inc.
[a]Actual increase from 1979 to 1982.
[b]Actually occurred in 1981 Tax Reduction Act.

the other tax terms, a point that was also stressed in chapter 4. Whereas lowering the effective corporate income tax rate through various tax preferences should be encouraged, it is essentially a small measure when compared with the swings in interest rates that have occurred during the 1973 to 1982 period. Indeed, while the tax advantages contained in the 1981 Tax Reform Act raised investment $8 to $9 billion per year, the increase in interest rates lowered investment $25 billion. Thus on balance the *net* effect of the first two years of the Reagan program was to diminish capital spending in real terms by approximately $17 billion.

With the tax increases contained in the 1982 legislation, the situation turned even bleaker for capital spending. Although the increase in accelerated depreciation will not be cut back until 1985, the 1982 changes not only wiped out safe harbor leasing, which was no great loss, but reduced the value of the investment tax credit from 10 percent to 8 percent; these two reductions reversed about $6 billion of the $9 billion increase that had previously been expected. In other words, the benefits of the tax bill remaining after August 1982 could be expected to raise investment by only $3 billion per year, compared to the burden of a $25 billion decline placed by higher interest rates. At this rate capital spending will remain in the doldrums for much of the 1980s.

Furthermore, as serious as was the 5 percent decline in total real capital spending for 1982, the reductions were much worse in key industrial sectors. Declines of 20 percent or more in real terms occurred for investment in the metals and transportation equipment industry, and of 10 percent to 20 percent for most categories of the machinery industry, particularly those sectors that make up "Smokestack America." The industries that were supposed to be helped the most by the tax bill were precisely those that were hardest hit.

This situation has led some economists to wonder out loud whether the whole procedure of generalized tax cuts is the proper way to stimulate the investment necessary for the United States to regain its competitive posture in world markets. They have suggested that instead of broad-based measures, such as the investment tax credit and accelerated depreciation, the government should target aid directly to those industries where the need is greatest and the financial capability lowest.[7] It is this topic which is now addressed in the final section of this chapter.

Targeting Investment: The British and the Japanese Experience

Proponents and adversaries of capitalism agree that its single most distinguishing feature is that investment is undertaken to bring the owners of capital the highest expected rate of return. To some, this is the genius of the system; to others, its despair. The advocates of capitalism argue, sometimes passionately, that only by choosing the highest rate of return can that scarce resource, capital, be allocated most efficiently; otherwise it will go into projects dictated by personal preference or political persuasion rather than economic necessity. On the other hand, the opponents argue that free-market choices cause railroads to buy amusement parks, steel companies to buy insurance firms, and oil companies to buy department stores instead of spending available capital resources on the improvement of their existing plant and equipment.

Both liberals and conservatives would agree, I think, that our present process of capital allocation has produced too few modern steel mills and too many bowling alleys and fast-food franchises. But they differ by 180 degrees on the way to fix the problem. The conservatives would argue that the market has not been free to move capital to its best uses because of the various tax and regulatory restrictions. The liberals, on the other hand, would argue that it is market forces that have produced this imbalance between steel mills and more frivolous activities, and hence the function has to be taken away from the market and turned over to the government, which thus should be empowered to direct scarce capital resources to their "best" uses.

In a perfect world without corporate taxes, inflation, suboptimal fiscal and monetary policies, government regulations, tariffs and quotas, and monopolists or monopsonists, including labor unions, it is clear that the market forces would make the best decisions, if only because the entire panopoly of investment decisions that have to be made is so great that even the most enlightened, well-motivated government bureaucrats cannot follow developments accurately in all markets.

However, that is not a very useful statement. For exactly this type of reasoning has heaped so much disgrace on the whole concept of supply-side economics. The steps that should have been taken to cure stagnant productivity, anemic growth, and high inflation were quite clear: cut taxes and increase saving, investment, work incentives, and productivity by switching resources from consumption to investment and from the public to the private sector. As an exercise in economic theory it was a magnificent triumph. As an exercise in political reality it was a virtual disaster because the politics of the situation permitted only token cuts in government spending and did nothing to stop the proliferation of unneeded tax preferences passed under the guise of accomplishing those noble economic objectives. So before dismissing investment planning out of hand as a knee-jerk conservative reaction, let us look at the political realities just a bit more closely.

In *some* countries targeted investment works well. Japan is one outstanding example. A country with an embryonic capital market that essentially depends on government decisions to distribute scarce capital resources, Japan has a growth record unsurpassed by any other major industrial country.

Furthermore, even the hard-core free marketeers are not above approving some government intervention. The targeting of government funds into research and development is unconditionally applauded because we realize that though the risks of R&D are generally too great for any one company to bear, the social rate of return on R&D is usually much higher than on comparable private investment.

Thus the major problem with targeting investment is not that it runs contrary to the principal of laissez-faire economics, but that bureaucrats, especially in the United States, invariably make the wrong decisions. Given a choice, the United States routinely opts to follow the experience of the United Kingdom rather than that of Japan.

What industries did Britain assist? The steel industry. The auto industry. The rail industry. The coal industry. The ship-building industry. The point of this aid was to provide enough modern capital plant and equipment to these industries so that they could regain their world competitiveness. The experiment has been a notorious failure. The British steel industry, succored by government aid so that it could return to its goal of forty million tons a year, is now down to fourteen million tons and failing rapidly. And have you driven a British car lately?

160

The Japanese, on the other hand, have directed their investment funds into high-technology industries: robots, miniaturized circuits, and now fifth-generation computers, which will pay off, if ever, in fifteen years or more.

If the U.S. government would invest more in the industries of the future and less in the industries of the past, we could make a fairly compelling case for some increase in government intervention in the capital markets. But the United States has shown a curious reluctance to meet the Japanese semiconductor and computer threat even halfway while voting billions of dollars in aid to the steel and automobile industries. This misallocation was briefly exacerbated by safe harbor leasing, for the major beneficiaries of this legislation are those companies that have no profits because of poor marketing or mismanagement.

The various tax incentive schemes that have been tried during the period from 1954 to 1980 have had very little effect over the long run on increasing the investment ratio of the U.S. economy. Although tax laws were indeed liberalized, the benefits were offset by the decline in profits, the increase in inflation, and the much higher cost of debt and equity financing. Short-term cyclical gains in the investment ratio were mitigated by the long-term secular upward trends in the cost of financing.

The U.S. experience of stimulating investment has been particularly disappointing when compared with the rest of the world, since this country is dead last in both the proportion of resources devoted to capital spending and in productivity growth, as is shown in figure 7.5. The large business tax cuts contained in the 1981 legislation reflected this realization.

The 1981 act did indeed reduce depreciation lives far enough that most firms would be shielded in the future from the ravages of inflation. Second, it provided important new incentives for personal savings so that more funds would be available, lowering the cost of debt capital. Third, it reduced capital gains taxes, thereby lowering the cost of equity capital to corporations. Whereas all of these moves combined would still leave the U.S. economy far behind Germany and Japan, it was at least thought that they would move the United States out of last place in the productivity derby and raise the investment ratio from 10 percent to perhaps the 15 percent level.

However, the Reagan program took away with one hand what it gave with the other. The increase in personal saving was more than matched by the increase in the federal budget deficit. The purpose of ACRS, to give firms lower tax rates if they invested more, turned out to reduce their tax rates even if they invested less, which they promptly proceeded to do. Consequently, total national saving declined, and interest rates reached historic highs instead of returning to their previous parity with inflation.

161

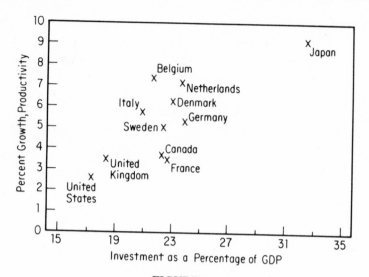

FIGURE 7.5

Productivity Growth and Investment Ratios

SOURCE: Prepared by Evans Economics, Inc.

When the economy recovers and once again approaches full employment and full capacity, there is still every reason to expect that ACRS will cause capital spending to be higher than would otherwise have been the case, although with the 1982 tax increases the benefits will be much smaller than originally anticipated. In the meantime, however, the investment ratio has already slipped further and is close to declining to new postwar lows. Because of the 5 percent rise in long-term interest rates, the Reagan business tax cut package was not able to deliver what its original backers had intended.

CHAPTER 8

The Key to Dynamic Growth:

Lower Capital Gains Taxes

The Importance of the Small Business Sector

The previous chapter dealt with the relationships between investment, the rate of return, and the cost of capital for large firms. However, it did not specifically address the issue of how the funds were raised. If the rate of return on a given investment is perceived to be well above the alternative uses of those funds, then it was assumed that the investment would be undertaken whether the funds were generated internally, borrowed, or raised in the equity markets. If external financing was needed, the firm was left to make its own decision about whether debt or equity financing was less costly.

For a firm in the top 1,000 (approximately 2,500 employees and $125 million in sales or more) this is a reasonably accurate description of how financing decisions are approached. However, the vast majority of firms in the country do not have this option. A small business, which is generally defined as 500 or less employees, almost by definition does not have this access to capital markets. It may borrow money from a bank or from personal sources, but tapping the capital markets in the way that large firms do is totally out of the question. For practical purposes, the only option available to most of these firms, outside of the personal financial resources of the owners and their friends, is the venture capital market.

Because the venture capital market represents such a tiny proportion of total investment in the U.S. economy—$1 to $2 billion compared to total capital spending of over $300 billion—some may denigrate the importance and the contributions of the small business sector in the overall economy. Since this author has started eight different companies at various times, perhaps the bias toward the importance of the small business community is already well established in what follows. Yet solid evidence also backs up these findings.

In a well-known study, David Birch of M.I.T. found that during 1960–76, 87 percent of all new jobs generated were in the small business sector, and 66 percent of all new jobs were provided by those companies with less than twenty employees.[1] These results, further subdivided by regions, are given in table 8.1, where it is seen that *more than 100 percent* of new jobs in the Northeast were provided by small business. If it were not for small businesses moving in when large firms departed, the economic viability of this region would have been largely destroyed. An update of this study for the period from 1978 to 1980 found an even more skewed result, with 96 percent of the net new jobs in that period occurring in the small business sector.[2]

To be sure, the variety of types of small businesses is as varied as the motives of the entrepreneurs starting them. Some are simply beauty parlors or luncheonettes, whereas others involve significant breakthroughs using the most modern esoteric technology. Obviously the desire to go into business for oneself is partially dominated by the desire to be one's own boss and to be graded on one's own efforts; as one entrepreneur put it, the P&L statement of your own company is "the ultimate report card." But just as clearly, self-ownership has as its reward the perception of greater after-tax rewards than would be possible working for someone else.

For the risks are so much greater; many small businesses do not make it past the first year, and 62 percent of them die in the first four years.[3] Although there is always some risk of being fired from even the largest firms, it is minuscule compared to the risk of one's own company failing, which entails not only loss of job but in many cases disappearance of life savings as well.

Thus anyone who believes in capitalism certainly would agree that the risk taker who starts his own small firm deserves rewards commensurate with that risk, and that the tax code should reflect this. Salaries are taxed at the same rate—with the minor exception of a small difference in social security contributions—whether one is self-employed or works for someone else. The self-employed may have the additional benefits of greater tax avoidance and, as will be shown in the next chapter, often neglect to report all of their income, but such schemes are certainly outside of the intent of the tax code. The major contribution that the tax laws can make to aid small businesses is in taxing capital gains at a much lower rate, thereby more amply rewarding the individ-

TABLE 8.1

Percentage of Total Jobs[a] Generated by Size and Status for Regions and the United States between 1960 and 1976

Region	Ownership	0–20	21–50	51–100	101–500	500–1000	Total
North-east	Independent	129.1	−11.2	−22.3	−21.1	24.3	98.8
	Headquarters	36.4	10.5	1.3	−6.6	−32.8	8.8
	Subsidiaries	11.6	7.2	3.6	−5.5	−24.4	−7.6
	Totals	177.1	6.5	−17.4	−33.3	−32.9	100.0
North Central	Independent	52.8	4.5	.3	−2.8	2.9	57.7
	Headquarters	12.4	5.8	3.8	4.9	13.1	39.9
	Subsidiaries	2.0	1.7	1.2	1.0	−3.5	2.4
	Totals	67.2	12.0	5.2	3.1	12.4	100.0
South	Independent	42.7	5.7	1.5	0.0	.4	50.1
	Headquarters	9.3	4.0	2.9	7.4	16.7	40.3
	Subsidiaries	1.5	1.5	1.1	2.0	3.3	9.6
	Totals	53.5	11.2	5.5	9.4	20.4	100.0
West	Independent	47.8	5.9	2.2	1.9	2.9	60.8
	Headquarters	10.0	4.3	3.0	6.2	8.6	32.0
	Subsidiaries	1.7	1.4	1.1	1.8	1.8	7.2
	Totals	59.5	11.6	6.3	9.3	13.3	100.0
United States	Independent	51.8	4.4	0.0	−1.5	3.1	57.8
	Headquarters	11.9	4.9	3.1	5.6	10.6	36.1
	Subsidiaries	2.3	1.9	1.3	1.1	−.5	6.1
	Totals	66.0	11.2	4.3	5.2	13.3	100.0

SOURCE: Reprinted by permission of the publisher from *The Job Generation Process*, by David L. Birch (Cambridge, Mass.: M.I.T. Program on Neighborhood and Racial Change, 1979), p. 9.
[a]Total jobs generated in each region are: Northeast (410,890), North Central (1,674,282), South (2,873,619), and West (1,800,112).

ual enterpreneur or the venture capitalist who takes these outsize risks in the first place.

Historical Treatment of Capital Gains Taxes[4]

In spite of the obvious importance of venture capital in providing funds to the small business sector, which in turn accounts for most of the job expansion in the economy, a lower rate of tax on capital gains has historically not been a particularly popular item. Part of this would appear to stem from the perception that it is just one more tax break for the "rich." Another problem, and

perhaps more germane from an economic point of view, is that a good proportion of capital gains do not accrue to those risk-defying entrepreneurs who
help young geniuses get started in their garages. For capital gains technically
cover any increase in price on any capital asset. Although that could indeed
be stock of a new business, it is often stocks or bonds of existing businesses,
real estate, gold and silver, objects d'art, oil wells, timber or orange groves,
beef cattle, or any one of a surprisingly large number of other assets. It might
also include—at least for tax purposes—a new book, record, film, or even an
econometric model.

We have always thought these distinctions rather easy to identify; after all,
one ought to be able to tell the difference between 100 shares of xygots International, currently employing three people in the neighbor's garage, and stock
in AT&T, an orange grove, or farmer Ben's prize bull. However, both friends
and foes of capital gains taxes alike have always decided not to set up different
tax rates among the various classes of capital assets, with the single exception
made with respect to the length of time that the asset is held before sale.

Many countries do not tax capital gains, especially long-term capital gains,
at all. Indeed, as is shown in figure 8.1, before 1980 the United States had the
highest combined short- and long-term tax rate on capital gains. As might be
expected, Germany and Japan have no long-term capital gains tax at all, but
neither do the Netherlands, Belgium, Italy, or Australia. That has never been
the case in the United States. Ever since the federal individual income tax was
imposed in 1913, capital gains have also been subject to some percentage of
income tax. This does not mean, however, that disagreement about how to
tax these gains was absent. In fact, the tax rate on capital gains changed much
more often than the underlying rate on other types of personal income.

Because of the substantial tax advantages that accrue to capital gains, it naturally follows that a considerable amount of time and energy have been spent
trying to classify various types of income as capital gains that simply did not
belong there, and it is undoubtedly these subterfuges that are responsible for
some of the antipathy toward the preferential rates on capital gains.

In particular, the loophole can be enormous if capital losses are deductible
in full against both capital gains and other income. For example, consider a
person with an income of perhaps $100,000 who wishes to pay no taxes. He
simply simultaneously buys and sells 10,000 shares of XYZ corporation which
currently has a market price of $100. Providing that the price of the stock
moves at least 10 percent at any time during the year—and presumably a fairly
volatile stock would be selected for this purpose—he could escape taxes entirely if capital losses were fully deductible against other forms of income.

Suppose the stock goes up in value 10 percent. At that point he merely takes
delivery on his short position, losing the $100,000, and the tax avoider then

Maximum Long-Term Capital Gain Tax Rate*

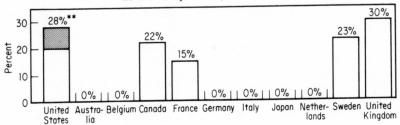

Maximum Short-Term Capital Gain Tax Rise*

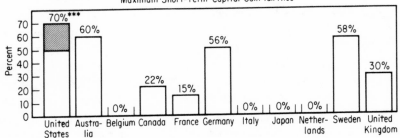

Minimum Holding Period to Qualify
for Long-Term Gain Treatment

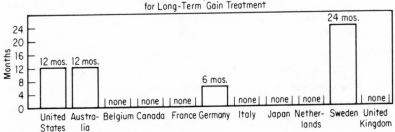

FIGURE 8.1

A Comparison of Individual Taxation of Capital Gains on Portfolio Stock Investments in Eleven Countries 1980

SOURCE: Calculations by Arthur Andersen and Co. for the Securities Industry Association, "Comparison of Individual Taxation of Long and Short Term Capital Gains on Portfolio Stock Investments and Dividend and Interest Income in Eleven Countries," December 15, 1980, p. 2. Illustration by Claire Sym, American Council for Capital Formation: Center for Policy Research. Reprinted by permission.
*State, provincial, and local taxes not included.
**In the U.S., the Economic Recovery Tax Act of 1981 reduces the maximum tax rate on the long-term capital gains of individuals to 20 percent for sales and exchanges after June 9, 1981. Under prior law, the top rate on long-term capital gains was 28 percent, second only to that of the United Kingdom in its severity.
***The 1981 Act reduces the maximum marginal individual tax rate from 70 to 50 percent, effective January 1, 1982. This cuts the maximum short-term capital gains rate from 70 to 50 percent, beginning in 1982.

resells short an equivalent number of shares immediately thereafter. Since until 1981 capital gains were never taxed until realized, the gains on the long position remain untaxed. Income can be passed from year to year and, with superior planning, even from generation to generation.

Since this type of tax dodge was clearly too good to pass up, it was in effect only from 1918 through 1923; after that the amount of capital losses that could be deducted steadily shrunk, and in general could be used only to offset capital gains rather than ordinary income. It is interesting to note that exactly the same sort of tax dodge grew up around commodity trading, and was so successful that the Treasury finally persuaded Congress in 1981 to close this loophole by taxing gains or losses on commodities at the end of the calendar year whether or not the position was realized—the first and only time that capital gains have ever been taxed before they were realized.

The idea of taxing capital gains at differential rates evolved as early as 1922, when short-term gains were taxed at regular rates but long-term gains, defined as those held two years or more, were taxed at a maximum rate of 12.5 percent.

During the Roosevelt years it is not very surprising to find that capital gains tax rates rose, but they still did not exceed 23.7 percent for long-term holdings. The major difference was in the stretch-out of the time periods. In fact, from 1934 to 1937 five different holding periods were specified. For holding periods of one year or less, 100 percent of the gains were included in income. For one to two years, the figure was 80 percent; for two to five years, 60 percent; for five to ten years, 40 percent; and for more than ten years, 30 percent of the total gain was included in income. Since the top maximum rate on other income was 63 percent in 1934 and 1935 and 79 percent in 1936 and 1937, the effective maximum rates for capital gains held ten years or more were 18.9 percent and 23.7 percent for these two time periods. Capital losses were deductible only to the extent of capital gains plus $2,000, so that the straddle impact was essentially wiped out.

The situation was simplified somewhat in the 1938 to 1941 period, where the number of holding periods was reduced from five to three. For assets held eighteen months or less, 100 percent of the gain was included in taxable income; for one and one half to two and one half years, two thirds of the gain was included, and for over two years, 50 percent of the gain was included. It might appear that the marginal tax rate had risen, since now 50 percent of the gain had to be included in income whereas previously only 30 percent was counted, but the tax code also introduced an alternative method that reduced the maximum effective rate on long-term gains to 15 percent.

The tax treatment of capital gains then settled down in 1942 and except for minor variations in the treatment of losses remained essentially unchanged until 1968. During these years, capital gains were divided into two categories:

short-term, which was six months or less, and long-term, which was over six months. The entire amount of short-term gains was included in income, whereas only half of long-term gains were included. However, taxpayers could use an alternative formulation in which long-term capital gains were taxed at a maximum rate of 25 percent, which became the standard for many years.

Thus for the first 55 years of the federal income tax, capital gains were always taxed much more lightly than ordinary income, with a maximum of 25 percent in any case. Obviously this period was not one long uninterrupted flow of prosperity; it did, after all, include the Great Depression. Yet from the end of World War II until 1968 the economy grew steadily, the general trend of the stock market was up, and indeed the annual rate of return from equities, including both capital gains and dividends, averaged over 14 percent per year over 1946–68, compared to a 2 percent average increase in the rate of inflation. It was a golden age for equities.

By 1968 the liberal flow was at high tide, however, and angered by the revelation that some of the rich paid virtually no taxes,[5] a concerted effort was made to raise capital gains tax rates. As can be seen in table 8.2, prepared by the Office of Tax Analysis, the combined changes eventually implemented were extremely complicated, but they had the net effect of raising the maximum capital gains tax rate from 25 percent to 49⅛ percent. The major changes were:

1. The 25 percent maximum rule was abolished. Hereafter half of long-term capital gains taxes would be included in ordinary income with no exceptions. When fully effective in 1972, this raised the maximum rate to 35 percent even without further complications.

2. In order to lash out against those alleged millionaires who paid no taxes, a minimum tax was applied to items of so-called tax preference, one of which was the excluded portion of long-term capital gains. True to form, the minimum tax could not touch those items that accounted for the great bulk of tax avoidance, such as tax-free municipal bonds. However, it did penalize someone who, for example, sold his company for a healthy capital gain, took the proceeds, and started another company which, as one might expect, had a large loss the first year. The loss could not be used to offset all of the capital gain, with the result that the overall tax rate was artificially high. The would-be entrepreneur obviously would be better off sticking with tax-free principals or "investing" in tax shelters than trying to start another company.

3. The worst part of the new tax code, however, had to do with something usually referred to as "poisoning." The idea is as follows.

Suppose that someone had an income of $250,000 from wages and salaries and $500,000 from capital gains in any particular year. One of the changes in the 1968 version of the tax code was to reduce the maximum tax rate on

TABLE 8.2

Maximum Marginal Tax Rates on Long-term Capital Gains, 1954–1978

Taxes Imposed	1954-63	1964	1965-67	1968[1]	1969[1]	1970[1]	1971	1972	1973-75	1976-78[2]
Alternative or Ordinary Tax	25	25	25	26.875	27.5	30.2375	32.5	35	35	35
Alternative or Ordinary Tax Plus Minimum Tax	25	25	25	26.875	27.5	32.21375	34.35	36.5	36.5	39.875
Alternative or Ordinary Plus Minimum Tax Plus Maximum Tax	25	25	25	26.875	27.5	32.21375	38.75	45.5	45.5	49.125
Alternative or Ordinary Plus Minimum Tax Plus Maximum Tax Plus Future Maximum Tax	25		25	26.875	27.5	41.51375	47.6	53.15	52.7	49.125
if there are sufficient foreign tax credits to eliminate the value of tax offsets under the Minimum Tax	25	25	25	26.875	27.5	45.57083	52.33333	58.5	58	52.5
Ordinary Tax, if extra long-term gain offsets short-term loss	91	77	70	75.25	77.0	71.75	70	70	70	70

Source: Office of the Secretary of the Treasury, Office of Tax Analysis, April 15, 1981.

Note: Due to interactions, the combined maximum rates from the various tax provisions are often lower than the sum of rates for the individual provisions.

[1] Includes the effects of the temporary surtaxes in 1968 through 1980: 1968, 7.5%; 1969, 10%; and 1970, 2.5%. In 1970 the surtax had the effect of reducing the minimum tax.

[2] Through October 31, 1978.

wages and salaries from 70 percent to 50 percent. Thus it would seem that the top marginal tax rate for this person would be 50 percent on labor income and 35 percent on capital gains.

This, however, is where life gets—or used to get—complicated. The excluded 50 percent of capital gains income became a so-called tax preference, and each dollar of tax preference reduced the amount of earned income subject to the maximum tax by an equal amount. Since $250,000 of capital gains was excluded from the computation of income, this essentially wipes out the lower tax rate on the wage income, and it too is taxed at the 70 percent marginal rate. The net effect is that the marginal rate on capital gains tax can be as high as 49⅛ percent instead of 35 percent.

Table 8.2 also presents certain arcane combinations where the tax rate on capital gains could be higher than 50 percent, but in fairness I actually know of no such actual cases and have always used the 49⅛ percent figure as the top rate. Even so, this meant that capital gains tax rates, after having been kept at 25 percent or less during the history of the Republic, suddenly increased to almost 50 percent. Capital gains, which in many cases encompassed an inordinate amount of risk, were now taxed at the same rate as wage and salary income.

It is not possible to measure directly the effect of this sharp increase in capital gains taxes on the small business sector or the overall rate of growth in productivity because of the long lags involved in nurturing a small business and its growth to maximum potential. However, it is possible to measure the effect that these higher tax rates had on venture capital and the stock market. As will be shown in the next two sections, in both cases the results were devastating.

The Revolt Against Higher Capital Gains Taxes

Whereas capital gains tax rates had increased steadily ever since 1968, the 1976 Tax Reform Act was the straw that broke the camel's back. With the maximum capital gains tax rate now equal to the maximum tax rate on wage and salary income, the financial rewards of working for oneself virtually disappeared. The venture capital industry could not shrink much more, but the stock market started falling, with a 15 percent decline in the popular stock market averages from January 1977 to March 1978. The economy improved somewhat as a result of Jimmy Carter's pump-priming measures, but unemployment remained high since these programs also resulted in higher inflation. Meanwhile productivity, which had shown some signs of recovering in 1976 with a 3.2 percent increase, actually declined in 1978—the first time in the postwar period productivity had ever fallen in a non-recession year.

With the stock market in the doldrums, the venture capital industry virtually extinct, and the level of productivity declining, a number of Congressmen decided that the time was ripe to undo the mischief caused by the 1976 tax reforms. The late William Steiger thus proposed that Congress "turn the clock back to 1968" on capital gains by reinstating the 25 percent maximum rate. Steiger later revised his position slightly, settling on a formula that would reduce the maximum rate to 28 percent by (a) increasing the exclusion of the long-term capital gains income from 50 percent to 60 percent, but more importantly, (b) getting rid of the minimum and maximum tax treatment of the excluded portion of capital gains. The qualifying time for long-term gains was also left at one year, as opposed to the six-month time horizon in effect from 1942 through 1968.

When the idea was first proposed, it is fair to say that none of us working on the bill ever thought it had much of a chance of being passed. Steiger firmly believed that the idea was meritorious, but he had introduced it more as an offset to the untoward proposal of the Carter administration to end the differential treatment for capital gains altogether.

The idea, however, spread like wildfire, not only in the House but also in the Senate, where Wyoming Senator Clifford Hansen quickly rounded up 60 co-sponsors. The broad-based support came not from those who wanted to provide a windfall for the rich; rather it came from those who felt that venture capital and entrepreneurship should be rewarded, and also those middle-class citizens who felt that they too might be able to participate in capital gains in the near future, particularly with the rate of inflation increasing so rapidly.

Naturally the Carter administration roundly opposed this tax reduction. Treasury Secretary Blumenthal testified that this was just one more giveaway to the rich; that it would dilute Treasury revenues without providing any offsetting benefits; and that it would have no positive impact on the stock market. Debate quickly degenerated to the mudslinging level with thinly veiled statements that those who testified in favor of the bill were merely opportunistic lobbyists trying to line both their own and their clients' pockets. Of course, a certain amount of this is usual for any tax reduction bill that benefits anyone other than the poor, but the decibel level of insults was a clear tip-off that the Carter administration had no economic or financial analysis to support their position and hence was reduced to ranting. I have always thought that their heavy-handed approach insured its defeat, but whatever the cause, the reduction was passed by overwhelming majorities in both houses and the lower tax rates became effective on November 1, 1978.

The claims made for the Steiger-Hansen capital gains tax rate reduction were:

1. It would increase the flow of funds into venture capital.
2. It would increase the number of firms going public and the total amount of equity financing.
3. It would raise stock prices, particularly those of smaller firms.
4. The net tax revenues to the Treasury would increase.

Each of these will now be considered.

The Effect of Lower Capital Gains Tax Rates on Venture Capital

The results relative to the first two points are beyond rebuttal. In 1968, the last year before capital gains taxes were raised, almost $1 billion of new private capital was committed to venture capital firms. When capital gains tax rates rose, the figure declined almost to nothing in the space of only two years and remained below $100 million per year for the entire period from 1970 to 1977, as is shown in table 8.3. As soon as the capital gains tax rate was lowered, the figure shot back to $1.3 billion in 1981. Seldom if ever has a clearer correlation existed between tax rates and economic activity.

The figures for the amount of public underwritings of small businesses, defined here as those with a net worth of $5 million or less, is similarly impressive. As is also shown in table 8.3, the pool of money thus raised declined from $1.4 billion in 1969 to less than $100 million in 1973–77. This source of financing took a little longer to dry up completely because public underwritings are usually undertaken for companies that have already received their first source of capital from venture capital firms and then, usually two or three years later, raise more funds for expansion by going to the capital markets. Similarly, the same two-year lag was observed on the upside; venture capital firms immediately raised their commitments in 1978, while stock market issues of small firms started to rebound in 1980.

The importance of venture capital and stock offerings for small companies

TABLE 8.3

Venture Capital Industry
Estimated Fundings and Disbursements
(millions of dollars)

Year	New Private Capital Committed to Venture Capital Firms	Estimated Disbursements to Portfolio Companies	Public Underwritings of Companies with a Net Worth of $5 Million or Less	
			Number	Amount
1969	$ 171	$ 450	(698)	$1,367

Capital Gains Tax Increase

Year	New Private Capital Committed to Venture Capital Firms	Estimated Disbursements to Portfolio Companies	Number	Amount
1970	97	350	(198)	375
1971	95	410	(248)	551
1972	62	425	(409)	896
1973	56	450	(69)	160
1974	57	350	(9)	16
1975	10	250	(4)	16
1976	50	300	(29)	145
1977	39	400	(22)	75

Capital Gains Tax Decrease

Year	New Private Capital Committed to Venture Capital Firms	Estimated Disbursements to Portfolio Companies	Number	Amount
1978	570	550	(21)	129
1979	319	1,000	(46)	183
1980	900	1,000	(135)	822
1981 (est)	1,300	1,200	(306)	1,760

Total Capital Committed to the Organized Venture Capital Industry
Estimate at December 31, 1981

Independent Private Venture Capital Firms	$2.6 billion
Small Business Investment Companies	1.6 billion
Corporate Subsidiaries (Financial and Non-Financial)	1.6 billion
Total	$5.8 billion

This pool remained static from 1969 through 1977 at some $2.5 to $3.0 billion (with new fundings more or less equal to withdrawals).

SOURCE: Reprinted by permission of Venture Economics Division, Capital Publishing Corporation.

can be seen in another perspective: in 1968 over 300 high-technology companies were formed in the United States, whereas not a single one was started in 1976. Though the companies that were already established in Silicon Valley and Route 128 continued to prosper in the lean years between 1968 and 1978, new business activity was virtually nil.

Virtually all sectors of the business and economics press were quick to draw the conclusion between the reduction in tax rates and the sudden wellspring of venture capital. The *Wall Street Journal*, of course, was in the forefront of praising this bill:[6]

The Key to Dynamic Growth: Lower Capital Gains Taxes

Venture capital is money raised by entrepreneurs whose only assets are their new ideas. Even if they turn out to be successful, investors must expect their capital to be locked up for 5 or 6 years. A decade ago venture capital was thriving. But along came the Tax Reform Act of 1969 which together with its subsequent revisions raised the maximum tax on capital gains from 25% to 49%, reduced the write-off of capital losses by 50%, and sharply curtailed the deduction of interest expense on borrowed funds used to make an investment. All in all, the rewards for success were cut in half, and the penalties for failure were doubled.

The effect on venture capital was devastating. The ability of small companies to raise equity capital by public stock issues declined drastically, and by 1973 small company issues had practically ceased. In 1977 when the maximum tax on capital gains hit 49%, equity capital from all sources dried up.

The tax reformers who sold this bad bill of goods to the Congress said the purpose of it was "to make the rich pay taxes." Congress expected to score some easy political points, not to dry up important wellsprings of economic progress. New small companies account for a disproportionate amount of new products and technologies, and they contribute substantially to the growth of the economy as a result of their own rapid growth and the productivity gains that they introduce into the economy.

By 1978 Congress realized what it had done, and Rep. Bill Steiger found majority support in both houses for his proposal to reduce the capital gains tax. In November the rate was reduced to 28%.

The response from venture capital was instantaneous and began in May before the law was passed when Senator Hansen rounded up 60 Senate cosponsors of the Steiger bill. By the end of the year venture capital raised by firms specializing in the activity rose eleven-fold over the previous year. In 1979 venture capital is back where it was 10 years ago.

The snapback is easy to understand. In 1969 Congress began adding to the costs of failure on risky new ventures, while reducing the rewards of success. With risk taxed at the same rate as corporate salaries, fewer people left comfortable employment to go off on their own with the ideas they couldn't sell to their employers. Those still willing could find few financial backers. In 1978 Congress restored incentives for assuming risk, and people began assuming risk once more.

However, this was not merely a case of the *Wall Street Journal* leading the parade. *Time* magazine stated that "in the early 1970s, . . . federal tax increases on capital gains almost dried up the venture capital market. The money faucets again began to open up three years later with the passage of a new tax bill that lowered the rate on capital gains from a maximum of 49% to 28%. The amount of fresh capital immediately jumped from $39 billion in 1977 to $570 million in 1978."[7] The *New York Times* added:

the venture capital spigot really began to open in November 1978, when the maximum tax on long-term capital gains was reduced from 49.5 *(sic)* percent to 28 percent. One indicator is a survey of 55 firms belonging to the National Venture Capital Association . . . which showed that the proportion of total investment devoted to

175

venture capital investment (where there was substantial principal risk, as opposed to investments in more mature companies or leveraged buyouts) increased from 37.5 percent in 1977 to 48.1 percent in 1978 and to 80 percent in 1979.[8]

As the *Economist* put it when the maximum effective tax rate on capital gains increased in 1969:

> The rich sought tax shelters—oil wells, football franchises, real estate. Conventional sources of venture capital for more productive investment all but dried up. . . . Then in 1978 the long-term capital gains tax was cut to a maximum of 28% . . . and new issues revived on Wall Street.
>
> The big financial institutions stick most of their money into bonds and the stock of the S&P 500. As these pension funds and endowments are tax-exempt anyway their decisions are not affected, directly at least, by tax changes. Individual investors . . . are ready to take quick and full advantage of tax cuts. It is they who traditionally gamble on the more speculative stocks that the "prudent man" rule of the Employee Retirement Income Security Act has persuaded many financial institutions to shun.[9]

In other words, prices of small stocks should have risen more than prices of large stocks in the aftermath of the capital gains tax cut.

Indeed, even those congenitally opposed to reducing capital gains tax rates would have to agree that the reduction in rates did spur the venture capital and new issue market. However, the effect of the tax cut on stock prices and actual revenues collected are much more controversial, and require more extended verification.

Capital Gains Taxes and the Stock Market

The biases of this author are going to become clear in a moment, if they are not already known, because I prepared a paper in April 1978 claiming that the reduction in the capital gains tax rate from 49 percent to 25 percent (which was the figure originally suggested by Steiger) would cause the stock market to increase 40 percent more than would otherwise be the case within two years after the tax reduction was passed.[10] Note that this would be "more than would *otherwise* have occurred," but this fine distinction was dropped in the general "popularization" of my views, although it turned out not to matter.

Of all the forecasts I have generated in the past twenty years, this one aroused the most controversy. Liberal members of Congress, of course, were furious, for they saw this as a set-up job merely to reduce capital gains taxes with wanton disregard for the truth. Members of the Treasury staff used slightly more professional language but came to the same conclusion, criticizing my work for containing autocorrelation, multicollinearity, and heteroscedascity (which simply mean I used incorrect statistical techniques). Ralph Bristol wrote that everyone should be "suspicious about . . . models that produce something from nothing," and concluded that "Econometric models should not be used to answer questions they were not designed to answer."[11] My results were labeled "fatuous" by tax committee staff members, and *Time* magazine stated that "Evans damaged his reputation last year when he predicted that the stock market would rise 40% over two years if the capital gains tax were reduced from 49% to 25%,"[12] and went on to explain how that "far-out conclusion" only bolstered critics who claimed my forecasts were too sensationalized anyhow.

Before we see how this all turned out, however, it is useful to review the theoretical and empirical underpinnings that led to this 40 percent forecast, since it is important to determine whether or not the increase was due to the economics of the situation or just a providential fluke.

One critical element of this argument, which many if not all its opponents seemed to overlook, is that it is not only the reduction in capital gains taxes *per se* which raises stock prices, but rather the increase in profits and decline in interest rates stemming from the tax cut which also have important secondary effects on the market.

To be more specific, the reduction in capital gains taxes stimulates economic activity and the stock market through the following combination of events. First, a reduction in capital gains taxes raises stock prices. These higher stock prices lead to a faster rate of growth in capital spending. They also lead to more equity financing, which reduces the debt/equity ratios of corporations. As a result, interest rates are lower than would otherwise be the case. The increase in investment stemming from the lower cost of financing creates higher levels of output, employment, and income, and reduces inflationary pressures by increasing productivity and raising maximum potential GNP. Finally, the increase in economic activity raises federal government revenues, thus reducing the budget deficit, which in turn leads to lower interest rates and lower rates of inflation.

The relationship between stock prices and capital gains can best be gauged by looking at figures 8.2 and 8.3. We know that stock prices will rise when profits increase and decline when interest rates increase, other things being equal. However, figure 8.2 clearly indicates that the correlation between the earnings/price ratio and the prime rate is not particularly robust.

Figure 8.2 indicates that before 1969, the earnings/price ratio was generally below the prime rate, which means that stock prices were higher than would be indicated by profits and interest rates. After the initial increase in capital

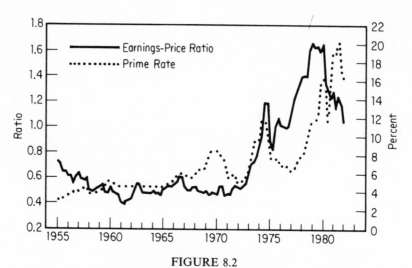

FIGURE 8.2
Earnings-Price Ratio and the Prime Rate
SOURCE: Prepared by Evans Economics, Inc.

gains tax rates, however (see table 8.2), the two curves more or less coincided. After the second major increase in capital gains tax rates, the earnings/price ratio moved well above the prime rate, which means that stock prices were depressed. They stayed depressed until late in 1978, when capital gains taxes were reduced, at which point the earnings/price ratio once again started to fall below the prime rate. Figure 8.3 compares the spread between the earn-

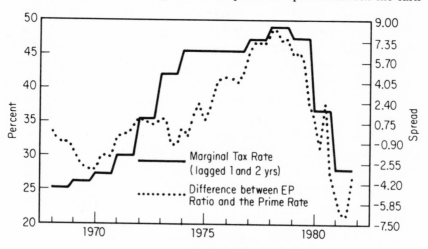

FIGURE 8.3
Marginal Tax Rate on Capital Gains
SOURCE: Prepared by Evans Economics, Inc.

ings/price ratio and the prime rate with the maximum effective capital gains tax rate for 1968–81.

Another factor to be considered is that the total change in stock prices caused by a change in capital gains taxes does not occur instantaneously because of the lock-in effect. Higher capital gains taxes reduce the number of individuals willing to sell their stock at any given time; since these capital gains remain unrealized, fewer new funds are available for purchases of other stock and hence prices gradually decline. This effect usually takes about two years to become fully operative. Thus the difference between the earnings/price ratio and the prime rate is compared with the average of the maximum tax rate on capital gains over the past two years.

Similarly, a reduction in capital gains taxes will not cause all individuals to sell their assets immediately. However, many investors will sell sooner; as this happens, more funds will be committed to purchases of equities. This will raise stock prices and cause an increasing number of investors to realize their capital gains, thus providing even more funds for equity financing.

The relationship between stock prices and investment is not particularly a supply-side theory; in fact, it is usually credited to James Tobin,[13] who used his Nobel laureate speech as a platform to deliver a ringing denunciation of supply-side economics. Tobin's theory is actually quite straightforward. When the cost of building a new business is less than buying an existing one, investment will increase; when the cost of buying is cheaper, firms will spend their money on mergers and acquisitions rather than investment in new plant and equipment. This ratio, which is more formally known as the ratio of market value (buying) to the replacement cost of assets (building), has declined more than 50 percent since 1965, as was already discussed in chapter 7.

A 40 percent increase in stock market prices would, according to our calculations, lower the volume of new corporate issues by about $5 billion per year, which would reduce long-term bond yields by about 50 basis points at any given level of economic activity. Since demand for loanable funds would rise as economic activity expands, interest rates would not actually decline this much; but the switch from debt to equity capital would lighten the burden in financial markets and would be critical in preventing crowding out. Hence an increase in equity prices lessens the burden of debt finance, permitting greater investment without corresponding upward pressures on interest rates.

An increase of $1 billion in spending will result in the creation of more jobs, which will raise individual and corporate incomes and thus result in more purchases of consumer and capital goods. Most economists agree that the investment multiplier is about two, which means that every $1 billion increase in capital spending caused by higher stock market prices will result in about $2 billion more in real GNP.

One of the tenets of supply-side economics is that the multiplier is much smaller for increases in spending that are inflationary, for the increases in prices and interest rates have a negative impact on consumer and capital spending. In general, increases in spending that do not raise productivity tend to have much smaller long-term effects on economic activity because of the backlash of higher inflation.

For this reason, the investment multiplier is usually higher than the spending multiplier for either consumption or government purchases. An increase in the amount of capital per unit of output improves the rate of growth in productivity and expands the total capacity of the economy, hence reducing the chances of bottlenecks and shortages. Since goods and services are now produced more efficiently, the rate of inflation does not rise as rapidly, and the gains in individual and corporate income stemming from more jobs and higher output are not eroded by higher inflation.

None of these links is particularly controversial, but the same cannot be said for my "brazen" prediction of that 40 percent gain in the stock market. But how did it all turn out? The best answer in this case is given by an excerpt in the October 21, 1980, *Wall Street Journal* editorial, "The 40% Solution":

The claims made in 1978 on behalf of the Steiger amendment have been uncannily accurate. Economist Michael K. Evans predicted that "a reduction in the maximum capital gains tax rate from 49.1% to 25% would raise stock prices about 40% by 1982 relative to what would occur if capital gains taxes remained at present levels."

The prediction was attacked by then Treasury Secretary Michael Blumenthal and other adherents to the theory that cutting a high marginal tax rate is the equivalent of a Treasury giveaway to the rich and greedy. The idea that allowing people to keep more of their capital gains would encourage investment and create more capital gains was ridiculed by the administration. Mr. Blumenthal argued that it would cost the Treasury $2.2 billion annually.

Well, what has happened since? Investment in venture capital firms, the financing of young and often innovative businesses, climbed to $1 billion in 1979 from the $300 million average for the years 1974 through 1977 and may hit $1.5 billion this year;

New capital raised through initial public stock offerings doubled in 1979;

Total equity financing in the first eight months of 1980, at $5.8 billion, was already $800 million higher than for the full year 1979;

The Treasury's capital gains receipts, instead of falling by Mr. Blumenthal's predicted $2.2 billion, are rising instead to the tune of some $900 million a year;

The New York Stock Exchange Composite stock average closed last week 44% above its level of November 1978, surpassing the gain that Mr. Evans had predicted in 1978.[14]

The Key to Dynamic Growth: Lower Capital Gains Taxes

Indeed, the increase in the overall stock market was actually even more dramatic. As shown in figure 8.4, the Dow Jones Industrial Average actually rose less than the 40 percent, since it is largely composed of stocks of large institutions bought by tax-exempt institutions. The American Stock Exchange index, on the other hand, increased 133 percent over the two-year period, although some of this was due to its overweighting with Canadian oil issues, which were helped by the second energy crisis. Not only did stock prices increase but the gain in the stock prices of smaller companies was substantially greater than in the largest ones.

How Lower Capital Gains Taxes Raised Revenues

The *Wall Street Journal* editorial refers to the fact that capital gains revenues actually rose after the tax cut was in place, a point not yet covered here. This is certainly not what the Carter administration had expected. Estimates made by the Joint Committee on Taxation on April 19, 1978, which were perhaps politically motivated, showed that revenue losses would range between $2 and $3 billion per year if the maximum capital gains tax rate were cut from 49 percent to 25 percent. These figures were later modified by the Office of

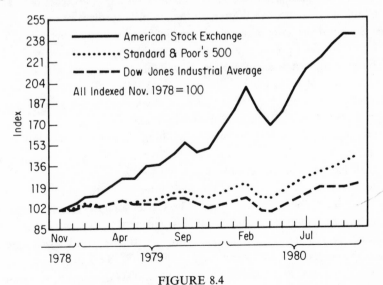

FIGURE 8.4

Stock Market Prices, November 1978–November 1980

SOURCE: Prepared by Evans Economics, Inc.

Tax Analysis at the Treasury to show only a $1 billion decline in revenues, taking into account the fact that some capital gains might actually be unlocked by lower rates and hence realized capital gains would actually increase by about $8 billion. However, with the average rate on capital gains declining from 15.4 percent to 10.8 percent, revenues would still fall by the $1 billion figure.

Throughout this book we have always been careful to argue that broad-based tax rate reductions in personal or corporate income taxes will not increase revenues. Federal government revenues account for approximately 20 percent of total GNP; thus in order for an income tax cut to leave the deficit unchanged, the spending multiplier would have to be about five—far greater than the investment multiplier of about two. While arguing throughout this book for a reduction in personal and corporate income tax rates because of their positive effects on productivity and incentives and their beneficial long-term effects in widening the private sector tax base, I have never claimed that such a move would actually decrease the size of the federal budget deficit without offsetting cuts in government spending.

The capital gains tax, however, is unique in its leveraged effect on the economy. The major reason for this, and the factor that distinguishes the capital gains tax from all other levies, is that the taxpayer can in large part determine whether or not he wishes to pay the tax. For most people who are unhappy with their high marginal tax bracket on other income, the only (legal) option, other than tax shelters, is to earn less income. However, the owner of a capital asset can delay his tax indefinitely by the simple expedient of not selling the asset. Such a decision is economically inefficient, for it restrains capital from flowing to its most productive use and hence retards growth in productivity and output. Nonetheless, this option is available to taxpayers with capital assets, and most of them use it.

The degree to which capital gains were unlocked was even greater than we had expected. Our preliminary estimate of a $0.9 billion increase turned out to be too low, as the actual gain was $1.8 billion. The effective tax rate, rather than falling 4.6 percent as estimated by the Carter Treasury analysts, declined less than half that much, as shown in table 8.4.

The significant differences between the Carter estimates and the actual figures turns out to be easily explained. The Carter analysts had assumed that the income distribution of capital gains would be the same after the tax cut as before, by which is meant the following. Consider two taxpayers: one has an income of $50,000 with capital gains of $5,000 taxed at a marginal rate of 20 percent; the other has an income of $500,000 with capital gains of $100,000 taxed at a marginal rate of 45 percent. The naïve assumption would

TABLE 8.4

*Total Capital Gains and the Effective Tax Rate
on Capital Gains for Returns with Net Capital Gains Only
(individual only, 1955–79)*

Year	Total Gains[a]	Taxes Paid on Capital Gain Income	Effective Tax Rate
	(in billions of dollars)		(percent)
1955	9.9	1.2	12.0
1956	9.7	1.1	11.8
1957	8.1	0.9	11.1
1958	9.4	1.1	11.1
1959	13.1	1.6	11.8
1960	11.7	1.4	11.6
1961	16.3	2.0	12.4
1962	13.5	1.6	11.8
1963	14.6	1.7	11.9
1964	17.4	2.2	12.7
1965	21.5	2.8	13.1
1966	21.3	2.7	12.8
1967	27.5	3.9	14.0
1968	35.6	5.2	14.5
1969	31.4	4.4	14.1
1970	20.8	3.0	14.6
1971	28.3	4.3	15.2
1972	35.9	5.6	15.7
1973	35.8	5.3	14.9
1974	30.2	4.3	14.3
1975	30.9	4.5	14.4
1976	39.0	6.2	15.9
1977	45.9	7.3	15.8
1978	51.5	8.3	16.1
1979[b]	72.1	10.1	14.0

SOURCE: Office of the Secretary of the Treasury, Office of Tax Analysis, March 20, 1982.
[a]Net long-term gain in excess of short-term loss plus short-term capital gain.
[b]Estimate.

be that a reduction in the capital gains rate schedule would increase realized capital gains of both taxpayers by the same 20 percent.

As a matter of fact that is a very silly assumption. Because the "poisoning" clause of the tax code affected upper-income much more than the middle-income taxpayers, the former were much more likely to unlock more capital gains in response to the lower rates. In addition, the upper-income taxpayer presumably manages his money much more carefully and hence was in a much better position to respond to the lower tax rate by adjusting his portfolio decisions, whereas the $50,000 a year taxpayer did not have the flexibility in tax and financial planning. Thus upper-income taxpayers responded much more than proportionately to the tax rate reduction.

Thus we find that the reduction in capital gains tax rates was an unequivocal success in all respects. It revitalized venture capital and new issues markets that had all but been given up for dead. It increased public underwritings of small companies by twentyfold. It increased stock prices more than 40 percent over a two-year period. And it even managed to raise an additional $1.8 billion for the Treasury in 1979 and 1980, one of the few cases where a tax cut has actually resulted in increased revenues.

The Aftermath of Lower Capital Gains Tax Rates

This would be a pleasant place to end the chapter, but something is not quite right, because by July 1982 the market was not only lower than in October 1980 but had tumbled even below levels of early 1978, before the capital gains tax cut was more than a glimmer in Bill Steiger's eye. So to be honest about it, we must analyze those factors that caused this sharp reversal of the market after it looked like the reduction in capital gains taxes was the equivalent of the goose that laid the golden egg.

With the landslide election of Ronald Reagan and the fierce controversy over his new fiscal program, the debate about the appropriate level of capital gains taxes quickly faded into the background. Indeed, the reduction in the maximum tax rate from 70 percent to 50 percent, which also had the effect of reducing the maximum long-term capital gains tax from 28 percent to 20 percent effective June 9, 1981, went virtually unnoticed in the financial press.

The decline in the stock market started in August 1981, only weeks after the lower capital gains tax rate went into effect. This plunge clearly was caused by the decline in economic activity, the sharp reduction in profits, the increase in interest rates, and the negative reaction of the financial markets to deficits forever. The relationship between the earnings/price ratio and interest rates themselves, which have already been presented in figure 8.2, clearly indicates that *relative* to profits and interest rates, stock prices were a good deal higher in 1981 and 1982 than in previous years. This development clearly can be attributed to the further reduction in capital gains tax rates in mid-1981. When profits and interest rates return to previous levels, stock prices undoubtedly will reach new highs as a result of lower capital gains taxes.

184

The Key to Dynamic Growth: Lower Capital Gains Taxes

Once again, however, the 1981–82 plunge in the stock market serves to emphasize the close interrelationship of all the coordinates of fiscal and monetary policy, and the need to combine them into a single coherent program. The decision of Congress to cut taxes but not spending during a period in which inflation was still near double-digit rates meant that the entire burden of stability was placed on the shoulders of the Fed, leading to the unprecedented high levels of real interest rates in the first half of 1982.

For in the long run, the level of stock prices is determined by the growth of the economy and the tax rate on capital gains. If increases in inflation are matched by increases in interest rates, then on balance stock prices do not rise, even in nominal terms. This explains the apparent paradox in which stock prices have advanced hardly at all since 1968 in spite of the fact that corporate profits have tripled over the same period. The phony increases due to inflation were offset by the tripling of interest rates.

During the next economic recovery, we expect both that profits will rebound sharply and that interest rates will decline; thus both these major factors will be working in favor of higher stock prices. Eventually the contribution of lower capital gains tax rates will once again help to propel the stock market to new highs. The lessons of 1981 and 1982, however, stand as a stark testimony to the fact that a reduction in capital gains tax rates, no matter how efficacious, cannot make a dent when the much greater magnitudes of income taxes and government spending combine to produce massive deficits, higher interest rates, and prolonged recessions.

CHAPTER 9

How Lower Tax Rates

Improve Work Effort

and Reduce Tax Avoidance

Evidence for Lower- and Middle-Income Workers

The question of whether tax rates affect work effort is even more controversial than the issue of whether they affect saving. For one thing, the answer is not even clear-cut on the theoretical level. Supply-side theory argues that people are motivated by rewards; at a higher real wage, they will work harder and more efficiently. Higher real wages can be obtained only by raising productivity or lowering taxes; otherwise they will simply be translated into higher prices. To economists this effect is known as the substitution effect, because the individual substitutes more work for leisure as the rate of pay increases. For example, at $1/hour most people would not feel like going out and washing windows, but at $100/hour the opportunity would undoubtedly appear much more enticing. Of course there are limits to this effect. Even at $100/hour, one can only wash so many windows before succumbing to complete exhaustion. Furthermore, at that income the would-be window washer would probably opt for more frequent vacations.

That is what is known as the income effect, which means that as individuals become wealthier they will spend more of their time on leisure. Someone who makes $200,000 a year is much less likely to take a second job to generate some extra spending money than someone who earns $20,000 a year. Furthermore, he is much more likely to take additional or extended vacations to enjoy his bountiful income.

The income effect also goes under the name of the backward-bending supply curve, for it implies that, after a certain income level, a higher wage will result in less than more work effort. This supply curve is contrasted with the normal upward sloping supply curve in figure 9.1. It is fair to say that if the backward-bending supply curve is important or even representative, much of supply-side economics is rendered vacuous. The whole approach of this book hinges around the central idea that productivity has been hampered by excessive increases in tax rates, which unquestionably include the effect on labor as well as deployment of capital.

For that reason, the reader will not be particularly shocked to learn that the evidence verifies that the substitution effect is stronger than the income effect. However, this evidence does not present itself in neat little packages: it must be amassed from studies of individuals at low-, medium-, and high-income levels; from IRS tax data; and from econometric studies of various movements in employment and productivity. The next few pages attempt to present an amalgam of this evidence without resorting to the drudgery of trudging through each individual study. The evidence can be synopsized thus:

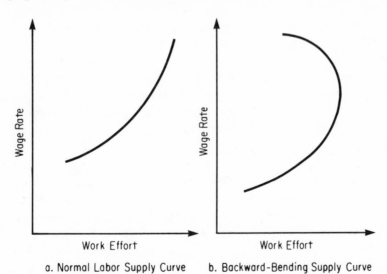

FIGURE 9.1
Normal and Backward-Bending Supply Curves
SOURCE: Prepared by Evans Economics, Inc.

187

1. Among what economists call the primary work force, namely those heads of households ages twenty-five to fifty-four, the substitution and income effects almost cancel each other out in terms of hours worked per year. However, the effect on productivity—in essence, how much each employee produces per hour—is more significant.

2. Among secondary workers, mainly teenagers, housewives, and those old enough to retire, the substitution effects are much stronger than the income effect. One reason for this may be that the leisure that primary workers give up to work harder may be genuine, whereas the "leisure" that housewives forego is likely to consist of housekeeping chores, shopping trips, or chauffering the children.

3. Among lower-income workers, higher tax rates definitely result in more dropouts from the labor force. For those who might claim that lower-income workers pay little if any income taxes in any case, it is once again the marginal rather than the average tax rate which is important. Under certain perverse circumstances, the marginal tax rate on poor people trying to work is greater than 100 percent—that is, the amount of benefits they lose upon accepting gainful employment is greater than the take-home pay on the newly found job.

4. Among middle-income workers, higher tax rates have only a marginal effect on the primary decision to work but do affect the decision to work overtime, to take a second job, and the rates of vacation and absenteeism.

5. Among upper-income workers, the effects are much more far-reaching although very difficult to measure empirically. To suggest that a corporate executive will leave for home an hour earlier because he has just been pushed into a higher marginal tax bracket is to make a mockery of supply-side economics. The evidence is more equivocal for independent professionals—doctors, lawyers, consultants, and the like; some take more time off to play golf when their tax rate rises, and others do not. Indeed, it is said that Ronald Reagan received his indoctrination into supply-side economics when he realized how many actors were refusing additional roles because of high marginal tax rates.

However, our argument does not hinge on such cases but reaches much more deeply into the economic fabric of society. Higher tax rates deaden initiatives, reduce risk taking and entrepreneurship, discourage the move to new job or career opportunities, and divert effort from improving one's skills in his or her chosen business and profession to figuring out how to avoid paying taxes.

As already mentioned, these effects are difficult to measure empirically. From a theoretical point of view, the definitive approach to segmenting the substitution and income effects was developed by Harvard Professor Richard Musgrave, who argued that the substitution effect was related to the marginal tax rate, while the income effect was tied to the average tax rate.[1] In other words, a decrease in the marginal tax rate would increase work effort, whereas a decrease in the average tax rate would diminish it.

If the Musgrave theory is correct, it presents a fascinating way to increase work incentive and productivity and to balance the budget at the same time: introduce a flat tax that significantly reduces high marginal rates but increases the average rate. Since the average rate is higher, it would by definition generate more revenues. Furthermore, if this flat tax were coupled with a law eliminating all deductions, the statutory average tax rate would be well below 20 percent.

Unfortunately, although such a tax does receive active consideration from time to time, it would be virtually impossible to accomplish politically; all the vested interests representing deductions would be lined up in one solid phalanx to oppose its introduction. Since the flat tax without deductions represents the best hope for reforming our tax structure and balancing the budget, more has to be said about it in the concluding chapter; at this point we merely point out that its theoretical foundations are at the heart of mainstream economics and not the work of the so-called fringe elements. From an empirical point of view, the marginal and average tax rates usually move together, making it quite difficult to separate the two effects. Thus most of what follows represents calculations based on the marginal tax rates.

Tax rates can affect work effort at several different decision levels. First, the prospective employee must make the decision whether or not to enter the labor force. This could involve several different alternatives depending on the situation. For the teenager, the choice could be a job, college, or military service; for married women, being a housewife or having a career; for those over sixty-five, whether to retire or continue to work. Second, having decided to enter the labor force, the employee decides how actively to pursue job opportunities. This depends as much on unemployment benefits as tax rates, for as long as benefits almost equal take-home pay, the incentive to find gainful employment other than in the previous occupation is severely limited. Third, having found a job, the employee still has to decide how many hours to work per year; such variables as overtime hours, vacations, and absenteeism rates are to a certain extent at the employee's discretion. Employees also decide whether or not to take a second job depending on the value of take-home pay in that job. Fourth and finally, once the number of hours to be worked has been decided, the question of efficiency on the job is still an important one in determining productivity. Except in the now largely obsolete case of piecework rates, one might not expect to find a direct correlation between the real wage rates and efficiency, but the next chapter shows that marginal tax rates do have a direct and significant effect on productivity.

Most of the empirical work done by economists addressing these questions has been done at the micro level, which means they have worked with the records of individuals rather than aggregate measures such as total hours worked in the private sector. In virtually all of this work a sharp distinction has been found between primary and secondary workers; response also varies by income level.

In particular, at the high-income level, the results may be disguised by several considerations.

1. Tax rates may have a bearing on the decision of what field to choose. For example, the rush of young talent to the high-technology industries in the 1960s stemmed from the realization that capital gains tax rates are far lower than those on ordinary income; and although moribund during much of the 1970s, this interest was reborn after 1978.

2. Tax rates may well determine how upper-income people spend their spare time. Many off-hours may be spent examining tax shelters instead of enhancing their knowledge of their particular business or profession. If they do not engage in such decisions themselves, the resources of other highly paid professionals are utilized.

3. High tax rates may cause highly paid managers to place a significant proportion of their compensation in tax-deferred pensions, which diminishes their mobility.

4. Independent professionals possess the ability to price their services individually. A higher tax rate may simply be reflected in an increase in the price of a visit to the doctor or lawyer.

5. Differential tax rates will have a major bearing on the form in which compensation is received: salary, capital gains, or tax-deterred pensions.

6. The question of tax avoidance becomes an overwhelming one when rates approach 50 percent.

These points will be examined after a review of the evidence for the lower- and middle-income groups.

Most of the studies for lower-income levels have been undertaken in conjunction with poverty programs and income maintenance schemes. During the 1970s the Department of Health, Education and Welfare (HEW) directed a number of studies examining the effects of differential tax rates for five New Jersey and Pennsylvania cities,[2] Gary, Indiana,[3] and Seattle, Washington, and Denver, Colorado.[4] In addition, several economists performed studies on the 1967 Survey of Economic Opportunity data base, and on a survey of 50,000 families receiving government payments under the Aid to Families with Dependent Children program.[5] The review of all these studies would be quite tedious and outside the scope of a non-technical book. And most of the studies

190

were undertaken using different assumptions and different methodological approaches, which makes comparison even more abstruse.

Given these problems, however, a surprising amount of agreement emerges from these diverse studies.[6] In particular, the results at the poverty level are not much different than for the labor force at large. The studies generally agree that a 1 percent change in tax rates would result in approximately a 0.2 percent change in labor force participation—an elasticity of 0.2. Furthermore, this elasticity appears to be about 0.1 for heads of households and about 0.3 for secondary workers, mainly wives. In particular, the relatively few heads of households who diminished their work effort because of higher marginal tax rates simply quite looking for jobs entirely; whereas for the wives the reduction was centered mainly in working fewer hours per week. In an interesting twist, female heads of households reduced their work input by less than either husbands or wives, a fact probably explained by differential availability of welfare programs to single heads of households.

The HEW studies specifically examined the question of what would happen if the government instituted a 50 percent negative income tax. Under such a program, people who did not work at all would receive a guaranteed annual income that would be reduced by $0.50 for each dollar of earned income. In the Seattle and Denver income maintenance experiments, HEW found that such a program reduced the labor supply of husbands by between 6 and 12 percent, for wives between 21 and 32 percent, and for female heads of families between 0 and 15 percent.[7] Taking the midpoint of the range in each case, this implies slightly higher elasticities than indicated in other regions: approximately 0.2 for heads of households and 0.5 for secondary workers. Furthermore, these studies also found that the availability of a negative income tax apparently resulted in a faster dissolution of marriages and the nuclear family.[8]

Some of the studies found even higher elasticities. According to Marvin Kosters, "The reaction of labor supplied by male primary workers is likely to be very small, especially for the hours of work component. However, the evidence suggests that for married women an increase in the tax rate . . . might be accompanied by as much as an *equal percentage decline* in the labor force participation rate"[9] (emphasis added).

At the lower end of the income scale, then, several reputable studies using different sets of data and different methods of calculation have all established that the elasticity of labor supply with respect to the tax rate is quite significant. Conservative estimates would suggest that, as mentioned above, these elasticities are about 0.1 for heads of households and 0.3 for secondary workers, although the Seattle and Denver studies generated significantly higher estimates. The idea that lower-income taxpayers do not pay very much attention to tax rates obviously deserves to be discarded along with so many other stereotypes about the poor and the uneducated.

Admittedly the solution for these lower-income people is not only the Reagan 25 percent across-the-board tax cut. Although such a reduction would help them as well as all other taxpayers, it would not eliminate the distortions of the welfare/workfare system which combine to create marginal tax rates of over 100 percent. Yet what had been the Democratic alternative, namely to increase the zero tax bracket and personal exemption even further, would do even less to increase work effort among the lower income levels. While that would lower the average tax rate, it would leave the statutory marginal rates unchanged and cause actual tax rates to rise through inflation.

For the lower-income workers, any sensible solution, it seems, must involve both the carrot and the stick. On the carrot side, more employment opportunities must be made available through an expanded economy. As this occurs, welfare benefits should not be immediately or completely withdrawn as the former recipient finds a job. Some phased withdrawal, both with respect to income and timing, would seem to be far superior to the all-or-nothing decision process favored by the Reagan administration. On the stick side, welfare benefits should be viewed as a temporary palliative until personal or business conditions improve once again, and not as a long-term crutch that discourages work effort. Those whose physical or mental disabilities preclude them from holding regular jobs would continue to be exempted from this short-term requirement, but those able-bodied people who could seek and find work under more profitable circumstances—and whose availability has been amply demonstrated by the HEW studies across the country—would be more highly motivated were it made clear that the welfare benefits were designed as temporary rather than permanent aid.

At the middle-income level, most studies again point to a much stronger substitution effect for secondary rather than for primary workers. A number of these studies have been collected, reviewed, and summarized by L. Godfrey.[10] He finds in general that the substitution elasticity for primary workers is only about 0.1, but for female workers it is almost unity. Since the elasticity from the income effect is about $+0.1$ for both groups of workers, the net effect is that a change in the tax rates has virtually no effect on primary workers but a very substantial one on secondary workers.

However, the primary worker effect for middle-income employees is understated because, unlike the lower-income workers where the primary decision is whether or not to enter the labor force, the tax-related decisions hinge on hours, overtime, absenteeism, and similar issues. In countries with higher marginal tax rates than in the United States, the effects are quite serious. In Sweden, where the marginal tax rates are far higher than in this country and rise to 85 percent at approximately $35,000 of income, lack of work effort is quite serious. During the period from 1960 to 1978, the average annual working time in that country for men in manufacturing has decreased 24 percent, overtime has declined 70 percent, and absenteeism has increased 63 percent.[11]

The evidence from the IRS tax tapes, discussed in greater detail below, corroborates with the microeconomic evidence very well and indicates that for lower- and middle-income individuals, a one percentage point change in the marginal tax rate (from 30 percent to 29 percent) would raise work effort by about 0.2 percent. Thus, for example, a 30 percent across-the-board tax cut, which would lower the marginal tax rate on wage income from approximately 30 percent to 21 percent, would increase work effort by approximately 1.8 percent over a three-year period, or 0.6 percent per year. This represents a very substantial proportion of the total growth of labor supply, which historically has averaged about 2 percent per year. Obviously an increase in this long-term growth rate of 30 percent cannot be considered unimportant.

Evidence for Higher-Income Workers

The evidence is scantier at the upper end of the income scale. For one thing, people at the upper end of the scale are more likely to be highly motivated. Someone who is capable of earning $100,000 a year is not going to quit work because his tax rate went up, providing he can still retain a substantial proportion of his income after tax rates. Of course, a true marginal tax rate of 98 percent would give a whole new meaning to the term the "idle rich."

Yet just because we do not see upper-income workers dropping out of the labor force or taking extended vacations because their tax rates have increased does not mean that high tax rates do not have an important, if sometimes concealed, effect on the economy. After all, it is in general the more economically valuable members of society who are affected by these higher tax rates. In the absence of non-market distortions, the worker is paid the marginal value product of his labor. Admittedly this calls into focus the question of whether a rock star who makes $50,000,000 a year is really 5,000 times as valuable as a garbage collector who makes $10,000 a year. But then again, every garbage collector has the option to try and become the Number One rock star and, as you may recall, one actually did.[12]

In any case, the evidence for the upper-income worker has to be dug out. A number of surveys have been taken in which managers were asked whether their work effort would change if their marginal tax rate did. Most, it turned out, did not know what their marginal tax rate was. Of these a goodly subset were insulted by the insinuation that they were not working as hard as they could. Even matters like vacations did not seem to be affected by tax rates.

The evidence is a little stronger in terms of the self-employed professionals: doctors, lawyers, consultants, and so forth. Several studies have shown that these people, who do enjoy greater flexibility in their work habits, do reduce their hours, take longer vacations, hire more assistants, and in other ways reduce their work efforts. One particularly popular way of beating the tax man which was associated with changes in the tax rates seemed to be "junkets"—conferences in exotic locations allegedly held in order to further one's knowledge of the field. The IRS eventually cracked down on this abuse, and more junkets now are held in the United States or its possessions.

But even these quasi-vacations and the occasional shorter hours do not really hit at the heart of the problem. The primary effect of high tax rates seems to be that these individuals will work just as hard as ever, but they will work at something else. To illustrate the point, consider for the moment a surgeon and a stockbroker, each of whom earns $200,000 a year before taxes. Initially, assume that all of the doctor's income is in wages; he does not yet know about tax shelters (an absurd point which we correct in a moment) and his top marginal rate including state and local taxes is 60 percent. Also assume that the stockbroker's income comes mainly in the form of capital gains, so his top marginal rate is 20 percent. Under such circumstances, there is eventually going to be a shortage of doctors and a surplus of stockbrokers, presuming that equal skills and training are involved in both professions (if it takes less skill to be a stockbroker, the mix will become even more unbalanced). If this keeps up, it will turn out that capital gets more care and attention than labor, which was presumably just the opposite intention of those liberals who wrote the tax laws.

Hence the first distortion is that high marginal tax rates shift the mix of labor into those areas where tax rates are lowest, thus depriving society of needed manpower in the professions. Doctors work just as hard as they always would have, but there would be fewer of them.

But as a matter of fact, we all know that most doctors, having spent the time and money on an education, do not in fact lay down their scalpels and become stockbrokers or money managers when the tax rates change. At least they do not do so directly. Yet after a long day, when the doctor is finally able to have some time to himself, does he read *Lancet* to keep up with the latest developments in his field? Or does he read *Medical Economics,* which explains the latest tax shelters designed (as it says there) especially for doctors and dentists?

Lower Tax Rates Reduce Tax Avoidance

While the case is perhaps most obvious in the medical professions, it is certainly true as well for other professions and high-salaried employees of major corporations. The time spent managing money in an attempt to reduce taxes could be spent much better, from a societal point of view, in keeping up to date on the latest advancements in one's own field. Thus the second distortion is that high marginal tax rates divert the individual's energy from keeping abreast of recent developments in his primary line of work into managing his financial affairs in an attempt to reduce his taxes.

The third distortion does not apply so much to independent businessmen as it does to managers at large corporations. In this case the issue is not so much the quantity of work but the quality. Basically, existing incentives actively discourage managers from producing radical new schemes that could significantly increase the profits of the corporation. After all, almost by definition, radical new schemes do not always work; most small business enterprises do not make it at all. On the average, however, new ideas are quite profitable, as can be seen from the average return of well over 20 percent in the venture capital industry.

Within the confines of a large corporation, however, a successful idea generates relatively little in terms of monetary rewards for its originator, whereas a bad idea can result in severe penalties up to and including the loss of job. The risk/reward ratio is clearly skewed in the wrong direction. If an employee's new idea works, he may at best be promoted and given a large raise, of which 50 percent to 60 percent disappears in higher taxes. He may be given more stock in the company, and indeed in the days when stock options could be used, this was a powerful incentive and one that diluted the negative effect of high marginal tax rates. However, the IRS changed this regulation so that the advantages of stock options in established firms became almost nil; although in 1981 the IRS did switch back again. Besides, unless capital appreciation is great, the dividends from the stock are worth relatively little on an after-tax basis, for until 1982 they were taxed at marginal rates as high as 90 percent when double taxation and state and local taxes are considered.

The escape hatch that exists for those with bright new ideas is to start one's own company and reap the rewards through capital appreciation of stock in that company. That is why venture capital is so critical to the entire growth process, and why productivity stagnated so much after that industry became moribund. But for those who are not able to follow this route, either because of lack of capital or because their skills in managing a company do not match their brilliance in inventions, the tax laws do not permit large corporations to reward incentives correctly. Thus although the executive puts in the requisite number of hours at a desk or in the field, far too much of the work done is in the direction of following past patterns of behavior rather than new developments that might lead to a major breakthrough in productivity and profitability.

The fourth distortion stems from lack of mobility. In an attempt to escape the taxman's clutches, many firms have awarded senior executives tax-deferred pay in the form of pensions that presumably will be taxed at a much lower rate after retirement; in the meantime, the pre-tax amounts can be used for capital accumulation. Another, not so benign reason for the creation of these generous pension plans is to keep the employee working at his present position. With full vesting this tie has become weakened, but in many cases the existence of pension rights and other benefits that accrue at retirement or on a tax-free basis keep the employee from seeking a job elsewhere, even when his talents could be better employed for another company or in a different industry. The necessity to shelter income in this manner thus inhibits job mobility and reduces productivity growth because labor resources are not available to the highest bidder.

Finally, the last major issue in this area is that of tax avoidance. In the narrow sense, tax avoidance deprives the government only of revenue that it does not rightly deserve, and in that sense no harm is done. In a larger sense, however, tax avoidance leads to shoddy or questionable practices which pervade the atmosphere of the entire corporation and lower the quality of work throughout the organization.

Everyone by now is familiar with the perquisites of the company car, the company airplane, the company dining facilities, the company retreat, and so on. Almost as well known are gimmicks such as buying an Oriental rug for the office, depreciating it as "carpet" over the next five years, and then taking the fully depreciated rug home and selling it for a handsome profit. While some might frown on these practices, little harm is done unless one is a fancier of Oriental rugs for their intrinsic values and is incensed by the fact that the prices seem to be exorbitant because so many people are buying them for tax reasons.

From a societal point of view, the line is crossed when the tax reasons for business decisions overwhelm the economic justifications. Money is put into a new corporate jet instead of new equipment because the tax incentives, both personal and corporate, are greater that way. Companies are bought and sold because the capital gains or losses are needed to balance the tax treatment of assets owned by senior executives in the industry.

Perhaps these examples might be considered rare because they seldom come to light in the business or financial press. That would be the optimistic view of tax avoidance. The more cynical approach would suggest that most companies do these sorts of activities but are not careless enough to have them come to light; or, alternatively, these activities come to light only when the company goes bankrupt and financial transactions are examined with a fine-tooth comb. But one does not even have to be a cynic to question whether much of the asset management of companies is not undertaken with a view toward improving the tax position of the high-level executives of those companies. This may not be true for the very largest companies that always seem to be under minute government supervision for everything from alleged antitrust violations to dirty bathrooms to failure to hire the correct proportion of paraplegic, alcoholic Aleutians, but is likely to exist in the mid-range companies where asset deployment is even more critical.

About the only statistically documented evidence available for the upper-income taxpayers stems from the work that this author did in his study for the Senate Finance Committee.[13] These results are based on individual income tax returns for 1962, 1964, and 1966, thereby bracketing the years of the Kennedy-Johnson 20 percent across-the-board income tax rate reduction. These results indicated that the elasticity of work effort with respect to changes in tax rates for the lower- and middle-income levels was about −0.2, closely replicating the microeconomic results. However, when calculated for the upper-income levels ($100,000 and above in the 1962–66 period, which would be roughly equivalent to $250,000 and above in 1981 dollars), the results at first seemed to go askew. The elasticities were generally larger than unity, and in some cases were greater than 2.

While these results are of course favorable to the supply-side point of view, they are "too good." A reduction in the maximum tax rate from 91 to 70 percent did not cause those individuals to work 40 percent harder. Not really. Yet the figures clearly did indicate that the proportion of total income received from work effort—as opposed to income from capital—did increase dramatically when tax rates were lowered. This finding is not just some econometric fluke but is buttressed by evidence, to be discussed shortly, showing that tax receipts in the top brackets doubled after the tax cut, even though the rate was slashed by over 20 percent.

It is no surprise to find that virtually no one paid taxes at the 91 percent marginal rate. Tax shelters for the rich proliferated then as now; donations of rapidly appreciating stock and other capital assets also eased the pain. One of the most popular escapes worked through the capital gains route, as follows.

Assume that the management of a corporation decided that a certain individual deserved a compensation of $100,000 per year. However, since that would subject him to very high marginal tax rates, the employee would be paid $50,000 in the form of the normal salary, while the other $50,000 would be paid to him in the form of stock options. Not stock options tied to his performance, or the performance of his division, or the entire company, although he might well receive those in addition. No, these were stock options determined in advance so that they would total exactly $50,000. It was just a way of avoiding taxes.

Independent businessmen, especially in the area of artists and writers, often converted their income into capital gains. General Eisenhower received an IRS ruling that the approximately $750,000 of income from the royalties of his best-seller, *Crusade in Europe,* should be treated as a capital gain because it was a once-in-a-lifetime source of income rather than a continuing flow. President Truman was furious at the ruling and got a law passed prohibiting this; however, when it came time to write his memoirs for *Life* magazine, he received his $600,000 payment spread over five years. Since he had written them in his house, he received generous tax write-offs for that being his principal place of business. In the area of economics, Paul Samuelson also converted the income from his best-selling economics textbook into capital gains.

The list of examples could go on and on; but this is not meant to be a primer on how people escaped high tax rates in the 1950s. By this time, however, the point should be clear: people simply do not pay taxes at ridiculously high marginal rates. To the extent that they arrange to have ordinary income transmuted into lower-tax capital gains income, no harm is done. However, to the extent that they engage in decisions that are economically inefficient in order to reduce their personal tax burden, all of society is harmed. The elasticities well in excess of unity show the degree to which tax avoidance schemes were rampant in the days before 1964.

Cutting Top Marginal Tax Rates Increases Tax Revenues

We do not need to rely only on this cross-section evidence, however, to show what happened to tax receipts when top marginal rates were reduced. Besides the Kennedy-Johnson tax cuts, top rates were slashed in the mid-1920s under Treasury Secretary Andrew W. Mellon. It is useful to examine both of these periods in some detail.

Before the United States entered World War I, the maximum tax rate on personal income was 15 percent, but this rate rose dramatically to a peak of 73 percent in 1918 and succeeding years. It was then cut to 55 percent in 1922 and 25 percent in 1926. It is instructive to learn what happened to taxes paid by millionaires as this occurred. To adjust for the differentials caused by inflation, let us consider those taxpayers with incomes over $300,000 in 1922 and

1927, although even this adjustment is an understatement of the true effects of rising prices. In 1922 this group paid taxes of $77 million, whereas in 1927, the year after the second reduction in rates, they paid a total of $230 million.[14] Not only did the economy benefit significantly, but the millionaires themselves paid three times as much in taxes with lower rates.

It could be argued that the Mellon tax cut results, while instructive, are not relevant today since the institutional structure and income distribution of the U.S. economy are far different now than they were in the 1920s. Yet we need not be restricted to this episode but can in addition rely on the figures before and after the Kennedy-Johnson tax cuts of 1964.

As was previously mentioned, the top rate was reduced from 91 percent in 1963 to 77 percent in 1964 and 70 percent in 1965 and later years. The figures for actual income tax paid for 1961–66 by taxpayers with incomes of $100,000 or more are taken from *Statistics of Income* and are reproduced in table 9.1.[15]

The results are so clear-cut that they really leave little reason for adverse interpretation. After virtually no growth in income taxes for incomes over $100,000 for three years, taxes paid rose dramatically beginning in 1964 even though income was taxed at significantly lower rates. In the case of individuals earning over $1 million per year, taxes collected *actually doubled* in the two-year span during which the tax rates were being *lowered.* For income classes under $100,000, taxes either fell or rose less than the average growth in total personal income.

These results, which represent a remarkable rebuttal of those who argue that upper-income tax cuts are a "raid on the Treasury," indicate that the further reduction from 70 percent to 50 percent under the Reagan economic program will not only spur economic growth and increase aggregate supply, but will actually assure the Treasury of greater tax revenues, which it sorely needs. The argument for upper-income tax cuts is almost as watertight as the argument for lower capital gains taxes.

It was the dawning realization that the rich do not really pay marginal tax

TABLE 9.1

Effect of Lowering Maximum Tax Rates on Tax Collections

	1961	1962	1963	1964	1965	1966
Maximum tax rate (in percent)	91	91	91	77	70	70
Taxes collected from incomes classes of[a]						
Over 1,000,000	342	311	326	427	603	590
500,000–1,000,000	297	243	243	306	408	457
100,000–500,000	1970	1740	1890	2220	2752	3176

[a]Adjusted gross income (in millions of dollars).

199

rates of 70 percent any more than they did at 91 percent, coupled with the knowledge that heavy utilization of tax-municipal bonds and other tax shelters was costing the Treasury a good deal more than the pound of flesh it was exacting from those high incomes, which led to the reduction of the top marginal tax rate from 70 percent to 50 percent with an absolute minimum of dissenting voices. Although allegedly quite controversial, this plank of the tax-cut bill was included and passed with little discussion and even less demagoguery.

The Shape of the Laffer Curve

The 50 percent figure for the top marginal rate was picked because that maximum rate had already been established for earned income and also, one suspects, because it has the sound of equity about it—half for you, half for the government. Yet except for this nice round-number quality, there would appear to be no particular reason to choose 50 percent. Indeed, it is logical to argue that the Treasury ought to set the maximum personal income tax rate no higher than the level that maximizes total revenues. It might want to set the rate lower for purposes of stimulating work effort and productivity, or even for reasons of equity. However, on economic grounds it is hard to support a rate above the revenue maximizing level—that is, in the backward-bending region of the Laffer curve. Perhaps one reason for keeping those high marginal rates is that the shape of the curve is generally considered to be unknown.

To determine the rate at which income tax revenues would be maximized, we have undertaken a large number of calculations, the most important of which are summarized in tables 9.2 and 9.3. These calculations utilize the Treasury estimates of the 1981 profile of income tax payments which were prepared for the across-the-board income tax cut. We conclude that income tax revenue would be maximized if the top rate were cut to at least 35 percent and possibly as low as 25 percent; now let us see how this conclusion was reached.

The first and noncontroversial part of the calculations simply consists of estimating the so-called static revenue loss under the assumptions of no offsetting gains at all—that is, assuming no increase in taxes from a reduction in tax shelters, less tax evasion, greater work effort, or any other factors. Even under this basis, the tax revenue lost by reducing the top rate to 35 percent is only $21.0 billion, compared to the Treasury Department estimate of $286.7

billion in 1981 tax receipts. This works out to be only a 7.3 percent cut, although of course it is concentrated exclusively in the upper-income levels.

Indeed no one really believes that there would be no offsetting revenue gains at all. These gains can be grouped into four categories: less tax-free interest income, a reduction in other legal tax avoidance schemes, an increase in work effort, and a smaller underground economy. In addition, it is reasonable to assume some dynamic gain from a more rapidly growing economy; these estimates are given separately in table 9.2. These calculations indicate that the 35 percent top rate is a conservative estimate of the rate that would maximize revenues, and that a rate of 30 percent or even 25 percent might indeed prove to be the optimal one in practice.

The first revenue-producing factor is the decline in tax-free or tax-sheltered income generated through municipal bonds and the holding of assets that generate capital gains rather than interest or dividend income. Because tax-free municipal bond income by definition need not be reported on 1040 forms, it must be estimated indirectly.

The figures for upper-income tax brackets can be dissected by examining the proportion of total income accounted for by wages and salaries, business and professional income, capital gains, dividends, and interest. Table 9.3 shows figures for 1963 and 1977 for those with income of $500,000 and over per year.

As shown above, wages and salaries and business and professional income—basically returns to labor—increased from 5.5 percent to 36.1 percent of total compensation over the period from 1963 to 1977. The reason is not very difficult to identify. When the top marginal tax rate was 91 percent on

TABLE 9.2

Revenue Gains and Losses with Lower Maximum Personal Income Tax Rates

	Top Rate of					
	50%	**45%**	**40%**	**35%**	**30%**	**25%**
Static tax loss	6.4	10.3	15.1	21.0	29.1	41.5
Gains due to:						
Less tax-free interest income	6.5	7.3	7.8	7.9	7.5	6.8
Other tax shelters	3.6	4.1	4.3	4.4	4.2	3.8
Smaller underground economy	0.0	1.7	4.5	6.6	7.9	8.5
Increase in work effort	0.0	0.3	0.5	1.7	2.7	3.8
Total gains	10.1	13.4	17.1	20.6	22.3	22.9
Net static gain or loss	3.7	3.1	2.0	−0.4	−6.8	−18.6
Dynamic gains[a]	2.6	4.1	6.0	8.4	11.6	16.6
Total gain or loss	6.1	7.2	8.0	8.0	4.8	−2.0

SOURCE: Calculated by Evans Economics, Inc.
NOTE: All figures in billions of dollars. All calculations based on 1981 levels of income and pre-tax cut rates.
[a]Assuming a multiplier of 2 and federal government revenues equal to 20 percent of GNP.

TABLE 9.3

Income by Type for Upper Brackets of $500,000 and Over

	1963	Percent	1977	Percent
Total	1,354	100.0	7,094	100.0
Capital gains and dividends	1,252	92.5	4,110	57.9
Wages and salaries	53	3.9	1,355	19.1
Interest	27	2.0	404	5.7
Business, professional, and other income	22	1.6	1,225	17.3

SOURCE: *Statistics of Income,* 1963 and 1977.
NOTE: Income figures in millions of dollars.

wage income and 25 percent on capital gains, many top-bracket employees were compensated primarily through capital gains. When the gap between the rates closed completely—in 1977 the maximum tax rate on wage income was 50 percent, while for capital gains it was 49.1 percent—few still received "hidden" compensation in the form of capital gains. Thus a 66 percent reduction in the spread on tax rates resulted in an increase in the ratio of labor/total compensation from 5 percent to 36 percent, or an elasticity of about 0.5.

It is true that one cannot make exactly the same calculation for interest income returning to taxable sources, for the Treasury statistics do not report how much income is currently placed in tax-free or tax-sheltered investments. As is shown in table 9.4, however, for incomes of $50,000 and above the proportion of income accounted for by dividends starts to increase dramatically, whereas the amount accounted for by interest income actually diminishes. It is clear that interest income is being diverted into tax-free municipal bonds and other shelters that do not have to be reported on 1040 forms at all.

If we assume as an approximation that interest and dividend income would represent the same proportion of upper-bracket income in the absence of distorting taxes, this provides an estimate of some $15 billion in interest income on which the government did not collect taxes for 1977. This figure would be at least $45 billion for 1981, since interest income has grown more rapidly than total taxable income during the past five years because of higher interest rates.

It would be foolish to assume that all of this interest income would return to taxable form if the maximum rate were cut from 70 percent to 50 percent. Using the elasticity of ½ calculated above, however, means that interest income would increase from 6 percent to 16 percent of total income over $100,000 per year. In 1977 total gross income for those making over $100,000 per year totaled $50 billion, of which taxable interest income was about $3 billion. We estimate that this $3 billion figure would have increased to $8 bil-

TABLE 9.4

Interest and Dividend by Income Class, 1977

Income Class	Total Adjusted Gross Income	Dividend Income	Interest Income	Percentage of Dividend Income	Percentage of Interest Income
$ 10,000– 12,000	66.8	0.79	3.31	1.2	5.0
12,000– 14,000	73.8	0.81	3.09	1.1	4.2
14,000– 16,000	76.0	0.82	3.06	1.1	4.0
16,000– 18,000	80.3	0.73	2.69	0.9	3.3
18,000– 20,000	78.1	0.79	2.45	1.0	3.1
20,000– 25,000	173.2	1.64	5.50	1.0	3.2
25,000– 30,000	118.8	1.48	4.41	1.3	3.7
30,000– 50,000	174.7	4.38	7.90	2.5	4.5
50,000– 100,000	74.9	4.99	4.67	6.7	6.2
100,000– 200,000	29.5	3.35	1.81	11.4	5.4
200,000– 500,000	12.9	2.51	0.80	19.5	6.2
500,000–1,000,000	3.5	0.97	0.20	27.7	5.7
1,000,000+	3.6	1.09	0.20	30.3	5.6

SOURCE: *Statistics of Income;* calculations of percent by Evans Economics, Inc.
NOTE: Income figures in billions of dollars.

lion at 1977 levels of income if the maximum tax rate had been reduced from 70 percent to 50 percent. This translates into an increase of $15 billion at 1981 levels of income.

Hence of the estimated $45 billion in tax-sheltered interest income, we estimate that $15 billion will move back into the tax base now that the top rate has been lowered to 50 percent. With this assumption, we are now in a position to calculate the net revenue gain. The Treasury would collect 50 percent of this additional $15 billion per year, or an additional $7.5 billion. From this we must subtract the reduction of the loss in revenue for those amounts now taxed at rates above 50 percent. This amount was $10 billion in 1977; using the same expansion factor it would be about $30 billion today. We estimate that the average marginal tax rate on non-wage income was 65 percent for income brackets above $100,000, so the decline to 50 percent would cost the Treasury about $4.5 billion. Thus on balance the revenue *gain* would be *$3 billion* per year.

Other tax shelters make up a catchall category which includes real estate, cattle, and other devices that shift income from one year to another as opposed to simply exempting it from taxes permanently. We do not have any specific estimates for this category but have assumed it to be about $25 billion per year. Market surveys indicate that there were approximately 12 million consumer units (individuals and families) with incomes of $50,000 or more in 1981. However, the Treasury estimates that only 4.1 million families had an adjusted gross income (AGI) of over $50,000 in 1981. The average AGI for all taxpayers with incomes of $50,000 or more is about $81,000. We have assumed that taxpayers shelter about 7 percent of their income, which implies a total of about $70 billion in tax-sheltered income (excluding interest income).

The calculation for the gain in tax revenues due to increased work effort involves several steps but is actually quite straightforward. The revenue gain is zero for a drop to the 50 percent marginal tax bracket because labor income—which includes proprietors' as well as wage earners' income—was not previously taxed at a rate above 50 percent in any case. A drop in the top rate from 50 percent to 45 percent would affect an estimated $69 billion of labor income; this figure is based on the proportion of labor income in the 45–50 percent marginal tax brackets relative to total labor income. A 5 percent drop in the tax rate would raise work effort by 1 percent of this $69 billion, or $0.69 billion. This figure must then be multiplied by 0.45 to generate the amount of increased tax receipts; similar calculations are used for further tax rate reductions. Note in particular in table 9.2 that the work effort generates the *least* additional tax revenue; the big gains accrue from reducing tax avoidance.

The underground economy figures are perhaps the weakest, since we do not have any firm numbers for the amount of income escaping taxation. However, the IRS has recently provided some estimates, which will be examined in the next section of this chapter. The income from illegal sources—drugs, prostitution, gambling, loansharking, and so on—would presumably never be reported at any positive level of taxation. More income from legal sources might be reported if tax rates were substantially lower, however, and we estimate that a reduction from 70 percent to 35 percent would generate an additional $6.6 billion per year in taxes.

When we compare total gains with static losses, the results are rather striking. A further decline in the maximum tax rate from 50 percent to 40 percent would generate an additional $2 billion in revenues relative to present tax laws. Even if dynamic gains are not considered, the Treasury would collect just as much revenue if it reduced the top marginal rate to 35 percent as it would with the present tax structure.

Furthermore, these figures are only static results; they do not take into account the rise in income and tax revenues due to higher economic activity. If personal income taxes are cut to a top rate of 35 percent, representing a static revenue loss of $21 billion, standard multiplier analysis would indicate that about 40 percent of this, or more than $8 billion, would be recaptured in higher receipts. With this added benefit, the government makes money even with a top marginal rate of 30 percent. Only when the rate slips to 25 percent and lower do we observe what is considered the traditional relationship between tax rates and receipts.

In fact, even the static revenue loss at 25 percent is only $41.5 billion, which is less than 15 percent of total personal income tax receipts. High marginal rates clearly account for only a very small proportion of total tax receipts. Below this, the revenue loss starts to balloon; it is about $65 billion at 20 percent and over $100 billion at 15 percent maximum tax rates. Below 25 percent, a reduction in tax rates clearly results in substantial revenue losses unless it is coupled with fewer deductions.

These results stress the crucial difference between average and marginal tax rates. A 50 percent reduction in average tax rates would cause a tremendous revenue shortfall. However, a 50 percent reduction in the top marginal rates would cause no shortfall at all once the offsetting gains and dynamic effects are taken into account. To put it another way, a reduction in the average tax rate from 20 percent to 15 percent would cost the government about $40 billion per year and would have only small positive effects on work effort, capital accumulation, and more honest reporting of income, while a reduction in the top marginal rate from 50 percent to 45 percent would actually raise the revenues to the Treasury.

Unfortunately, the politics of upper-income tax cuts overwhelm the economics. A cut in the maximum rate to 35 percent means that no one with an adjusted gross income of under $40,000 would get a tax cut at all; those with incomes between $40,000 and $50,000 average an $80 cut, whereas those with income of over $200,000 would get an average tax cut of $65,520 per year. At 25 percent the disparities are even greater, although this case does encompass a wider range of the income distribution scale. Those with incomes of $25,000 would receive a tax cut of $20 per year; the $50,000 class would move up in respectability to a $2,190 annual tax cut, and the "fat cats" at $200,000 or more would average a tax reduction of $88,140 per year.

The economic advantages of reducing top marginal rates are indisputable. A reduction in the top rate to 25 percent or even 35 percent would eliminate most of the those distortions due to misallocation of resources caused by the tax system. It would also attract the best and the brightest from other countries, thus improving our technology for that reason as well. The inherent economic advantages of such reductions, coupled with the fact that virtually no revenue would be lost, are obvious. The only way that maximum tax rates of 25 percent could ever be implemented, however, would be in conjunction with a major broad-based value-added or consumption tax, which in the past has proven to be very politically unpopular. The flat tax of 15 percent to 20 percent with no deductions, which is also an excellent idea, faces the same insurmountable political hurdles.

Tax Avoidance and the Underground Economy

Our estimates of the beneficial effects of cutting the top marginal tax rate to 25 percent so far have been primarily based on responses in the legal sector—fewer tax shelters, a move away from tax-free municipal bonds, and an increase in work effort. However, the single biggest source of tax leakage is probably illegal tax avoidance—failure to declare all of one's income from legal sources, overstated expenses and deductions, and income generated in the illegal sector. All of these are commonly coupled together under the rubric of the "underground economy." Casual observation has tended to indicate for years that this sector is not only an important and significant proportion of GNP but is growing about twice as fast as reported income.

Stories about the size of the underground economy are, of course, not new; the major work has been done by Peter Gutmann[16] and Edgar Feige.[17] Most of these stories have been based on anecdotal evidence, some crude ratio of currency in circulation to GNP, or the ratio of self-employed to total labor force. Quasi-official estimates from the IRS used to indicate that the underground economy was not more than 5 percent of GNP, and it was not increasing in relative terms.[18]

Many economists have long suspected that the IRS underestimated these numbers in order to give the impression that most people paid all their taxes, but only the IRS had the files and all other attempts were thus based on secondary data. In March 1982, however, IRS Commissioner Roscoe Egger testified before Congress with a completely different story.[19] The IRS estimated that the total "tax gap"—the amount of unpaid income taxes—approached $100 billion in 1981. Although Egger did not say so, this implies, as we will show, that the underground economy represents well over 10 percent of GNP. Furthermore, he also presented figures, which are reproduced here as table 9.5, indicating that the tax gap as a proportion of GNP has steadily increased over the past decade.

Complete methodology is not yet available from the IRS in order to compare and cross-check its methods with its earlier studies, and a cynic might wonder if the IRS had not raised its estimates in order to push for legislation to reduce unpaid taxes, specifically by expanding the types of income subject to withholding. However, since the earlier estimates always seemed unduly low, it is more likely that the IRS finally came to grips with the seriousness of the situation and decided to admit how widespread the problem really is.

The Egger Report divides the tax gap into five classifications: underreporting on individual tax returns, overstated expenses and deductions, nonfilers,

TABLE 9.5

Gross Tax Gap from Legal Sector, Nonfilers,
Corporate Tax, and Illegal Sector in Tax Years 1973, 1976, 1979, and 1981

	1981	1979	1976	1973
Legal Sector	87.2	66.5	42.6	29.3
Individual income tax returns	83.3	61.8	39.0	26.5
Filed returns	78.4	58.4	36.8	25.3
Income underreported:				
Wages	2.5	1.8	0.7	0.6
Tips	2.3	1.7	1.4	0.9
Dividends	3.6	3.1	1.5	0.9
Interest	4.1	2.9	1.3	0.9
Capital gains	9.1	8.5	5.1	2.0
Nonfarm business	26.2	17.5	11.6	9.6
Farm business	1.4	1.7	1.7	1.5
Pensions	2.8	2.3	1.1	0.7
Rents	1.5	1.2	0.6	0.4
Royalties	1.3	0.8	0.4	0.1
Partnerships	5.5	3.1	2.5	1.5
Estates and trusts	0.5	0.4	0.3	0.2
Small business corporations	1.7	1.2	1.2	0.4
State income tax refunds	0.4	0.3	0.1	0.1
Alimony	0.1	a	a	a
Other	3.1	2.4	1.0	0.6
Total	66.1	49.0	30.6	20.5
Overstated expenses, deductions, credits[b]	12.3	9.4	6.2	4.8
Nonfilers[b]	4.9	3.4	2.2	1.2
Corporate tax[b]	3.9	4.7	3.6	2.8
Illegal sector[b,c]	6.1–9.8	4.6–7.4	2.5–4.0	1.8–2.9
Drugs	4.5–8.1	3.2–6.0	1.4–2.7	1.0–2.0
Gambling	0.6–1.2	0.5–0.9	0.4–0.7	0.3–0.5
Prostitution	0.4–1.2	0.3–1.0	0.3–1.0	0.2–0.7
Total (using maximum estimates for illegal sector)	97.0	73.9	46.6	32.2
Memo: Income taxes actually paid	361	305	202	158
Tax avoidance as percentage of taxes paid	26.9	24.2	23.1	20.4

SOURCE: Statement of Roscoe Egger, March 22, 1982, before Senate Finance Committee except last two lines, which are from *Survey of Current Business* and EEI calculations.
NOTES: All figures in billions of dollars. Details may not add to totals because of rounding.
aLess than 100 million.
bThese are preliminary IRS figures and have not been reviewed by the Office of Tax Analysis.
cTotal of three items below and does not include any other illegal activities.

corporate taxes, and the illegal sector. The illegal sector tax gap is estimated by the IRS to be somewhat less than $10 billion, which implies perhaps $20 to $30 billion in total illicit income. In view of the casual evidence available from drug busts and gambling reports, this figure sounds much too low, and in fact the most recent IRS estimate for 1976 is lower than its earlier calculation. But we can all agree that lowering marginal tax rates is not going to cause drug dealers to declare any more of their income, so in that sense the illegal sector is not germane to this discussion.

The overstated expenses and deductions area is akin to the problem associated with tax shelters; we will reintroduce our own estimates in conjunction with the IRS figures later in this section. Very little information is available on the sources of corporate tax avoidance except that its underreporting is primarily restricted to small firms similar to those subchapter S corporations* included in individual income tax returns.

The biggest single category contributing to the tax gap is the small business sector. The IRS has split this into several categories—nonfarm business, farm business, partnerships, and small business corporations—but the idea is the same for all of these categories: most of these businesses do not declare all of their income.

According to the IRS, the tax gap from these categories (excluding corporate tax) was estimated to be approximately $35 billion in 1981. Based on a marginal tax rate of about 35 percent, about $100 billion of income from this source was undeclared. According to Department of Commerce statistics, proprietors' income was $134 billion in 1981, but that is a net figure; to come up with a gross receipts figure, the costs of doing business must be added. Assuming gross margins of about 50 percent would imply about $300 billion in reported gross receipts, this means that about 25 percent of total receipts are not reported. As a proportion of net income, *almost half* is unreported.

The other area that the IRS has singled out for massive underreporting is capital gains. Its estimates show that only 56 percent of all capital gains transactions are properly reported, but even this figure is too high. Perhaps this proportion had some justification when commodity prices were stable and the vast majority of capital gains represented equity appreciation, but not in recent years. We would estimate that the only time capital gains on coin and stamp collections, paintings and sculptures, vases or Oriental rugs ever get reported is when the individual is donating his collection to a worthy cause and claiming a tax deduction. Capital gains on real estate not put back into another residence may be reported at a somewhat higher rate, but we would estimate that the vast majority of these transactions also go unreported—particularly when the house is sold to a foreign national or member of the illegal sector of the economy at a fictitiously reduced price. Hence underreporting on capital gains probably creates a tax gap twice what the IRS has estimated.

The way in which the IRS generates its estimates of the tax gap is through something known as the Taxpayer Compliance Measurement Program (TCMP). The general idea is that the IRS selects 50,000 tax returns and audits

*Subchapter S corporation refers to closely held corporations for which the income accrues directly to stockholders; hence it avoids double taxation.

them very thoroughly, finding evidence of underreporting and possibly other errors. This percentage of underreporting is then applied to the total population of taxpayers to obtain global estimates of the tax gap.

It is probably fair to say that if your return is selected for audit under TCMP and you have received income for which a so-called "paper trail" exists but has not been declared, your underreporting will be detected. On the other hand, if you received payment in cash and spent it directly without depositing it in your bank account, or at least any bank account that issued a 1099 and thus alerted the IRS to its existence, the underreporting will remain undetected.

Thus, for example, the IRS finds that compliance on wages and salaries has remained steady at 99 percent in recent years, and that half of the noncompliance represents an underestimate of tips. In other words, only ½ percent of wage and salary income is not reported to the tax authorities.

With all due respect to the IRS and TCMP, one need think only of the unreported income to the gardener, the baby-sitter, the maid, or the handyman to seriously question this low percentage (note that cash payments to the doctor, lawyer, plumber, and so on fall under the category of small businesses, which we have already discussed).

The IRS has tried to come up with alternative measures of this tax avoidance, which it quaintly calls the "informal" economy. Its earlier estimates, based on BLS consumer surveys, indicated that approximately $33 billion was spent in the "informal economy" in 1976, a figure comparable to $60 billion in 1981 assuming straight proportionality. The IRS then estimated that about 75 percent of this income was unreported.

Many of the providers of these services have incomes low enough so that they would not otherwise be liable for taxes in any case. Hence, the average marginal tax rate for these kinds of income probably would be no higher than 25 percent. Even so, this indicates a tax gap from this sector of about $15 billion, compared to the IRS estimate of $2.5 billion.

The other major area that the IRS does not consider is the barter economy. However, we doubt whether this is very large; estimates made in 1976 by the Roper poll placed this figure at between $2 and $4 billion. Even using the upper estimate and assuming it has tripled, instead of doubled like the rest of the economy, would yield no more than $12 billion, or perhaps a $4 billion tax gap.

We have no particular quarrel with the IRS estimates of other returns from capital—dividends, interest, pensions, rents, royalties, and so forth—since most these payments can be traced by records, thus providing an audit trail for TCMP. That tax gap totaled approximately $13 billion in 1981.

In its most recent figures, the IRS also estimated that the tax gap from underreporting of legal income has increased sharply as a proportion of taxable income, as can be seen in the following comparison.

	Total Personal Tax Gap[a]	Total Personal Taxable Income Reported	Tax Gap as Percentage of Personal Income
1973	26.5	822	3.2
1976	39.0	1,046	3.7
1979	61.8	1,455	4.2
1981	83.3	1,767	4.7

[a]Legal sources of income only.

The reasons for this steadily increasing proportion are not hard to fathom. When the average American family paid a top marginal tax rate of perhaps 20 percent, tax avoidance was something for the rich or perhaps those whose ethics were questionable. However, as many of the same families progress to the 40 percent and 50 percent brackets, the world looks somewhat different. Even if middle-income taxpayers do not know all the details, they are well aware of the fact that the rich, through tax shelters, are paying a far smaller proportion of their income in taxes than are those whose average incomes are derived from wages and salaries.

The strong sense of injustice thus engendered has already led to the beginning of a breakdown in the efficacy of the entire tax system—a feeling of cynicism reinforced by the breakdown of other "pillars of society," particularly the often seemingly whimsical and random nature of criminal justice. Once the foundations of civil and criminal justice are perceived by the average citizen to have eroded, the self-imposed constraint to pay one's taxes disappears, leaving in its wake a new morality that considers tax cheating an acceptable societal game that benefits the majority of the population. Just as prohibition was unenforceable during the 1920s, so too tax compliance runs the very strong risk of becoming an endangered species if our tax code continues in its present form.

For underreporting of income or overstatement of expenses and deductions is not the only form the taxpayers' revolt has recently taken. Indeed, legal tax avoidance through tax shelters, tax-free municipal bonds, and other similar instruments have accounted for an additional $60 billion in the tax gap for 1981.

Table 9.6 summarizes the results from all the sources of underpayment of individual income taxes. The results are not a very pretty picture for those who claim that our tax system still works well. For every $1.00 paid in individual income taxes, $0.57 is not paid. To put it another way, if everyone declared all of his income and did not use tax shelters, the tax bill for the remaining taxpayers would be reduced 36 percent.

TABLE 9.6

Underpayment of Individual Income Taxes in the Legal Sector, 1981

Source of Income	Amount of Income	Average Marginal Tax Rate	Tax Gap
Business and professional practices	100	0.35	35
Capital gains	100	0.20	20
Interest, dividends, rents, royalties, and pensions not reported	50	0.25	13
Informal economy	60	0.25	15
Barter economy	12	0.33	4
Miscellaneous sources of other legal income	28	0.25	7
Overstated expenses, deductions, and credits	36	0.33	12
Tax-free municipal bonds	45	0.40	18
Legal and quasi-legal tax shelters	100	0.40	40
Total	531		164
Memo:			
Total adjusted gross (taxable) income		1,767	
Tax avoidance income as percentage of total adjusted income		30.0	
Gross national product		2,926	
Tax avoidance income as a percentage of GNP		18.1	
Personal income taxes paid		289	
Tax gap as a percentage of personal income taxes paid		56.7	
Total federal taxes paid		626	
Tax gap as a percentage of total federal taxes paid		26.2	

SOURCES: IRS and Evans Economics, Inc.
NOTE: All figures except tax rates in billions of dollars.

These figures can also be compared to a flat rate income tax with no deductions at all. Adjusted gross (taxable) income reported for 1981 was $1,767 billion. Adding the $531 billion of income that we estimate was not declared produces a total of approximately $2,300 billion. To generate $290 billion in taxes, which was the amount collected last year, would require a 12.6 percent flat tax on all incomes—with, of course, no deductions.

The proportional income tax plan most commonly mentioned includes some progressivity, such as a $2,500 personal exemption. Under this modification, the flat tax rate would rise to 16.7 percent. Still not bad compared to what we have today.

According to the elasticities discussed earlier in this chapter, a reduction in the marginal tax rate on labor from 33 percent to 17 percent would increase work effort by approximately 3.3 percent. It would also lower the tax rate on saving from 44 percent to 17 percent, which would raise the aftertax rate of return by 3.2 percent, assuming a 12 percent interest rate.

The increase in labor and capital generated by lower tax rates would raise the productive capacity of the economy about 2 percent per year, or approximately $60 billion per year in 1981 dollars. This flat rate tax would thus generate about $15 billion in additional tax revenues the first year, $32 billion the second, and so on up to $100 billion the fifth year, by which time the additional growth from the tax incentives would have largely run its course. Clearly this would offset some of those gigantic government budget deficits. Unlike the current Reagan tax cuts, this one would involve no *ex ante* loss of government revenue and thus would not cause monetary restraint to drive interest rates higher and choke off recovery. Indeed, the strong inducement to save more would eventually result in a substantial decline in interest rates.

In this author's opinion such a tax would do more to solve the current problems of the economy than any tax legislation introduced by the Reagan administration. Within the framework of political reality, however, it is very doubtful that it will ever see the light of day. All the vested interests that currently profit by tax shelters—financial institutions that invest heavily in municipal bonds; the state and local municipalities themselves; the oil industry and other natural resource industries that utilize the depletion allowance; the stock market industry which receives favorable tax treatment for capital gains; and of course the myriad lawyers, accountants, and lobbyists who owe their very existence to the current tax laws—will stridently denounce such legislation. In addition, the so-called consumer groups who favor maintaining the deduction for mortgage interest, for charitable contributions, for health care, or for state and local taxes will have no trouble being heard. Once this happens, the entire tax bill will turn into another bidding war and the result will be fewer tax revenues, an even larger deficit, and even higher interest rates. And at that point someone will figure out that the upper-bracket income should be surtaxed, and we will end up right back where we are now—only worse.

For if the 1981 tax reduction act contained one lesson, it is that bidding wars can turn even the most sensible and presumably optimal economic tax laws into an unholy mess. That bill was supposed to include a straightforward 30 percent reduction in personal income tax rates and a 40–50 percent reduction in depreciation lives. These were indeed passed, but look what else came with the package! Indexing of tax rates. Reduction in the marriage penalty. Lower taxes for Americans working abroad. Additional deductions for charitable contributions. Higher limit for investment tax credit on used equipment. R&D tax credit. Increase in investment tax credit on old buildings. Safe harbor leasing. Incentive stock options. All Savers certificates. Expanded IRAs and Keogh plans. Exemptions from the windfall profits tax. Lower estate and gift taxes. And more—much, much more.

The evidence presented here on tax avoidance by individuals, coupled with results presented in chapter 7 on the negative tax rates in the corporate sector, provide some fairly good clues to the puzzle of why the Reagan program did not work. Although the tax cuts were supposed to provide both incentives for saving and improvement of work effort, the programs that were passed were so porous that the deficit grew much faster than expected, interest rates rose, and the beneficial effects of supply-side economics were submerged in a sea of red ink. We conclude that the deficit problem—and hence the high interest rate problem—cannot be solved within the framework of our present tax structure, and that radical revisions to plug these loopholes represent the best, if not the only, chance to revitalize the economy without re-creating inflationary pressures.

CHAPTER 10

The Determinants

of Productivity

Why Productivity Declined

The record of productivity growth in the U.S. economy during the past fifteen years has been one of the country's sorriest chapters. For the period from 1947 to 1968, productivity increased at an annual rate of 3.2 percent. Since then, however, its performance has successively deteriorated. As has already been noted, productivity has grown on an average of only 1 percent per year since 1968 and actually declined from 1977 to 1982.

So far I have concentrated on the importance of tax rates on saving, investment, productivity, and real growth. It remains my contention that the growing tax burden and its distorting effects on the optimal use of labor and capital have been the primary reasons for the demise of productivity growth since 1968. However, it would be quite narrow-minded to argue that the increase in taxes has been the only factor which has caused this dramatic reversal in productivity.

Certainly the benefits of the tax cut are not restricted to increasing saving and investment; the improvements in work incentives and labor productivity are also important. Nonetheless, even under an optimal program where tax rates and spending are reduced in tandem, the full complement of the Reagan tax package would increase productivity by only about 1½ percent per year—less than half of the 4 percent decline that has taken place since the late 1960s.

It would be similarly inaccurate to argue that the demise in productivity has stemmed primarily from the reduction in the investment ratio. Capital stock growth has shriveled from about 6 percent per year during the investment boom years of 1965–68 to 3 percent per year recently. Yet this decline has accounted for only 1 percent of the 4 percent decline in productivity growth that has occurred since 1965. Clearly other causes have been at work as well.

The major factors causing the decline in productivity growth since 1965 are:

- Level of the saving and investment ratio
- Change in education, training, and demographic mix of the labor force
- Degree of government regulation
- Level of relative energy prices
- Availability of venture capital
- Spending on research and development

The numerical importance of each factor, both on a historical basis from 1965 to 1980 and the expected improvement during the 1980s, is given in table 10.1.

The figures given in this table indicate that the traditional methods of increasing productivity—an increase in saving and investment, and higher R&D—will provide *no contribution* to productivity growth during the first half of the decade. The reasons are quite simple. Venture capital and R&D generally impact the economy with a four- to nine-year lag; hence the benefits

TABLE 10.1

Factors Affecting Change in Productivity Growth

	Decrease from 1965 to 1980	Increase from 1980 to 1985	Increase from 1985 to 1990[a]
Saving/investment ratio	−1	−½	½
Change in demographic mix of labor force	−½	½	¼
Change in marginal tax rates	−1	1	0
Cost of government regulation	−½	½	0
Relative price of energy	−½	½	0
Venture capital/R&D	−½	0[b]	½
Total change during period	−4	2	1
Level of underlying productivity growth at end of period	−½	1½	2½

SOURCE: Calculations by Evans Economics, Inc.
[a]Relative to 1980–85. In other words, the entries in this column are zero unless this factor contributes *more* to productivity growth in the 1980 to 1990 period than it did in the 1980 to 1985 period.
[b]0 in this period because average lag is 4 to 9 years.

of the Reagan administration will not be apparent until 1985 at the earliest. Whereas the improvements due to higher saving and investment could appear with a lag as little as one year, both have dropped sharply since Reagan took office. The investment ratio has declined from 11.7 percent in 1980 to an expected 10.2 percent in 1983, hardly the type of progress originally envisioned by the Reagan team. Although some improvements in 1984 and 1985 are still expected, the ratio will remain well below the level of the 1970s.

Yet we do expect an increase in productivity growth of 2 percent during the first half of the decade. These gains, then, are to be found exclusively in the non-investment areas of productivity: higher labor productivity, lower energy prices, and less government regulation. For by definition, productivity growth refers to gains in output per employee-hour from all sources. In the broadest sense, productivity can improve because:

1. Labor has more or better capital with which to work.
2. Labor decides to work harder because of better training or motivation. The latter may be caused by higher pay, better management practices, or simply fear of job loss.
3. Government regulation provides less interference or more help in the production process.

The first factor, namely that the amount of capital per worker increases, is the traditional case of higher saving and investment leading to greater productivity and has already been covered in some detail.

The second factor has more to do with the motivation of workers themselves; it is not a response to more or better capital. Chapter 9 focused on how lower tax rates raise incentives; this chapter discusses how education, training, and change in the demographic mix of the labor force affects work effort. Obviously a poorly schooled ghetto youth on his first job will not be as productive as a college graduate with twenty years of experience. We have estimated that about ½ percent per year of the decline in productivity over the past fifteen years has stemmed from decline in work effort due to these factors.

The third factor given above involves neither the quantity nor the quality of labor and capital but refers instead to the role of the government in supporting or hampering commerce. To take an extreme example, suppose the government ordered all workers to spend one hour per day reading government manuals. Productivity would immediately drop by one eighth, since the time spent would be subtracted from the production of goods and services. This is clearly an extreme example, but by requiring labor and business to follow certain counterproductive regulations, the general effect is much the same. The government can also determine the level of productivity more indirectly through policies on energy, on transportation and communications, and on foreign trade. In addition, the degree to which government encourages R&D will in large part determine the growth of technology in future years.

The remaining sections of this chapter discuss the importance of each of these three non-investment determinants of productivity.

Factors Affecting Labor Input

The determinants of productivity that impinge directly on labor can in turn be subdivided into two main groups: work incentives, as reflected in tax rates; and education and training of the labor force, which is our present focus.

The effect of education and training are difficult to measure even under optimal circumstances since even very substantial changes do not become apparent until many years later. A cutback in education today might diminish students' ability to read and write—but not affect their job efficiencies until ten or twenty years later. Similarly, cutbacks in aid to higher education could lead to a shortage of specific job skills—engineering, physicists, language teachers, and so forth—but the overall loss to society would not become apparent until those with existing skills had retired and their replacements were not readily available. This process could also take ten to twenty years before its full effect was felt.

In addition, the quality of education may be inversely proportional to its quantity. Open admissions to colleges and universities, for example, may not raise the overall level of education at all if the new students thus accepted do not have the necessary background for absorbing higher education, are not offered remedial courses on the grounds that that would be insulting and/or racist, and are taught and graded on a double standard.

There is little question that education is very highly correlated with income on a cross-section basis. In fact, many studies of the permanent income hypothesis (see p. 121) have actually used the level of education as a proxy variable for permanent income itself, with very significant results. Although there are some anomalies, such as an MBA in general being worth more than a PhD, income and educational level are very closely correlated in all ranges except the very top of the income scale.

Nevertheless, the evidence is not at hand either to support or reject the hypothesis that a decline in the level of education over the past fifteen years is one of the factors responsible for the demise of productivity growth. This is undoubtedly due to (a) the long lags involved, as mentioned above, and (b) the problems with measuring the degree of education. The quantity of higher education certainly increased from the mid-1960s to the mid-1970s, which would on balance work against the argument of lower productivity.

The training issue is somewhat more clear-cut, particularly for secondary workers in the labor force. Primary workers can be defined as heads of households between the ages of twenty-five to fifty-four. Secondary workers are all others, thus including teens and near teenagers, older workers, and working spouses.

For the most part, primary workers are fairly well trained when they enter the labor force. Most of them have had professional training—in teaching, law, accounting, business, medicine, or related fields—and many others have attended various trade schools or other vocational programs or have served apprenticeships. Of course many youths enter the labor force right out of high school, but by age twenty-five most have either had substantial job training or experience, and hence can provide a net contribution to labor productivity.

Secondary workers, however, initially are often poorly educated and ill-trained, or are entering the labor market after years of homemaking and have neither polished skills nor familiarity with the routine of regular work. The near-retired often can work only at a slower pace or may offer skills that are outdated relative to today's market requirements. Of course there are exceptions to these generalizations. However, the idea here is not to concentrate on those exceptions but rather to point out that an increase in the proportion of secondary workers in the labor force initially causes a decline in productivity. In general, the productivity of these employees tends to improve as they become more familiar with their new jobs—particularly for teenagers and working wives. Thus once the proportion of secondary workers in the labor force stabilizes at its new higher level, productivity should not be adversely affected. Yet, during the years when this proportion is still increasing, there is little question that aggregate productivity growth is slowed by this factor.

Until 1964 the proportion of secondary workers in the labor force declined on balance. Teenagers were encouraged to get more education. As real family incomes grew, wives were "retired" from the labor force because they could afford to stay home and spend more time with their families, especially younger children. It was often a source of pride, at least to the man, when his wife was no longer forced to work to make ends meet. People retired earlier as Social Security benefits improved and as firms paid more generous pensions. More teenagers were able to afford to go to college. In general the reduction in the proportion of secondary workers in the labor force was viewed as one of the benefits of an affluent and enlightened society.

However, this declining trend in labor force participation reversed itself shortly after 1964. A truly dedicated supply-sider might even claim this too was due to the Kennedy-Johnson tax cut, but clearly other factors were also at work. We have shown that a reduction in tax rates does cause increased labor force participation at the margin. Yet the Kennedy-Johnson tax cut has long since been wiped out by bracket creep and higher Social Security taxes, while labor force participation rates rose most rapidly during the 1970s when marginal tax rates were increasing.

The changes in the proportion of secondary workers in the labor force follows two divergent paths. First, the total population from ages sixteen to twenty-four will actually decline by six million during the decade of the 1980s, as is shown in figures 10.1a to 10.1d. This means that the ratio of 16- to 24-year-olds to the total population will decline from 15.9 percent in 1980 to 12.6 percent in 1990. Since these employees are generally the ones with the lowest productivity—at least when initially entering the labor force—productivity growth should increase somewhat during the 1980s as a result of this strictly demographic factor alone.

The second major component of the secondary labor force, working wives, will probably continue to rise substantially during the 1980s, although not at quite as fast a rate as it did from 1965 to 1980. Part of the reason for the slowdown is simply that if this participation rate continued to increase at 1965–80 rates indefinitely, it would hit 100 percent before the end of the century; obviously the asymptote must come into effect sometime before then. Furthermore, it is unlikely that more than 80 percent of wives would ever be in the labor force at any given time; some have small children to be cared for, and a few will still choose not to work even when small children are not at home. After all, the labor force participation rate even for men ages twenty-five to fifty-four has remained around 96 percent for many years.

The third group, the older workers, is much more problematical. Under the original Reagan plan to cut spending, it was thought that Social Security benefits would gradually diminish through a combination of slower growth in benefits for the retired and a gradual increase in the retirement age. At the present that does not seem to be a very realistic possibility, with the congressional antipathy to voting even token cuts in Social Security. Hence participation rates of older workers are expected to continue falling, although at a somewhat slower pace.

An optimal supply-side program, coupled with the decreasing number of teenagers in this country between 1980 and 1990, should raise productivity and cut unemployment during this decade. However, as the economy plunged into the most prolonged stagnation in forty years, followed by a sluggish recovery dominated by high interest rates and oversized government budget deficits, many of the incentive efforts of lower tax rates were wasted. At the same time that lower marginal tax rates provided more of an incentive for employees to

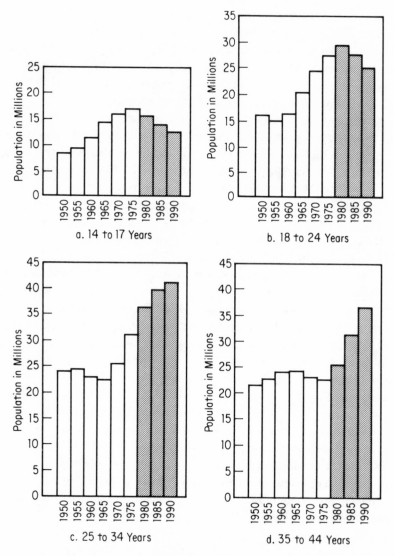

FIGURE 10.1

Age Distribution, 1950–1990

SOURCE: *Population Reports,* Bureau of the Census.

work more overtime, reduce excessive absenteeism and vacations, and seek employment more assiduously, the opportunities disappeared before their very eyes. With plants closing down and more and more companies going out of business, the number of available jobs shrank significantly. While this is of course part and parcel of every downturn, the supply-side incentives were simply wasted in the siege of recession.

The Determinants of Productivity

Though the economy will show greater strength later in the 1980s, much of the advantage that would have accrued from the supply-side tax cuts is thus annulled. It will not be necessary to attract as many new entrants into the labor force because the demand for jobs will be lower. The declining number of teen-agers will improve productivity but clearly that has nothing to do with sup-ply-side programs. To a certain extent the tax cuts will still improve incentives, particularly relative to the situation that would have existed if the Carter tax rates and inflation policies had remained in place and the marginal tax bracket for the average worker had climbed to 60 percent by the end of the decade. Indeed, the 25 percent across-the-board Reagan tax cut will increase produc-tivity growth by 1 percent per year for the 1980–85 period. Yet without a ro-bust economy, the chances of productivity growth returning to the 3 percent mark look dim.

We have not yet discussed the negative impact that unions have had on pro-ductivity growth. Everyone is familiar with the restrictions which limit how many bricks the mason may cement, how many shingles the roofer may place, and how many boards the carpenter may saw. In industrial unions, jobs are classified as non-interchangable, creating the need for redundant labor. In other areas, the combination of government regulation and union work rules have conjoined to limit the amount of work that may be performed by airline pilots, truck drivers, or railroad workers. Certainly lifting of these restrictions would substantially improve national productivity.

Although these imperfections obviously do exist, they have not been respon-sible for the diminution of productivity growth during the past 15 years. By comparison, the importance of unions in the private sector has diminished sharply over the postwar period. Whereas roughly one job in three was union-ized in the late 1940s, this figure has now slipped to one in five and almost certainly will slide further during the 1980s. By insisting that real wage gains outpace the rise in productivity, the unions have essentially cut the number of jobs available for their members in half.

In the manufacturing sector, restrictive work practices of the unions have resulted in jobs being transferred to non-union plants in this country or, more often, overseas. The construction trades succeeded with their restrictive prac-tices longer because of the commitment toward housing by the government, and also because of the fact that for a while inflation made real estate a good investment in spite of—or because of—the rapidly increasing prices. In the transportation sector, the power of the unions is clearly being eroded by de-regulation of the trucking, railroad, and airline industries. In the public sector, it took a taxpayers' revolt to keep the unions from feeding so voraciously at the trough, but this revolt recently has become quite effective at the state and local, if not the federal, level.

Certainly there will continue to be union abuses, crooked union leaders, racketeering, and pension fund abuses, just as a more conservative administration in Washington will not rid the world of business crooks or tax cheats either. Yet it is so often the case that government rules and regulations, rather than private sector bargaining, have created the imbalance of power toward unions. The construction unions have been significantly aided by the Davis-Bacon Act—passed during the Hoover administration—which essentially sets the floor for non-union labor on government contracts at the prevailing union wage. The strong transportation unions were helped for years by the knowledge that higher labor costs could be fully passed along to the consumer in the form of higher regulated fares and other charges. Of course weak management and a belief that wage increases could be passed along to the consumer also helped shape many management decisions. The so-called open-door policy, where unions felt as if they were pushing against an open door because their raises would be passed along to the consumer, is also an all-too-familiar phenomenon, particularly in the steel industry.

On balance, I believe that most of the union abuses present today were created during the 1930s and the 1940s, when the power of the unions was the greatest, and that few have been added in the past fifteen years. The combination of greater foreign competition, a prolonged period of economic stagnation, the decreasing importance of heavy industry, and the decline in government regulation should result in a more flexible union sector in the forthcoming decade. Although the overall level of productivity would undoubtedly be higher in the absence of unions, this is not a realistic or even particularly worthwhile goal for future government policy. Instead, the emphasis clearly ought to be placed on letting private sector business and labor reach mutually acceptable contracts with the firm assurance that the government will no longer provide any crutches for either side, with its only role reduced to minimizing intervention that would either reduce productivity or raise inflation.

Government Regulation and Productivity

Big government has always had the potential to have an overwhelming effect, whether good or ill, on productivity and the real growth of the economy. This power extends far beyond the confines of the tax code. By assigning monopolistic privileges it can favor one industry or sector at the expense of the rest of the economy. By juggling procurement procedures and other benefits, it can make some rich and others poor and thus determine their ability to contribute to the advancement of society. By establishing tariffs and quotas it can advance or retard international commerce. By controlling the supply of scarce natural resources it can control the sectoral growth patterns of the economy. By regulating various industries with a light or heavy hand it can dictate whether they will prosper or wither. The list continues indefinitely but even this introduction should make it clear that any serious discussion of productivity cannot disregard the role of the government in non-tax issues.

From the growth of the Industrial Revolution until the Great Depression, laissez-faire capitalism was widely believed to be the system that worked best. This can be seen by the prodigious growth of countries where capitalism was actively practiced compared to those countries with a lack of industrialization and economic advancement where other forms of economic systems remained in force. Even then, however, various segments of the business sector were governed by federal regulation.

The foremost regulations in the pre-1914 era of capitalism governed the dissolution of monopolies, the railroads, and purity in food and drugs. Admittedly little antibusiness legislation was passed in the 1920s, but even during this conservative decade the number of federal regulatory agencies continued to increase, as is shown in figure 10.2. The Great Depression shook capitalism to its roots, resulting among other things in another proliferation of federal agencies, many of which were designed to correct the evils of speculation of the 1920s. While many of the New Deal laws still remain on the books today, the worst excesses of this legislation, such as price fixing, were shortly thereafter declared unconstitutional; and in any case antibusiness sentiment retreated with the onset of wartime activity, resulting in virtually no increase in regulatory authority during the 1940s or the 1950s.

After World War II, the economy ran smoothly for the next twenty years, deluding many into believing that the situation was permanently under control. As we have remarked several times, productivity grew at an average rate of 3.2 percent per year, the economy was generally at full employment although mild recessions did continue to occur on a regular basis, and inflation averaged only 2 percent. Not so coincidentally, the growth in federal regulatory authority was quite modest.

Almost in tandem with the increased activism in fiscal policy management and fine tuning, however, arose the clamor to improve the Quality of Life through legislation. While an outburst of legislation during cyclical waves of liberalism is hardly a surprise, this variety was unique in the sense that it focused on the range of decisions which had heretofore been considered the private preserve of individual companies.

The thrust of previous regulatory legislation for business had been to con-

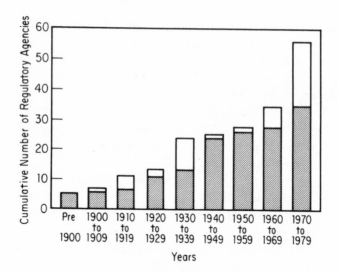

FIGURE 10.2

Historical Perspective of Federal Agency Growth

SOURCE: Center for the Study of American Business. Reprinted by permission.
NOTE: Agencies do not total 57 since some agencies have split regulatory functions between two or more spin-off agencies. The date that the parent organization was established was used to create the chart.

strain or diffuse the power of what were seen to be the behemoths of industry. Large corporations were restricted in terms of size and scope, in terms of the markets they could enter, from selling goods too cheaply (Robinson-Patman), from collusive behavior in setting prices, and in the case of financial institutions, from expanding across state lines and from serving both as a bank and an agent to sell securities. Yet the legislation of the 1970s had an entirely different focus—to improve society by providing a cleaner, healthier, safer, and more equitable environment. This was accomplished by changing the methods individual firms used in the manufacturing, processing, or distribution of goods. Besides representing an unprecedented expansion of the regulatory arm of the federal government, the increase went far beyond sheer numbers, bringing whole new sectors of the economy under regulation. Previously regulation had been primarily constrained to the natural monopolies—transportation, communications, and utilities—and to financial services.

This time, however, the business community was told that it must reduce the amount of pollutants it spews into the water and the atmosphere. It must meet certain safety standards, which on automobiles would include the design of the bumpers and the eventual installation of airbags. Certain transportation equipment and home appliances must be made more energy efficient. Business could be held liable for misfeasance of their product even if it was manufactured many years ago and no longer in the possession of the original owner.

224

The Determinants of Productivity

Workers must be guaranteed cleaner, safer, and quieter working conditions. And a certain proportion of women, blacks, Hispanics, and other minorities (although not Jews or Orientals) must be hired.

All this is familiar enough ground. What is perhaps not so well known is the cost that this imposes on the U.S. economy, although the Reagan administration has done much to publicize these costs. Tables 10.2a and 10.2b show the growth of these agencies during the 1970s and the budget for each major agency as of 1981. In that year, the federal government spent over $7 billion and employed 89,000 bureaucrats to monitor the business dealings of the private sector.

These figures, while large enough by themselves, represent less than the tip of the iceberg as far as the costs imposed on the private sector. To see this, consider the relative public and private sector burdens for the cost of pollution abatement and control. As is shown in table 10.2, total direct government costs ran to about $2.2 billion in 1981. Nevertheless, the Department of Commerce estimated that total pollution control costs to the private sector ran a staggering $55 billion that year, as is shown in table 10.3.

Using this ratio of public/private sector costs for the remaining regulatory agencies, which do not issue any figures on the cost to the private sector, would generate a total cost of regulation of approximately $175 billion for 1981. The reason for this multiplier is not hard to understand. It takes only one bureaucrat, with a salary of perhaps $50,000, to order the automobile industry to install fuel-efficient pollution control devices of dubious value that will ultimately cost consumers billions of dollars. The private/public cost ratio is probably highest for pollution control, since that area is most heavily weighted with capital expenditures. However, Murray Weidenbaum and his colleagues at the Center for the Study of American Business have undertaken a more thorough study and have estimated that the cost of regulation in 1981 was between $125 and $150 billion. Thus it would appear that approximately 5 percent of total GNP is being utilized for regulatory purposes.

One of the most egregious examples of the effect of federal regulations can be found in the automobile industry, as is shown in table 10.4. The increase in the retail price of automobiles due to federal requirements—safety, emission control, and fuel economy—has risen to $1,600 per car in 1982 dollars according to estimates published by the Bureau of Labor Statistics. Assuming a normal year of approximately 10 million sales, these standards are thus seen to cost the American public some $16 billion per year. However, the economic impact is far greater than that. Assuming that the price elasticity for new cars is approximately -0.7, then a $1,600 price increase, which is approximately 20 percent of the total price, would result in a 14 percent decline in the number of cars purchased, or an additional decline of $11.2 billion in output. Further-

SOURCE: Center for the Study of American Business. Reprinted by permission.
[a]Percent change cannot be calculated since no staffing figures were available for 1970.

TABLE 10.2a

Expenditures on Federal Regulatory Activities

(Fiscal years, in millions of dollars)

Area of Regulation	1970	1971	1972	1973	1974	1975	1976	1977	1978	1979	1980	1981 (estimated)	1982	Percent Change 1970–79	Percent Change 1981–82
Consumer safety and health	392	593	948	1059	1251	1347	1464	1772	2261	2474	2903	3022	3217	+531	+6
Environmental and energy	85	146	493	585	759	967	1026	1047	1296	1517	1926	2242	2516	+1685	+12
All other	389	483	544	642	824	954	1108	1243	1359	1527	1697	1938	2047	+293	+6
Grand total	866	1222	1985	2286	2834	3268	3598	4062	4916	5518	6526	7088	7780	+537	+8
Percent of annual nominal increase		41	62	15	24	15	10	13	21	12	18	10	8		
Total in 1970 dollars	866	1163	1814	1976	2231	2348	2456	2627	2963	3066	3326	3322	3283		
Annual real percentage increase		34	56	9	13	5	5	7	13	3	8	0	−1		

TABLE 10.2b

Staffing of Federal Regulatory Activities

(Fiscal years, number of permanent full-time positions)

Area of Regulation	1970	1971	1972	1973	1974	1975	1976	1977	1978	1979	1980	1981 (estimated)	1982	Percent Change 1970–79	Percent Change 1981–82
Consumer safety and health	5786	6212	22274	28518	28066	28333	29193	32282	32113	32494	31339	31072	31392	+462	+1
Environmental and energy	n.a.	240	8282	8830	11271	11872	12314	12846	16175	16353	17718	18642	17787	[a]	−5
All other	21875	22653	23797	29612	31360	33801	35812	36877	38029	38562	39058	39736	39622	+76	0
Grand total	27661	29105	54353	66960	70697	74006	77319	82005	86317	87409	88175	89450	88801	+216	−1
Annual Percent Increase		5	87	23	6	5	4	6	5	2	1	1	−1		

TABLE 10.3
Costs of Pollution Abatement and Control

	1972	1973	1974	1975	1976	1977	1978	1979	1980
Total, current dollars	18.2	21.9	26.3	30.9	34.7	8.0	3.0	49.2	55.7
Consumption	1.5	2.1	2.7	3.5	4.0	4.3	4.6	5.5	7.0
Business, investment	5.5	6.8	7.5	8.9	9.5	10.1	10.8	12.0	13.1
Business, operating	5.3	6.3	8.0	9.3	10.9	12.7	14.6	17.5	20.9
Government	5.9	6.7	8.1	9.2	10.4	10.9	13.0	14.2	14.7
Total, constant dollars	18.4	20.6	21.3	23.0	24.3	24.8	26.1	26.4	26.7
Percent change	—	12.0	3.3	8.0	5.7	2.1	5.2	1.1	1.1

SOURCE: February 1982 *Survey of Current Business.*

more, this loss has resulted in a decline of approximately 300,000 jobs in the automobile and related supplier industries. It is clear that federal regulations have had a tremendous impact on employment and output patterns in the automobile industry as well as on consumer expenditures for private transportation.

In large part it is fair to say that this quality-of-life legislation, at least in its original form voted for by Congress before having been distorted by the various regulatory agencies, has been quite popular with the American voters. Indeed, repeated attempts to water down the pollution abatement laws have met with remarkably little success.

The problem, then, with this new spate of legislation is not so much that it tried to build a better society but rather that the costs are both enormous and hidden. The programs, which the American public was told would be free or at worst come out of excess profits, now amount to about $150 billion per year compared to total corporate profits of $117 billion for 1982.

The problem is exacerbated by nonsensical statements of the sort that prices cannot be put on clear air or water, or safer equipment or products, or equal opportunity, or fuel efficiency, or better working conditions (including portable toilets for cowboys). It is this kind of alleged logic that is largely responsible for the current set of economic distortions. Certainly there is a price that people would not pay for clean air and water: if, for example, they did not have enough to eat, a place to sleep, or clothes to wear. Improvements in the quality of life are very expensive, and a luxury to many.

Theoretically, the whole program was justified on a so-called cost/benefit basis, and the pledge that the costs of the program would at least be compared if not equalized with the benefits. Indeed, the government was supposed to prepare an Economic Impact Statement for each set of government regulations. Unfortunately, although predictably, the entire exercise turned into a giant political football. Nonexistent or marginal benefits were assigned to vari-

TABLE 10.4
Increase in Retail Price of Automobiles Due to Federal Requirements

Year of Regulation	Government Mandated Equipment	Initial Price Increase	Estimated Current Cost in 1982 dollars
1968	Seat and shoulder belts, standards for exhaust emissions	31.97	61.71
1968–69	Windshield defrosting systems, door latches, etc.	9.92	18.74
1969	Head restraints	19.27	35.45
1970	Reflective devices and further emission standards		19.55
1968–70	Ignition locking and buzzing systems, etc.	10.34	16.44
1971	Fuel evaporative systems	20.65	36.55
1972	Improved exhaust emissions and warranty changes; seat-belt warning system	30.71	54.66
1972–73	Exterior protection	69.06	122.92
1973	Reduced flammability materials, etc.	6.32	11.25
1969–73	Improved side-door strength	15.20	26.90
1974	Interlock system and improved exhaust emissions	102.51	172.22
1975	Additional safety features and catalytic converter	122.06	189.19
1976	Hydraulic brakes, improved bumpers, etc. (less savings from removal of interlock system)	36.71	53.59
1977	Leak resistant fuel system, etc.	19.86	27.41
1978	Redesign of emission controls	9.99	12.89
1979	Emission and safety standards	17.85	21.42
1980	Redesign of emission control, bumper damage standards	131.33	144.46
1981	Emission controls and improved fuel economy	470.91	489.75
1982	Improved fuel economy	84.68	84.68
	Total		1,599.78

SOURCE: Bureau of Labor Statistics.

ous projects and assumed to have enormous importance, while costs were systematically understated and in any case failed to take into account the negative effects on productivity in the private sector.

Even this, however, did not faze some of the most ardent devotees of government regulation. In one landmark case, the Occupational Safety and Health Administration (OSHA) lost an important Supreme Court decision, which is likely to set a precedent that can be used to deny the more outrageous requests by environmentalists. The question at issue was whether the allowable amount of benzene pollutants should be reduced from 10 parts per million (ppm) to 1 ppm. A federal government cost/benefit study indicated that this reduction would cost $500,000 per year and would save one life every fifteen to thirty-eight years. This trade-off was good enough for the extremists but not good enough for the Supreme Court. Furthermore, high OSHA officials went out of their way to state that this was a test case and that if they lost it would be a grave setback to safety and health regulation. This decision has reintroduced some reasonableness into OSHA rulings, particularly when coupled with the change in administration.

Perhaps it is unrealistic to have ever expected "truth-in-legislation" estimates. After all, voters are seldom told the true cost of programs by their congressman. Instead they are told, for example, that Social Security represents a return on the money they have "contributed" to the fund during their working days, whereas it is patently obvious that those payments are nothing more than intergenerational transfers—and very badly financed at that—since the old-age and survivors fund has already gone broke and the disability fund will do so sometime in 1983. So perhaps we should not expect any difference for quality-of-life legislation—particularly when the costs are much harder to assess because so many of them are hidden.

The major inflationary aspects of increased federal government regulation do not even stem from the measurable costs of having to buy more capital equipment or, in the case of utilities, having to use higher-priced but less polluting fuels. Instead they stem from the loss in productivity that is implicit in the entire regulatory atmosphere. Firms are told that they must use scarce funds to purchase a machine that reduces pollution—not one that allows them to produce goods more efficiently. Capital expenditures to produce more fuel-efficient cars and trucks must be undertaken over a much shorter time span than would ordinarily be compatible with the replacement of the necessary machine tools, thus diverting funds which might be used for other improvements. OSHA regulations about noise requirements mean that equipment is redesigned to reduce the decibel level, not utilize labor and raw materials more efficiently. Affirmative action quotas often mean not putting the most qualified person in the right job. Where regulations prohibit the building of a new plant, it does not matter how great the tax incentives if the actual construction is not permitted in the first place. Thus the distortion of capital flows reduces productivity and expansion of the total capacity of the U.S. economy, both of which diminish the total supply of goods and services and hence cause a higher rate of inflation.

Unlike most trade-offs involving various government programs, no one benefits by the deadweight loss in productivity. Programs that favor monopolies, for example, result in consumers being charged higher prices, but at least the owners of those companies benefit even though consumers are worse off. Programs that strengthen the hand of unions also raise prices, but at least members of the labor unions gain, albeit at the expense of the rest of society. Larger transfer payments to the aged and the indigent obviously benefit them directly, as well as the physicians who minister to their needs. Programs to assist various industries—housing, agriculture, automobiles, steel, and so forth—invariably raise prices and distort capital flows, but the designated beneficiaries generally are better off. In the case of the decline in productivity caused by overregulation, however, no one benefits. The deadweight loss in efficiency is the burden paid by all of the society, and it is not recouped by anyone.

By far the single largest cost of regulation is in the area of pollution abatement and control. This is also the area in which the most complete econometric studies have been performed. In work done by this author for the Council on Environmental Quality (CEQ) while at Chase Econometrics in 1976, it was reported:

Over the period 1970–1983, the wholesale price index will have risen 5.8% more, the consumer price index will have risen 4.7% more, and the implicit GNP deflator will have risen 3.6% more than would have been the case in the absence of pollution control expenditures . . . during the three-year peak period (from 1975 through 1977) the WPI rises 1.9% more, the CPI rises 1.4% more, and the GNP deflator 0.8% more.

The stimulus of increased expenditures on pollution control growth offsets the negative effects of higher inflation and lower productivity growth in the early years of the period. By 1983, however, real GNP is projected to be 2.2% below the baseline forecast.

The unemployment rate . . . gradually rises to a level of 0.2% above the baseline forecast by 1983. The increase in unemployment is somewhat less than might be expected for the decline in real GNP because of the lower level of labor productivity.

The CEQ cost estimates indicate that incremental pollution control investment will reach a peak of approximately 3½ percent of total private plant and equipment expenditures in 1977. Depending on such general economic factors as the rate of unemployment and interest rates, this investment is expected to result in somewhat lower levels of other types of plant and equipment expenditures . . . the Aa corporate bond yield rises 1.1% above the base line in 1977, and, in response, housing starts drop by over 20% the following year.[1]

As might be expected, the effect on prices varied significantly by industry. The Chase Econometrics study estimated that by 1983 the price of services offered by utilities would be 27.8 percent higher because of pollution abatement, due both to the extensive amount of pollutants released by utilities and the fact that installation of scrubbers to reduce these pollutants would also diminish the efficiency of the power-producing plants. Next on the list were nonferrous metals at 8.1 percent, paper at 6.2 percent, chemicals at 4.8 percent, and iron and steel at 4.1 percent.

Based on these and other estimates, it would appear that during the peak years pollution abatement and control added about 1 percent per year to the inflation rate, and adds about ½ percent per year now that the peak retrofitting of existing plant and equipment has passed. The losses in productivity growth were about ½ percent per year at the peak and ¼ percent per year presently.

Even these estimates might be too low because they take into account only the direct effects of regulation. As has been already mentioned, it is quite likely that a firm, forced to install an expensive piece of equipment that will reduce the emission of pollutants, will forgo purchasing another piece of machinery that would increase its overall productivity. The Chase Econometrics study did try to take this into effect, estimating that every $1 spent on pollution control would result in a $0.40 decline in productive investment, based on increases in the cost of capital (as was discussed in chapter 7). However, even this calculation does not take into account the prohibition in building new plants at all in certain locations where the concentration of pollution is already thought to be too high, which may result in less efficient plants eventually being built that are not near raw materials, transportation facilities, or major markets.

No firm figures on the economic impact of the other major regulatory agencies are available except for the amount spent by the government, which tells us little about their total cost to the private sector. Using the same rule of thumb as before—applying the same public/private sector cost ratio to the other areas of regulation—would imply that the total negative effect of government regulations on the economy has been to raise inflation about 1 percent per year and lower productivity about ½ percent per year. These are conservative estimates, which could just as easily be doubled with more expansive assumptions.

To relate even a small fraction of the quirks and abuses these agencies have heaped on the private sector above and beyond the mandate with which they were originally entrusted by Congress could easily double the size of this book.

In particular, industry has generally considered the "Bad Six" to be the Environmental Protection Agency (EPA), the Consumer Product Safety Commission (CPSC), the National Highway Traffic Safety Administration (NHTSA), the Federal Trade Commission (FTC), the Equal Employment Opportunity Commission (EEOC), and OSHA; and although many would add ERISA to that list, it is more a case of bad law rather than over-eager regulators overstepping their prescribed mandate. Rather than discuss the excesses of each of these agencies in detail, we will present a brief smorgasbord of "horror stories" from the 1970s, when these agencies were at their heyday.

A Smorgasbord of Horror Stories

The Monterey Abalone Farm Experience

Monterey Abalone Farms (MAF) was founded in 1972 to domesticate the abalone. Its goal was commercial production of abalone for U.S. and foreign markets. MAF was started with $250,000 of seed capital invested by ten individuals. The firm was unable to interest professional sources of venture capital because it expected a long lag between initial investment and profitability. It found that public debt markets were essentially closed to it as well. An offering of upward of $500,000 would have cost over $200,000 in registration costs. The lack of funds has slowed the rate at which the firm has been able to expand.

Since MAF was founded, it has dealt with 42 different federal, state, regional, county, and municipal government agencies. The president of the firm, who is also the chief scientist and engineer, estimates that he spends 50 percent to 70 percent of his time dealing with various units of government. He has spent over 1,000 hours litigating OSHA appeals and variances. OSHA was overruled in 70 percent of the cases. He has consistently found that regulators have no idea how to categorize an aquaculture firm and tend to lump aquaculture in with wholly different species of industries. While the federal government usually gets the blame as the major source of regulatory mischief, MAF has found examples throughout all levels of government. When in doubt, employees of regulatory agencies prefer to err on the side of overprotection.

Since aquaculture is a new field, MAF has been subject to a number of regulations designed for other industries that are totally inappropriate for a seafood farm. All levels of environmental protection agencies have tried to treat MAF as a sewage treatment plant because its abalones defecate in the water. A great deal of time was spent in explaining the differences between aquaculture and sewage treatment to regulators at local, state, and federal levels of government.

MAF's divers go to depths of 40 feet to check lines, collect breeding stock, and collect scientific data. OSHA decided that MAF must comply with the deep-sea diving standards designed specifically for diving associated with off-shore oil drilling in the Gulf of Mexico. The divers in offshore oil drilling go as deep as 1,000 feet. Eventually, the California Aquaculture Association was able to obtain a one-year exemption so that MAF could prove how its operations were different from offshore drilling. The burden of proof was on the industry to demonstrate why it was different.

State and local governments are not about to be outdone by the federal agencies in making life rough for new industries. The California state government requires all sixty-eight zoning jurisdictions within the California Coastal Zone to develop precise development plans for all lands under its jurisdiction. The California Aquaculture Association (CAA) requested that aquaculture be allowed access to clean water. It was told that it could have access to areas zoned as industrial. However, water conditions in the industrial areas are poor and generally incompatible with raising seafood that meets FDA guidelines. Thus, the CAA applied for access to rural areas where water quality is better. The CAA was told that the oil companies had made the same request, and it had been up to them to show why they were different. Again, the burden of proof was on the industry. The CAA could not afford to plead its case in all sixty-eight jurisdictions, and thus was unable to gain access to some of the clean water that is vital to its operation.

Wheelchair Access

The Rehabilitation Act of 1973 specified that "no otherwise qualified handicapped individual . . . shall . . . be excluded from participation in . . . any program or activity receiving federal financial financing assistance." This simple statement turned out to have very costly implications for urban mass transit. The Department of Transportation issued final regulations to implement the Rehabilitation Act in May of 1979. These regulations require that existing mass transit systems be retrofitted to allow wheelchair users access to these facilities. The Congressional Budget Office (CBO) has estimated that the program will cost about $7 billion (in 1979 dollars) over the next 30 years. For this $7 billion, about 17,000 wheelchair users would gain access to the bus and subway systems. This comes out to about $400,000 per new rider. CBO has calculated that this figure is equivalent to $38 per bus or subway ride. The comparable cost of a taxi trip or dial-a-ride bus/station wagon is $7 per trip.

While handicapped-rights groups make claims to the contrary, it seems that the handicapped would much prefer a continually expanded dial-a-ride program to greater bus and subway access. Many of them cannot get out of their houses to go to the subway or bus stops without assistance. When the weather is cold or wet, many handicapped people, particularly the elderly, do not want to spend time outside traveling to transit stops and waiting to be picked up. Also, many feel that they are vulnerable to mugging when out alone and for this reason would rather be picked up at home.

The statistics for the two subway train systems best equipped to serve the handicapped (BART and Metro) bear out the qualitative evidence that the handicapped do not flock to accessible transit systems. In 1978 only an average of 100 handicapped persons per day used BART—out of a total daily ridership of 145,000. A survey in May 1979 of Metro ridership showed thirty-four wheelchair users out of a daily ridership of 200,000.

The story for buses is even more clear-cut than that for subways. In 1978 Brock Adams issued requirements and awaited bids for a "Transbus" which would offer much greater access than conventional buses equipped with lifts. No one would bid on his requirements. He ordered the National Academy of Sciences (NAS) to investigate and expected it to vindicate the Department of Transportation (DOT) bid requirements. NAS studied the specifications and concluded that the Transbus could not be manufactured, even with modest changes in the required design.

Meanwhile, cities began to purchase buses equipped with wheelchair lifts. These lifts added about 10 percent to the cost of the buses. The 158 buses in St. Louis provide round-trip service for eight to ten wheelchair users per week. The buses have experienced a high incidence of mechanical failure. The unplanned maintenance costs on the buses have averaged nearly a quarter of a million dollars per year. Milwaukee equipped 100 of its 548 buses with lifts in 1979. It averaged a whopping 1.5 rides per day in the summer. And as the weather turned cold, ridership declined to a total of six in October and nine in November. The total cost of outfitting the buses was about $1.5 million. If the useful life of the lifts is five years, and ridership continues at its current pace, the average cost per trip would be just less than $1,000.

Tris Flame Retardant[2]

The CPSC banned the chemical Tris as a flame retardant in children's sleepwear. The effect of the Tris ban on the small, family-owned independent cloth cutters and sewers was critical. While the commission felt it had to ban the use of a carcinogen in children's sleepwear, it certainly did not have to place the full economic burden of the recall on sleepwear manufacturers. A plan was worked out to diffuse the economic impact of this recall, but textile mills were exempted in July 1978 from any responsibility to buy back Tris-treated material, hence dumping the entire cost back in the laps of the apparel companies.

In this regard, the mayor of Cohoes, New York, testified before the House Committee on Small Business that the Tris product recall could force the closing of Swanknit Corporation, which employs 150 people in Cohoes and has a total payroll of nearly $1 million. The mayor suggested that since the CPSC had first indicated that material treated with Tris met its own flammability standards, the federal government should purchase the inventories of treated sleepwear. President Carter subsequently vetoed legislation that would have provided government funds to reimburse the manufacturers for their estimated losses of nearly $51 million due to the Tris ban.

EPA Cleans the Air

EPA mandated that Armco steel must install a scrubber to reduce iron oxide dust emissions. While the scrubber removes 21.2 pounds of pollutant per hour, the motor that runs the scrubber emits 23 pounds of sulfur and nitrogen oxides per hour. Thus, the net effect of the regulation is that the air is dirtier by 1.8 pounds of pollutant per hour.

The Ace Hardware Story

The CPSC filed suit against the Ace Hardware Company because Ace was attempting to sell 1,494 containers of windshield washer that did not have childproof caps and were not labeled "cannot be made nonpoisonous." Rather than have the caps replaced and the warning statement added, CPSC ordered that the windshield washer be destroyed. Ace volunteered to either destroy the material or give it to the CPSC. However, pollution laws barred the destruction of the material by Ace, and CPSC did not have the legal authority to accept the condemned fluid. A court order was obtained after several months of legal maneuvering, and the CPSC finally acquired the offending bottles.

Winter Sports

In 1973 the CPSC issued a bulletin entitled "Safety Tips on Winter Sports." Among the useful advice offered by the document: "Skaters should never skate close to open bodies of water."

Flutterball and Birdieball

Marlin Toy Products, Inc., produced two children's toys, Flutterball and Birdieball, both of which contained plastic pellets. In 1972 the Food and Drug Administration (FDA) banned the two toys because children could swallow the pellets if the toys cracked. Marlin recalled the toys and redesigned them without the plastic pellets. Marlin expected the toys to be removed from the ban list. However, it was 1973, and the infant CPSC, not the FDA, now had the jurisdiction. The CPSC apparently used outdated FDA records as the basis for its ban list, and the Marlin products continued to be banned. Marlin complained to the CPSC that the ban list was in error. The CPSC responded that they would not recall a quarter of a million lists merely because two toys were banned erroneously. Marlin Toys was forced to lay off 75 percent of its work force as a result of the federal intransigence.

How to Crash Safely

Highway safety regulations are the source of many tales of regulation gone amok. In the mid-1970s, NHTSA proposed making highways safer by eliminating hazards such as rigid signs, lightposts, embankments, and barriers. It funded the replacement of these hazards with "breakaway" road signs, breakaway lightposts, and the cushioning of other highway barriers. Unfortunately, those responsible for the design specifications failed to notice two crucial factors: imports of lightweight foreign cars were climbing and domestic manufacturers were downsizing their fleets. The result of this error was that the "safer" signs and lightpoles replaced at taxpayers' expense did not break away when struck by many newer, lighter cars. They are no safer than the fixtures that they replaced. The man responsible for the error in design specifications later received a $20,000 special achievement award from President Carter.

Home Sweet Home

A court ruled that the Department of Housing and Urban Development (HUD) could not sell any of its existing stock of houses in Philadelphia without stripping them of all lead-based paint. The cost of removing the paint was so high that the houses were never stripped. The houses were left vacant and vandals eventually destroyed them. HUD concurrently ordered the Federal Housing Authority (FHA) not to grant any mortgages for Philadelphia houses that were not certified to be free of lead-based paint. As most of the remaining low-priced houses in inner Philadelphia were built when the use of lead paint

The Determinants of Productivity

was common, the HUD directive served only to eliminate most of the qualified houses from the FHA program. Thus, government concern for children's health caused HUD to curtail federal assistance to low-income individuals who wanted to buy houses. Better no housing than unsafe housing.

OSHA Quickies

- OSHA specified the number of knotholes per foot permissible in wooden ladders.
- OSHA specified the appropriate angles at which various kinds of ladders could be used safely. It then stated how to estimate the angle by calculating the sine of the angle between the ladder and the ground by looking at a sine table.
- OSHA defined "exit" in about 150 words.

And finally, probably the most famous of all:

- Caution! Horse manure may be slippery.

The Impact on Small Business and Individual Incentives

The impact of regulation, while damaging to all sectors of business, has been especially hard on the small business sector. Historically, a considerable portion of the innovation that took place in the U.S. economy originated in small, high-risk, high-technology firms. Recently, the pace of innovation, except for the microcomputer revolution, seems to be slowing. The deleterious effects of the increase in capital gains taxes between 1968 and 1978 have been discussed. These effects were exacerbated by increased federal intervention in capital markets and increased regulatory activity at all levels of government.

During the 1970s, three actions by the federal government have inadvertently reduced the flow of venture capital to small business. Changes in tax treatment of other forms of investment, federally mandated pension regulations under ERISA, and increased cost of dealing with government agencies appear to have effectively dried up key parts of the venture capital market. Higher capital gains taxes were a fourth inadvertent conspirator until their reduction in 1978.

Liberalized tax treatment of essential segments of our economy has long been a part of our tax structure. However, the indirect negative effects of seemingly laudable tax breaks can be considerable. Starting in 1976, the federal government allowed income placed in individual retirement accounts (IRAs) and Keogh plans to receive preferential tax treatment. These funds go to centralized institutional investment pools that are precluded by law from investing in high-risk ventures. As a result, savings that had been available to local small businesses are now channeled to centralized funds and invested in low-risk securities. A source of high-risk seed capital has been lost. The favorable tax treatment of investments in real estate, oil and gas drilling, and agriculture has also served to siphon money away from the venture capital market.

The tax breaks available for investment research and development expenditures are more useful for established firms than for new innovative firms. Established firms can take the investment tax credit immediately. New firms rarely have large profits, so they must carry the investment tax credit forward before they see any benefits. A refundable investment tax credit for firms in the first few years of operation would serve to eliminate this inequity. Canada currently allows a 25 percent tax credit for research and development expenditures by small firms. Relief for new, small firms is justifiable since they do not have internal sources of capital (which carry an immediate 46 percent write-off) as large established firms do and are effectively excluded from the debt market.

ERISA regulations have also helped to stem the flow of venture capital to small businesses. ERISA requires conservative professional management of pension funds according to the "prudent man" rule. As pension fund managers are held legally responsible for being prudent, they are not about to squander their portfolio on high-risk funding of young innovative businesses. The result of society's desire for greater retirement security has been the elimination of seed and start-up capital for small business. This dilemma would be alleviated in part if ERISA could be modified to allow up to 5 percent of pension fund portfolios to be invested in small business.

Finally, the cost of dealing with the regulatory agencies, filing and litigating appeals, and lobbying for regulatory relief are relatively greater for new small firms than for established large firms. The established firms can afford the array of attorneys and specialists necessary to contend with regulatory agencies. In turn, the regulatory agencies seem to cope better with established firms than with new innovative firms. They know where to classify the established firms but often seem to have no idea where new kinds of business fit under regulations tailored to a different species of business.

Before leaving this section, the EEOC deserves additional brief mention, if only because its mission is unique in economic terms. In the case of all the other major regulatory agencies, the goal is at least theoretically to improve the quality of life for everyone concerned, although it clearly raises prices and reduces efficiency. In the case of EEOC, however, much more of an adversary position is involved; for given the size of the job pool, for every winner there is a direct loser, and the costs are not diffused over all of society.

Clearly discrimination is a bad idea whose time never was, and the passing of this blot on American civilization is endorsed by the overwhelming majority of society. However, setting up quotas—thinly disguised under the euphemism of "affirmative action"—has turned out to be a cure hardly better than the disease.

Decriers of supply-side economics often dispute the assertion that people are primarily motivated by money; that is why they claim that a tax cut has no effect on work incentive and productivity. Obviously we think otherwise. Yet money is not the only motivator; pride of a job well done, a chance for advancement and increase in power, or a strong commendation from one's supervisor are certainly other factors that motivate many workers as well. In the case of companies bound by affirmative action clauses, many employees know that no matter how well they perform on the job, the steps toward advancement are reserved for someone from a particular minority group. Nothing kills initiative and willingness to do a good job more quickly.

Furthermore, productivity suffers when the best person for the job is bypassed and the position is given to someone less qualified. Whereas it is virtually impossible to measure this effect quantitatively, the convoluted logic that many large organizations must go through in order to meet their quotas definitely results in mismatches and an overall reduction in total productivity growth. Beside squelching the morale of those who have been passed over, putting unqualified people in important jobs decreases the efficiency of the entire organization.

The solution to the problem, as hinted at in the previous section of this chapter, is to provide higher-quality education and training to all, particularly to the disadvantaged—which calls for more government funding, not less. Shifting the burden over to the private sector and assigning quotas by whatever name causes lower productivity, more sluggish growth, and eventually fewer jobs for everyone.

Progress of the Reagan Administration on the Regulation Front

However, we do see some improvement in lowering the cost to society of regulatory programs during the 1980s. One of the major campaign promises of Reagan was to reduce the role of the federal government in regulation, and some signs of success are already evident. It is true that he has not had much better luck than any of his predecessors in removing entrenched bureaucrats. Furthermore, an allegedly conservative Congress showed little interest in pruning the laws, although it did successfully overturn the FTC ruling that used-car dealers had to reveal the condition of the cars they were selling. Consequently, the budget figures for regulation are declining very little, and it is hence an odds-on bet that fundamentally the same regulatory functions that are in place now will survive until the next wave of liberalism in the 1990s.

However, that does not mean that the costs of regulation to the private sector will necessarily be as large, since this is one area in which the president, either directly or through the key appointments to various agencies, can modify the most onerous regulations. Indeed, the FY 1982 budget did reduce the level of federal regulatory costs in real terms, although the declines were admittedly very slight.

The major beneficiary of these changes will undoubtedly be the automotive sector. According to estimates prepared by Murray Weidenbaum, the Reagan plan would save $9.3 billion in the cost of new cars over the next five years and free up $1.3 billion in capital to the automobile manufacturers over the same period. These changes are being accomplished without gutting the standards for pollution, safety, or fuel economy—they are the result of simple commonsense applications of existing standards. For example, automobile manufacturers will now be allowed to meet exhaust emission standards by using sales-weighted averages of results from different model lines instead of being required to meet the standards for each individual line. Other changes have to do with the streamlining of testing and reporting criteria, and they include items such as permitting self-certification programs for vehicles to be sold at high altitudes.[3] All in all, Weidenbaum identified thirty-four areas in which regulations were modified, delayed, or dropped altogether in 1981 for the automobile industry alone.

The two other major changes in the regulatory environment in 1981 were chemical labeling in the workplace and the energy efficiency standards for household appliances. In the first case, the Carter administration proposed that each piece of equipment in the workplace—a factory, warehouse, and so forth—be labeled if it contained or carried any toxic substance. As a result, virtually millions of pieces of equipment would have to be labeled, even if the chemicals were not exposed and the probability of damage was nil. It is estimated that rescinding this labeling requirement will save $643 to $900 million initially, and $338 to $473 million per year thereafter in 1981 dollars. The major beneficiary of this is obviously the chemical industry, but implementation would have cut across a wide swath of American industry.

The Reagan administration also has withdrawn the proposed standards for minimum energy efficiency of household appliances. Here was another case of a good idea run amok. After the first energy crisis, manufacturers were required to estimate how much energy various appliances would use per unit of running time. Such a comparison helped to make consumers aware of the probable annual energy costs of given appliances and also spur them to look for the most energy-efficient brands. So far, so good. However, that did not satisfy those same legislators who resolutely refused to raise the price of energy to free-market levels. In addition, appliances had to meet certain energy standards, and those manufacturers that could not comply would be out of business. Such a move would clearly be counterproductive in the sense that it would eliminate a major part of competition in the household appliance area by causing smaller firms to cease operation entirely. Now the labeling standards will stay, but not the mandatory requirements. Besides improving the competitive posture of this sector of the economy, this move is estimated to save consumers about $500 million per year.

To summarize this section, the new round of regulatory activities started in the 1970s are probably here to stay as much as are the social welfare state programs of the 1930s and the 1960s. The major cost of these programs, namely the retrofitting of existing plant and equipment for pollution and the shutdowns and job displacements which that entailed, is for the most part behind us. In addition, the excesses of the program that mushroomed under the Carter program are back under control at least for the remainder of this decade.

Hence, of the burden that these programs imposed on society during the 1970s—1 percent per year in inflation and a loss of ½ percent per year in productivity in the U.S. economy—about half should be rescinded during the decade of the 1980s. Yet these costs still represent, in a very real sense, an additional tax of some $30 billion per year on the public. The benefits in terms of cleaner air and water, healthier working conditions, and safer products are more difficult to quantify; but it does appear that, with the notable exception of so-called equal opportunity, the average voter is satisfied with the additional regulations. Hence these costs and benefits to society can reasonably be expected to continue into the indefinite future and must be included in the calculation of any future trade-off between productivity, real growth, and inflation.

Part IV

Policy Implications

CHAPTER 11

How Supply-Side Economics

Could Lead to Balanced,

Non-inflationary Growth

Offsetting the Trade-off Between Inflation and Unemployment

Even if supply-side programs are used correctly to shift resources from consumption to investment and from the public to the private sector, thus generating the requisite increases in productivity, one final hurdle must still be faced. Throughout the postwar period, an improvement in economic activity has always led to a higher rate of inflation. It is often claimed that higher growth results in lower unemployment, which leads to higher wage gains, an increase in unit labor costs, and more inflation. This trade-off between unemployment and inflation is usually known as the Phillips curve.

Supply siders have always reserved some of their most virulent attacks for the concept of the Phillips curve, since it was precisely this trade-off between unemployment and inflation that they claimed could be buried with the proper mix of monetary and fiscal policies. Besides, they argued, the curve had already become invalid, since high unemployment and high inflation occurred at the same time during the previous three recessions. By trying to reduce inflation through recession, they claimed, the economy ended up with more of both.

The Phillips curve itself, it seems to me, is not the sort of item that one embraces or discards on faith. It is a very simple empirical relationship between the rate of inflation and last year's unemployment rate. It has no philosophical bias in one direction or another; either the relationship can be verified empirically or its cannot. The sound and the fury about whether this curve does in fact exist is easily determined simply by graphing the relationship and seeing what correlation, if any, exists. This has been done in figures 11.1 and 11.2. What is seen there, of course, is a family of Phillips curves. The trade-off between inflation and unemployment is significant but is dwarfed by the upward drift of the curve over the past 30 years.

The cause of the steady upward drift of the curve has been subject to much controversy and speculation. At one time, it was thought that this shift was caused by demographic changes in the labor force. With more women and teenagers in the labor force, the equilibrium rate of unemployment has increased over time from 4 percent to 6 percent, which implies that pushing the unemployment rate all the way down to 4 percent in the 1970s would have entailed a great deal more inflation than would have been the case in the 1950s.

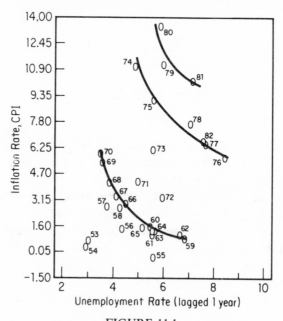

FIGURE 11.1

The Phillips Curve

SOURCE: Prepared by Evans Economics, Inc.

246

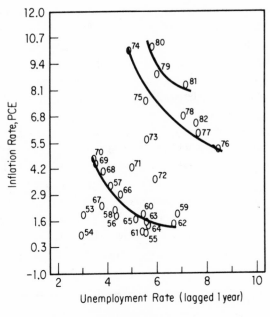

FIGURE 11.2

The Phillips Curve

SOURCE: Prepared by Evans Economics, Inc.

However, graphing the Phillips curve using the unemployment rate for married males makes no difference; the shifts are, if anything, even more clearly marked. Changes in demographics cannot explain the upward movement of this curve.

In fact, most of this upward drift represents the long-term deterioration in the underlying growth rate of productivity.* Indeed, declines in this underlying rate did occur in 1969, 1974, and 1978, years which correspond fairly closely to the shifts of the Phillips curve. The stability of the curve from 1957 to 1970, when underlying productivity growth was close to 3 percent, also supports this hypothesis.

In addition, however, we believe that some of the upward movement in the curve represents the change in inflationary expectations. The evidence for this is not as overwhelming, but we do notice a sub-curve for 1953–56 which is below even the 1957–70 experience. The inflation that did occur in 1956 moved long-term bond yields up from 3 percent to 4½ percent, and while this rise seems minuscule now, it did represent the first step in the realization that the

*This term indicates the average productivity growth excluding changes caused by cyclical fluctuations.

247

postwar economy was moving away from stable prices to one with continuing secular inflation. The second major upward shift in the curve occurred during the period of the wage-and-price freeze and controls, which worsened long-term inflationary expectations, a point of view that is certainly consistent with the long-run global history of such controls. Not so incidentally, the controls also worsened the underlying rate of productivity as misallocation of resources steadily worsened.

Whether due to productivity or expectations, the fact of the matter is that in the longer run inflation will diminish if and only if unit labor costs rise less rapidly. Figures 11.3 and 11.4 show a near-perfect correlation between unit labor costs and both (a) the CPI and (b) the implicit consumption deflator (PCE). In both cases the difference between actual inflation and the increase in unit labor costs has averaged only 1 percent over the past 30 years.* In spite of all the noise made over the years about how inflation is caused by energy crises, crop failures, worldwide commodity shortages, wage

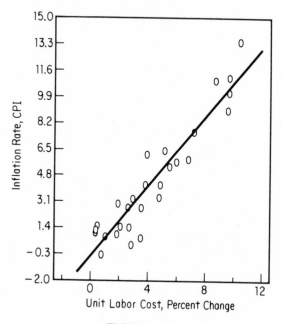

FIGURE 11.3
Unit Labor Cost and Inflation
Source: Prepared by Evans Economics, Inc.

*In more precise statistical terms, the standard error of the regression of inflation on unit labor costs is only 1 percent.

and price controls, and so forth, it is an unassailable fact that the change in unit labor costs on average accounts for all but 1 percent of the fluctuations in inflation.

The latter-day apologists for demand-side economics continue to concentrate on the movements along each one of the individual Phillips curves. There is in fact little question that such movements have occurred in the past and will continue to occur in the future. As a rough rule of thumb, the trade-off that a 1 percent decline in the rate of unemployment will lead to a 1 percent increase in the rate of inflation is still accurate—*providing* that the factors that shift the curve itself, namely productivity and inflationary expectations, remain unchanged.

To concentrate on that trade-off, however, is to neglect the forest for the trees. A decline in unemployment all the way from 10 percent to 5 percent would raise inflation by about 5 percent, *assuming* the economy remained on the same Phillips curve. By comparison, the upward shift in the curve over the postwar period has accounted for approximately a 10 percent increase in the rate of inflation for any given level of unemployment. Thus it should be obvious that the rate of inflation can decline at the same time that unemploy-

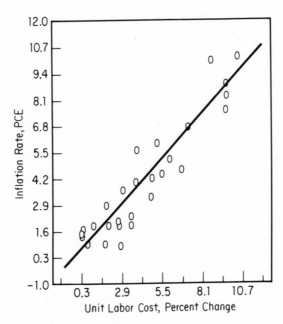

FIGURE 11.4

Unit Labor Cost and Inflation

SOURCE: Prepared by Evans Economics, Inc.

ment diminishes if we can increase productivity and reduce inflationary expectations.

Previously this claim could be ridiculed as a pipe dream, since the curve always seemed to shift in only one direction. Yet 1982 marshalled fresh evidence that the upward drift of the curve can be reversed. In particular, the 1982 point is aligned with the 1974–78 Phillips curve rather than the 1979–81 curve. Granted that it will be a long time before the economy returns to the 1957–70 curve, for the first time progress has been made in the downward direction.

Few would disagree that much of the disinflation during the first year of the Reagan administration was caused by exogenous factors, since wage rate gains did not initially moderate and recession-sodden productivity continued to fall in 1981. However, wage rates moderated significantly in 1982, increasing 6.4 percent compared to approximately 10 percent in both 1980 and 1981. Such a downward flexibility in wage rates had not occurred since the early 1950s and could not have taken place without a significant change in expectations, recession or not. Thus, the Phillips curve for the U.S. economy is clearly shifting back down again—one positive sign amidst the increasing gloom of other indicators.

Another factor that influences the position of the Phillips curve is the marginal tax rate on labor income. Wage earners bargain on the basis of their after-tax incomes; if tax rates are increased, they demand larger wage increases, whereas if rates are reduced, they are satisfied with somewhat smaller increases. This was dramatically illustrated in the case of the 1964 tax cut and the 1968 tax surcharge. Average hourly earnings in the total private nonfarm sector increased only 2.8 percent in 1964, the lowest increase in the entire postwar period. It is hardly coincidental that 1964 was the year of the Kennedy-Johnson tax cut. Wage gains then remained modest until 1968, when they jumped to 6.1 percent, the largest increase since the highly inflationary days at the beginning of the Korean War. Whereas other factors, such as the rate of unemployment and inflation, also clearly influence wage rates, the marginal tax rate cannot be disregarded.

Hence the three-year 25 percent tax rate reduction has a salutary effect on diminishing wage gains for the 1982 to 1984 period. Admittedly the experiment is somewhat clouded because of the high rates of unemployment which have accompanied the tax cuts. However, if unemployment were the only factor causing lower wage rates, the economy would have remained on the same branch of the Phillips curve. The downward movement, besides being due to lowered inflationary expectations, is also partially due to lower tax rates. Thus we see another way in which a properly structured supply-side program can lead to lower inflation along with increased prosperity.

In some cases, the Phillips curve could even have a positive slope—higher unemployment leads to higher inflation. This is not quite as bizarre as it first sounds since we have good reason for expecting changes in productivity to offset changes in wage rates in either direction. For example, a contractionary policy designed to slow aggregate demand might have the unintended side effect of reducing investment as well. As a result, the decline in wage rates would be matched by the decline in productivity, and inflation would remain the same. Similarly, a stimulative policy might encourage enough additional saving and investment that the gain in productivity would outweigh the hike in wage rates, and inflation would actually diminish.

On a secular basis, a long-term decline in productivity usually leads to a narrowing of the differential between wages and prices, which often results in an attempt by labor to receive larger nominal wage gains. This of course leads to more inflation, lower productivity, and hence higher unemployment. This is particularly true for open economies, where swings in foreign trade are largely governed by relative prices and hence faster inflation leads to lower exports and productivity growth.

International Comparisons of Phillips Curves

Based on these observations, it is likely that the close empirical relationship between inflation and unemployment that existed in the United States between 1955 and 1970 is the exception rather than the rule. In order to test this hypothesis, we have calculated Phillips curves for the other leading industrialized countries of the world: Canada, the United Kingdom, France, Germany, the Netherlands, Belgium, Sweden, Italy, and Japan. These are shown in figure 11.5. Only in the case of the Canadian economy, which follows the United States most closely, is there even a remote resemblance to the standard Phillips curve.

It could be argued that this comparison is not quite fair because it covers the period from 1956 to 1980, whereas even the U.S. curve went off the track after 1970. In order to test this hypothesis, we also graphed all of the Phillips curves for the 1956 to 1970 subperiod as well, as is shown in figure 11.6. Again, virtually no trace of the trade-off exists between inflation and unemployment. In the case of Germany, the curve seems to be horizontal, whereas in the United Kingdom and France it seems to have a slight positive slope, which would indicate that the shifts in productivity overwhelmed the underlying changes in wages and prices.

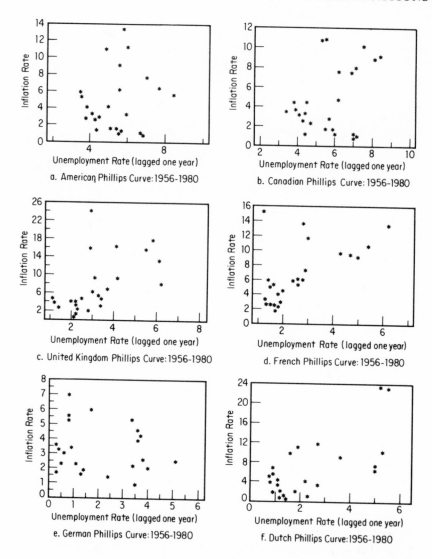

a. American Phillips Curve: 1956-1980

b. Canadian Phillips Curve: 1956-1980

c. United Kingdom Phillips Curve: 1956-1980

d. French Phillips Curve: 1956-1980

e. German Phillips Curve: 1956-1980

f. Dutch Phillips Curve: 1956-1980

We realize that the dogma about the trade-off between inflation and unemployment will not be put to rest simply by showing that such a relationship did not exist in the postwar period anywhere outside of North America, but it certainly makes the case for predicting this trade-off to be more difficult. If fiscal and monetary policies are correctly utilized to reduce interest rates and raise incentives, productivity will increase apace and the Phillips curve will be invalidated for the U.S. economy in the 1980s. Higher growth need not be accompanied by higher inflation as long as the gain in productivity is greater than the increase in wage rates.

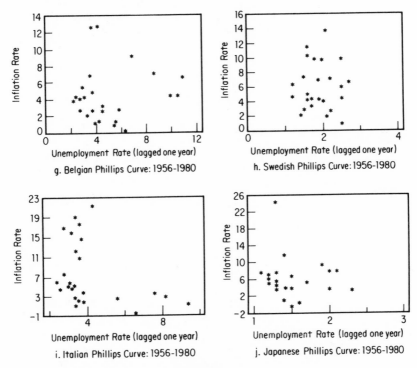

FIGURE 11.5

International Comparison of Phillips Curves

SOURCE: All figures prepared by Evans Economics, Inc.

The Benefits of a Properly Structured Supply-Side Program

Under a balanced supply-side program, which includes personal income tax rate cuts, corporate income tax rate cuts, government spending cuts, and a decrease in the amount of government regulation, the following steps generate an improvement in economic conditions.

1. A reduction in personal income tax rates increases the incentive of individuals to save by raising the rate of return on assets held by these individuals. This higher saving leads to lower interest rates and higher investment.

2. A reduction in corporate income tax rates, whether through a direct reduction in the marginal statutory tax rate or through indirect measures, such as a higher investment tax credit or shorter depreciation lives, will improve investment by increasing the average aftertax rate of return.

3. Higher investment leads to an increase in productivity, which means that more goods and services can be produced per unit of labor and capital

253

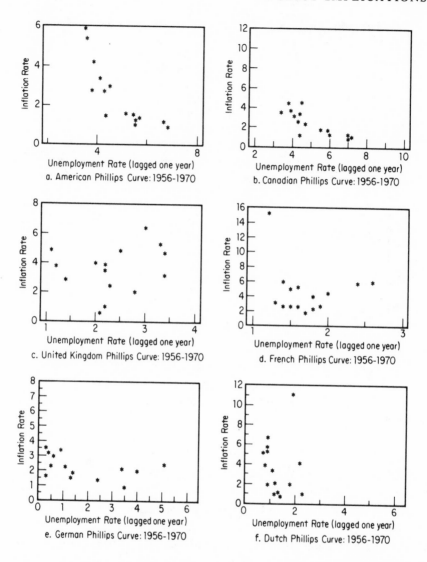

a. American Phillips Curve: 1956-1970

b. Canadian Phillips Curve: 1956-1970

c. United Kingdom Phillips Curve: 1956-1970

d. French Phillips Curve: 1956-1970

e. German Phillips Curve: 1956-1970

f. Dutch Phillips Curve: 1956-1970

inputs. As a result, unit costs do not rise as fast and the rate of inflation diminishes.

4. The transfer of resources from the public to the private sector, which is accomplished by reducing the growth in government spending, increases productivity, since productivity gains in the public sector are small or nonexistent.

5. Higher productivity provides the needed capacity to produce additional goods and services demanded because of the tax cut, thus leading to balanced growth without bottlenecks or shortages.

254

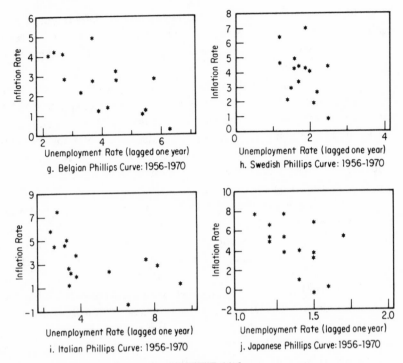

FIGURE 11.6

International Comparison of Phillips Curves

SOURCE: All figures prepared by Evans Economics, Inc.

6. Lower tax rates result in more modest demands for wage increases, since real income has risen by virtue of the tax cut and hence workers do not suffer a loss of real income by moving into higher tax brackets.

7. Lower inflation leads to an increase in real disposable income, and hence a rise in consumption, output, and employment.

8. Lower tax rates also improve work effort and individual incentive, which result in an increase in the quality and quantity of work. This in turn raises productive capacity still further, thereby contributing to still lower inflation.

9. The reduced rate of inflation causes an increase in net exports, which strengthens the value of the dollar. This leads to further reductions in inflation as the prices of imported goods rise more slowly.

10. The increase in capacity also permits the production of more goods for export as well as domestic consumption, thereby providing additional strength for the dollar and less imported inflation.

It is clear that few of these benefits were apparent during the first two years of the Reagan administration, for reasons that have been enumerated and described throughout this book. The unbalanced approach—tax cuts but no spending cuts, with the entire burden of restraint tossed in the lap of monetary policy—brought about continued stagnation and the first double-digit unemployment rate since 1940.

Having said this, however, I still believe that supply-side economics—the use of fiscal policies to shift resources from spending to saving and from the public to the private sector—represents the best hope for curing the ills of the economy in the longer run. In particular, the abandonment of supply-side principles—shifting resources back to the public sector and diminishing saving through tax increases—can only lead to stagnant or declining productivity and an eventual return to double-digit inflation.

Whereas high interest rates clearly depress investment initially, that situation could continue indefinitely only if the Fed took overt action to raise rates in the face of declining money supply and negative real growth. While the Fed's policy from 1980 through 1982 has been quite uneven, it has clearly moved in the direction of lower interest rates during times of economic decline, and since July 1982 has moved aggressively in the direction of further ease. Hence if the economy remains weak, nominal interest rates will diminish even if real rates would be rising due to lower inflation. Although personal saving depends on the real rate of interest, capital spending depends on the nominal rate, since depreciation allowances are valued in historical instead of replacement terms. Furthermore, ACRS will eventually boost investment, although some of this will be offset by the reduction from 200 percent to 150 percent declining balance.

Thus *eventually* a sustained increase in private sector saving would cause interest rates to decline significantly, since the *ex ante* increase in saving would be greater than the *ex ante* rise in investment. Though this would indeed entail an extended period of sluggish growth, the economy would eventually start to rally as interest rates declined. The personal income tax cuts would provide additional funds to financial markets, which would keep the downward pressure on interest rates. The resulting increase in business activity stemming from lower rates would increase tax revenues and lower interest costs, thereby moderating the government deficit.

In addition, the tax cuts would eventually lead to higher productivity as the economy recovers, both because capital formation increases and because work effort is increased. This higher productivity is translated directly into smaller price increases, which raises real income and consumption. Hence both aggregate supply and demand are expanded. Aggregate supply rises because of the increased inputs of labor and capital, and aggregate demand rises because real income is higher and interest rates fall further. Labor may share in some of the fruits of higher productivity, in which case real income would receive an additional boost; but even if this does not occur, real disposable income rises as inflation declines.

These linkages are indicated by the flowchart shown in figure 11.7. The top left-hand side of the chart indicates how supply-side economics would have worked if the tax cuts had been accompanied by *lower* interest rates. In this case the economy, led by higher capital spending, would respond quickly. The top right-hand side of the chart indicates what happens when the tax cuts are accompanied by *higher* interest rates. In this case capital spending does not initially advance, but the sharp increase in the real rate of interest boosts personal saving enough that interest rates eventually decline. After interest rates

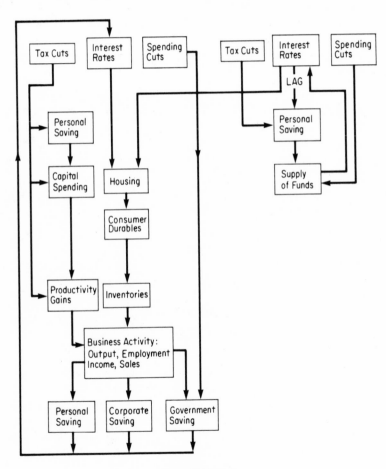

FIGURE 11.7
Causal Flow of Supply-Side Economics

SOURCE: Prepared by Evans Economics, Inc.

start to descend, the second case merges into the first one, which explains the double arrow connecting the two parts of the diagram.

However, this relatively sanguine conclusion about supply-side economics is far from sufficient to rescue it from the gladiators in the political arena. For the problem with these relatively promising comments is that such reactions often take several years to materialize. In the meantime, the body politic becomes extremely restless over extended bouts of double-digit unemployment and triple-digit budget deficits. As a result, it would be nonsensical to consider the long-term beneficial economic aspects of supply-side economics without acknowledging the importance of political reality. This interaction is now analyzed in the concluding chapter.

CHAPTER 12

Supply-Side Policies for the 1980s

Can Supply-Side Economics Be Salvaged?

The great experiment of Reaganomics has failed. Does that mean we give up on supply-side economics?

One option, of course, would be to turn the clock back to the 1970s. Roll back all the tax cuts, reverse those cuts in government spending, and reflate the economy back to double-digit rates so that increases in the tax revenues can once again be used to balance the budget.

Even die-hard, lifelong political adversaries of President Reagan seem to have little interest in following this approach. Indeed, the Democrats have distinguished themselves primarily by their uncharacteristic lack of ideas about how to improve the economy. Although some may rail at the Fed, many of them have an underlying queasy feeling that perhaps the tenfold increase in transfer payments that they voted in since 1965 has something to do with the current problem.

The ultimate goal of both economists and politicians is to create full employment with no inflation. Strictly speaking, the last time this was accomplished was the 1920s, and even that decade contained three mild recessions before the stock market crash triggered what eventually became the Great Depression. However, during the first twenty years of the postwar period the unemployment rate averaged less than 5 percent and the rate of inflation averaged just under 2 percent. This is, in my opinion, the best we can realistically expect to accomplish. But getting the economy back on the track to reach these goals is obviously no mean feat, and the question is whether this can be accomplished better with or without supply-side economics.

Reducing the unemployment rate from 10 percent to 5 percent represents a Herculean task. To put this in perspective, consider the period from 1962 to 1966 when the economy grew at an average rate of 5.4 percent per year—the fastest five-year growth period in postwar history. Even during that "Golden Age," the unemployment rate fell only from 6.7 percent to 3.8 percent. Thus a replication of that tremendous effort, which would represent a complete turnaround from the four-year stagnation of 1979–82, would reduce the unemployment rate only to 8 percent. Besides, with this unusually rapid growth, it is extremely unlikely that inflation could be reduced to 2 percent at the same time.

Yet a 5.4 percent growth rate for five years in a row would be well nigh impossible under the current imbalance of the total national saving rate in general and the government budget in particular. Even conceding that the economy is indeed emerging from its four-year recession, a five-year average growth rate of between 4 percent and 5 percent is probably the best we can reasonably expect. Similarly, productivity growth cannot be expected to exceed 2 percent per year, which means that the underlying rate of inflation probably would not drop below 4 percent.

Even these goals, however—8 percent unemployment and 4 percent inflation—will not be attainable unless interest rates return to their historical parity with inflation. The consumer durables, housing, and capital spending sectors of the economy simply return to previous levels if interest rates remain 5 percent or more above the rate of inflation. As was previously mentioned, the last time this was tried was in 1930–33, with somewhat less than sparkling results. But given the current state of financial market expectations, lower interest rates combined with above-average growth cannot occur with the present mammoth budget deficits.

The Reagan program was theoretically designed to reduce if not eliminate the deficit, while at the same time reducing inflation and raising productivity, thereby returning the economy to a path of balanced, non-inflationary growth. However, there are few politicians of any political persuasion who do not want to accomplish exactly the same thing. The roads of Hell are paved with good intentions; the question is how much optimal fiscal and monetary policies could actually accomplish.

It must be clear that even if "optimal" has the same connotation to all economists, it certainly has different meanings to politicians. For if we leave out the vacuous strategy of cutting taxes without cutting spending, at least four different alternatives can be considered:

Supply-Side Policies for the 1980s

1. Cut taxes and government spending proportionately
2. Cut government spending first, delaying tax cuts until the budget is balanced
3. Keep taxes and government spending growing at the same rate and use monetary policy to reduce inflation
4. Keep government spending growing at the same rate but cut marginal tax rates while raising average tax rates

The first plan is of course what the Reagan administration told the voters it would do. If followed, I still believe that such a plan would have been highly successful. The demand-side effect would have been approximately zero, given that both taxes and spending were reduced the same amount. Since the budget position would have been relatively unchanged, the monetary effect would have also been approximately zero. The supply-side effect—an increase in productivity, work effort, and individual incentive—would have eventually produced a lower underlying rate of inflation. We would not have initially had a strong recovery and a balanced budget, as some of the ideological supply siders promised, but it would have been a workable long-run solution that produced as its end product a healthy economy.

The second plan is essentially what the Eisenhower administration did: cut government spending without changing taxes very much. Eisenhower did introduce accelerated depreciation in 1954, terminate the excess profits tax, and introduce a small tax credit for dividends, so he did not leave all taxes unchanged. But all of these tax cuts were specifically directed toward saving and investment; no broad-based tax cuts were seriously considered at the time. The cuts in defense spending did lead to a mild recession in 1954, but they also resulted in an actual decrease in prices in 1955—the last time that ever happened—and the economy remained healthy until monetary policy was called on to stem what was viewed as a disquieting inflation rate of 4 percent.

The third plan has little to recommend it. Essentially the coward's solution, it requires no specific action on the part of Congress and tosses the ball entirely into the lap of the monetary authorities. It also is suboptimal because the exclusive use of the monetary tools for restraint means high interest rates, which lead to less capital formation. Although it does keep inflation in check in the short run, it retards real growth and prohibits the increase in productivity gains which in the long run is the only enduring solution for reducing inflation.

The fourth plan may at first sound bizarre; cut tax rates without cutting taxes. Perhaps this is just another mutation of the discredited Laffer curve. Yet couched in somewhat different terms, it does not seem at all outlandish. In fact, as a national sales or value added tax, the general idea is currently in widespread use in most European countries. A variant of this tax would be to apply it only to energy by posting a substantial tariff on each barrel of imported oil or gas. Finally, the most radical but at the same time beneficial change in the tax structure—a flat-rate income tax—could also be instituted.

Throughout this book we have stressed reduced government spending as the best way to right the imbalances of the economy as manifested in high inflation, high interest rates, and low productivity. From an economic point of view this remains the optimal solution. However, as mentioned at the end of chapter 11, any economic program makes sense only if considered within the confines of a political solution. If the American voters and the Congress do not wish to cut existing government benefits, which by the end of 1982 was eminently clear, that does not necessarily mean throwing in the towel on improving the state of the economy. Thus now let us turn to a discussion of alternative measures from the tax side of the picture.

Alternative Methods of Taxation

The most common criticism of the Reagan economic program is that the three-year 25 percent across-the-board personal income tax rate cut was too radical, too far-reaching to be successful within the confines of existing economic and political limitations. Nothing could be further from the truth. The Reagan program failed because it was not radical enough.

The whole essence of supply-side economics is to reconfigure the tax structure so that the high marginal tax rates that lower productivity and distort saving and investment decisions are reduced to a minimum. To most economists and politicians, cutting marginal tax rates also means reducing average tax rates. There is nothing wrong with reducing average tax rates providing that government spending is also reduced proportionately. But reducing average tax rates is not the heart of supply-side economics. If voters would rather maintain their current standard of government benefits, then supply-side economics can still function well with unchanged average tax rates providing that the high marginal rates are cut.

From the viewpoint of economic efficiency, it would be best if average tax rates, marginal tax rates, and government spending were all reduced, for increased reliance on the public sector for income maintenance payments and investment decisions does indeed reduce incentives and productivity. However, cutting marginal tax rates while keeping average tax rates and government spending levels constant is far better than cutting both marginal and average tax rates and leaving government spending levels unchanged, thereby increasing the deficit.

In general, the average American voter is surprisingly lukewarm when asked if he would like his federal income taxes cut. In polls taken shortly before the 1980 election, voters repeatedly confirmed that they preferred keeping levels of taxes and government benefits intact rather than cutting both of them proportionately. The parts of the tax code that most upset the average American are the high marginal tax rates and the perceived inequities that allow the rich to pay only a negligible proportion of their total income in taxes.

The average voter does not want to cut Social Security benefits, unemployment insurance, Medicare and Medicaid, or other retirement benefits. He is somewhat more enthusiastic about reducing welfare payments to the poor—as opposed to the middle class—but even here no clear-cut consensus exists for terminating these benefits. Presumably few are in favor of welfare cheats and able-bodied people who choose not to work at all, but purging the roles of all such cases would still save far less than one year's tax cut.

In view of the mandate from the American voter not to tamper with popular government spending programs, and given the need for increased defense capabilities, massive reductions in the average tax rate can only lead to huge budget deficits, resulting in either interest-rate induced recessions or deficit-fueled inflation. Thus the appropriate policy must revolve around cutting marginal rates while leaving average rates unchanged. This could be accomplished by several alternative measures, some of which are discussed next.

A national sales or consumption tax is the simplest to explain and to implement. Under such a plan, most goods and services sold to the final user would be taxed at some flat rate, say 10 percent; naturally there are some exemptions. The purchase or sale of a house is taxed at a much lower rate because a 10 percent tax would drastically reduce mobility in real estate transactions. Interest payments are not taxed, nor are medical payments, tuition, legal fees or charitable contributions. In many states "necessities," which are defined in various ways, are also exempted. Purchases of capital equipment by businesses are usually tax-exempt, and nonresidential structures are virtually always tax-exempt, although New York City recently imposed a transfer tax on office buildings. Even so, under a national sales tax almost all goods and services purchased by the final user are subject to the tax. Even with all these deductions, a 10 percent tax would raise over $100 billion per year in additional revenue.

The major disadvantage of the tax is that its initial impact is inflationary. In the long run the increase in saving, investment, and productivity would lower costs and hence more than offset the rise in prices due to the sales tax. Yet this will not be true in the short run for, as has been pointed out several times, demand-side effects occur more quickly than supply-side effects. Furthermore, the increase is immediately reflected in the CPI, whereupon it is incorporated into all the union contracts and cost-of-living indexes, which generates a further inflationary spiral.

Some have suggested that the move to a national sales tax be accompanied by legislation specifically exempting from the CPI the increase in prices due to this tax. This move, it is argued, would short-circuit the inflationary spiral just described. It simply will not work. The Thatcher government lowered marginal income tax rates and offset them by higher value-added tax rates in order to remain revenue neutral, and the U.K. price indexes were then recalculated to show no increase, but no one, least of all the unions, was fooled. Labor received wage increases proportional to the total increase in the cost of living, including the higher taxes. No evidence exists to suggest that such a scheme would work any better here.

This author once suggested a compromise solution—back in the days when the budget was approximately in balance and a sales tax was being considered as revenue neutral, that is, accompanied by an income tax cut, not as a revenue raiser. I suggested that the income tax cut of 10 percent take place all in the first year, while the increase in sales tax take place in five annual 2 percent increments. That way, the inflationary impact of the higher consumer prices would be offset by the supply-side effect much sooner, and hence inflation would not increase at all.

The idea was quickly laughed out of the room. It was explained to me in words of one syllable that if Congress ever tried such a hare-brained scheme, the majority would vote for the 10 percent income tax cut, the first-year 2 percent sales-tax increase—and that would be it; no further tax increases. Hence this idea was quietly dropped. But somehow a direct descendant of that Congress forgot the basic lesson in August 1981 when it voted for tax cuts now and spending cuts "later."

The value-added tax is really quite similar in concept except that it is applied on the value added at each step of production instead of all at once on the final sale. For example, suppose a firm manufactures tires. The cost of labor to make the tire is $15 and the cost of capital—interest, depreciation, rent, and profit—is another $5. The tire is then sold for $25 to an automobile manufacturer. The tire manufacturer pays tax on the $20 difference between the price at which it sold the tire and the cost of the raw materials, which were purchased from someone else. The value which the manufacturer added to the product is what gets taxed at each stage of production. If the automobile dealer then puts a price of $35 on the tires it sells with the new car, its value-added is $10 and the tax it pays is so apportioned.

The advantage of the value-added tax, it is sometimes claimed, is that it lessens the chance of tax evasion. If the tax is levied only once on the final product, some retailers could simply avoid recording their sales and hence pay no tax, perhaps splitting the difference with the buyer. In the case of a value-added tax, however, every step in the chain forms a cost basis for the next step of production. Thus tax avoiders at one step would cause someone else to pay more tax, and hence the system is "self policing." For this reason, many economists prefer the value-added tax, although for this country the difference would be relatively minute.

The value-added tax is used in virtually every country in Europe, with base rates ranging from 8 percent to 15 percent. In most countries so-called luxury goods have a higher value-added tax than the base rate, but this is primarily to tax conspicuous consumption; the additional tax itself brings in virtually no additional revenue. The tax is generally accepted and cannot properly be considered even a remotely radical idea. As a substitute or replacement for the existing tax code, it would definitely be a big improvement, although the gains to growth and efficiency are smaller than would be the case under the flat-rate income tax.

The other major change in the tax laws that is economically efficient is a $10/bbl tariff on imported oil. Such a tax would discourage the use of all petroleum products, but would fall disproportionately on suppliers of foreign oil, thereby contributing to exploration and development of domestic resources. Such a tax would initially be inflationary but in the long run would lead to lower rather than higher oil prices since it would remove the OPEC leverage to double oil prices again if worldwide supplies ever again became tight. Just as the Reagan decision to deregulate the domestic oil industry led to a decline rather than an increase in oil prices, so too would this tariff eventually lead to less inflation. Such a tax would also raise about $40 billion per year since, with the windfall profits tax as it is currently structured, the Treasury gets between 75 percent and 80 percent of any increase in domestic oil prices. An increase in the gasoline tax would also generate many of the same benefits, although it would not drive a wedge between domestic and foreign production.

The Advantages of a Flat-Rate Income Tax

Both the national sales or value-added tax and the tariff on imported oil and gas would improve economic performance, for they would reduce the deficit and lower interest rates without raising marginal tax rates. However, both have two major disadvantages. The first is that the initial impact is inflationary. The second is political; the American public does not want to face another tax in addition to the current burden. Whereas lower deficits would of course be welcome, the average consumer would view the combined effect as more taxes with insufficient offsetting benefits. In addition, the taxpayer revolt at the distortions and inequities of the current income tax system is likely to become an increasingly serious problem in the near future if the tax code is not significantly revised.

Even if average tax rates had not been reduced by the Reagan administration, far-reaching changes in the tax code would have been necessary, for the present tax system is one huge mess. Indeed, with the combination of the tax reductions contained in the 1981 fiscal policy act and the proliferation of tax avoidance schemes that now threaten to become a permanent feature of the economic landscape, it is likely that, for the first time since the establishment of the modern social welfare state, tax receipts are likely to grow *more slowly* than nominal GNP in future years. The reasons are threefold.

First, indexing of personal income taxes removes bracket creep from the personal income taxes.*

Second, the loopholes spawned in the Tax Reduction Act of 1981 essentially mean that corporations and the rich will be able to pay an even lower proportion of taxes than in previous years. Some of these loopholes, such as safe harbor leasing, were closed in the Tax Equity and Fiscal Responsibility Act of 1982 but most still remain intact.

Third, the damage done by bracket creep during the 1970s has pushed so many people into the 40 percent and 50 percent brackets that, in spite of the tax cut, both legal tax avoidance and the underground economy will continue to grow much faster than nominal GNP.

If we also consider the indirect tax of the deficit, as expressed in higher interest rates, the actual effect of the total Reagan tax cut package has paradoxically been to shift the burden of taxes *even further* onto the backs of the middle class, who will in turn respond by greatly increasing their tax avoidance.

Furthermore, with the economy in a semi-permanent state of underutilized resources, the important secondary effects of lower tax rates—increased individual incentives, greater work effort, and higher productivity—are likewise lost. All these benefits were based on the underlying assumption that the economy would be operating near full employment and capacity so that the increase in labor supply would in effect lift the production ceiling. Certainly a system was not envisioned where aggregate demand was significantly below existing capacity, and where the increase in incentive would be met by a reduction in job opportunities. For under this scenario, the gains from increased labor input are never realized.

---

*This may eventually be reversed by Congress, but at the time of writing no serious move in this direction had yet been attempted.

Supply-Side Policies for the 1980s

The shift from the public to the private sector was supposed to get people off the welfare rolls and on to the employment roles; at the upper end of the age spectrum, a decreased reliance on Social Security would mean that older workers would stay in the labor force longer. But with fewer jobs available, these motivating factors have a hollow ring. *With an underutilized economy, the advantages of supply-side economics completely disappear.*

The combination of the 25 percent personal income tax rate reduction and indexation thereafter will work to stabilize the marginal federal tax rate at 30 percent, instead of soaring to 45 percent as would have been the case if conditions had continued as they were during the Carter years. Similarly, the average tax rate by 1990 will decline to 13 percent, compared to 22 percent under an extrapolation of the Carter conditions.

If personal income, like GNP, increases 8 percent per year throughout the decade, this would push average family income close to $50,000 by the end of the decade, which means that taxes would be $4,500 lower with Reagan than under the projected Carter tax rates. This sounds quite impressive—until we ask the question of whether the consumer is better or worse off with the combination of tax cuts and higher interest rates.

Under a 5 percent rate of inflation, the mortgage rate should eventually decline to about 8 percent. In the first half of 1982 it averaged over 17 percent, about 9 percent higher than normal. If the average consumer lives in a house which costs two and one half times his annual income—currently the figure is 2.8 times but we expect housing prices to fall in real terms over the rest of the decade—then by 1990 the cost of the higher mortgage rate would be $10,000 per year, far overshadowing the $4,500 gain from the tax cut. The staggering burden of high interest rates negates the tax cut of its essential benefits for the middle-class consumer who borrows to buy a house or other assets and cannot afford to save very much because such a large proportion of his income is gobbled up by mortgage payments.

Thus the tax-cut induced deficits have robbed the middle class of any improvement in real disposable income by raising interest rates. However, in closing the deficit gap, we must be very careful not to raise marginal rates, which would permanently mutilate any supply-side benefits that might occur once the economy does start to recover. Thus what is needed is a tax system which (a) raises the total amount of revenue collected relative to the present system; (b) continues to keep pace with the increase of GNP; (c) eliminates counterproductive deductions and loopholes; (d) lowers marginal tax rates in order to encourage work effort and individual incentive; and (e) increases the proportion of personal income saved. The flat-rate income tax accomplishes all of these goals.

The flat-rate tax at one stroke would end all loopholes; decisions would once again be made for economic reasons rather than because of whimsical decisions of Congress, the IRS, or the tax courts. With a top rate of 17 percent, virtually no one would have the incentive to spend the time and money seeking tax avoidance schemes. Hard work and risk taking would once again be rewarded instead of penalized. This would be true supply-side economics; not welfare for the rich.

A flat-rate tax would of course have to be accompanied by an end to most deductions. Otherwise the resulting structure would remain as riddled with loopholes as the present force, and the deficit would continue to increase apace. Such a move would be certain to incur great wrath from all the vested interests that currently profit by tax shelters—financial institutions that invest heavily in municipal bonds, the state and local municipalities themselves, the oil industry and other natural resource industries that utilize the depletion allowance, the stock market industry that receives favorable tax treatment for capital gains, and of course the myriad of lawyers, accountants, and lobbyists who own their very existence to the current tax laws.

Such a proposal is bound to upset the average taxpayer who thinks that the deductions for mortgage interest, charitable contributions, catastrophic medical or casualty expenses, and state and local taxes should be maintained. However, even keeping all these basic deductions and including a $2,500 personal exemption would only raise the necessary tax rate to 17 percent. In other words, even with these deductions a 17 percent tax would raise as much revenue as does the current personal income tax code, even without taking into account any of the manifold benefits of such a tax.

The benefits of such a modified flat-rate tax would be enormous. The increase in the rate of return on saving and the improvement in work incentive stemming from a lower marginal tax rate would increase real growth by 2 percent per year, which would generate about 1.3 million new jobs each year. The higher levels of economic activity would generate $100 billion per year in additional tax receipts after five years. The mushrooming of tax avoidance would come to a sudden and irreversible halt. Perhaps most important, the long trek back to a more lawful and equitable society would begin.

The reduction in the budget deficit is not without its short-term drawbacks. The flat-rate income tax will bring in more revenue, especially among tax avoiders, than the current graduated schedule. Of course this money must come out of someone's pocket; it does not come out of thin air. Thus some people will initially suffer a reduction in real disposable income, which will in turn cause some further reduction in consumption. In other words, the initial response of the demand-side reaction will be negative, not positive. Yet on balance the government's gain in saving will be greater than the consumer's loss.

268

The massive switch to saving and investment would result in a sharp increase in the investment ratio. This would not be a pipe dream like the Reagan business tax cuts, which were nullified by higher interest rates; in this case interest rates would go down because total saving really would increase.

Thus productivity would rise both because of an increase in capital formation and greater labor incentive as a result of lower marginal tax rates. This would lead to further reductions in inflation. As that happened, the Fed could gradually ease monetary policy, as a given rate of money supply growth would support a larger increase in real growth with a lower rate of inflation. Thus the economy would slowly be nursed back to full employment. But it certainly would not happen overnight, and for the first year before those lower interest rates were translated into higher investment, GNP might even decline further.

The flat-rate income tax, while retaining the essential elements of supply-side economics, thus finesses the problem of the early 1980s: that the higher budget deficits have led to increases in the real rate of interest, essentially choking off the expected rise in aggregate demand. This program in essence salvages the useful elements of supply-side economics while solving the contradictions. Perhaps this is the right note on which to end the book.

But that is not at all what I propose to do, for the solution just proposed, while economically logical and internally consistent, has a very doubtful political future. Just as supply-side economics foundered on the shoals of political expediency when Congress was unable to cut government spending, so too would the concept of a flat-rate income tax be rejected by the coalition of special interests wanting their pet deductions saved; of liberal economists demanding that the rich pay more when it is perfectly obvious that they use tax shelters to pay less; and the general public, who does not realize corporations in the long run do not pay taxes at all but merely pass them along in the form of higher prices or backward in the form of lower wages, and hence everyone, including rabid critics of corporations, would be better off without this additional layer of taxes. One cannot in fact draw a useful conclusion without considering the superimposition of political and economic forces.

The Superimposition of Political and Economic Cycles

In 1945 Arthur Schlesinger, Sr., pointed out that ever since the Civil War, American political movements had followed a 15-year cycle of alternatively liberal and conservative views. Schlesinger's proximate reason for that comment was to point out that the 15 years of liberalism under the New Deal were about to come to an end and that the country should brace itself for a wave of conservativism.

Schlesinger did not predict beyond that immediate changeover, but if he had it would have been one of the more remarkably accurate forecasts of the century. The 1945–60 conservative era was indeed followed by the liberal era beginning in 1960, which reached its heights in the late 1960s and early 1970s and then burned out by 1975. By 1980 the country was ready for both a conservative president and Congress; and in many respects the 1980s seemed to mimic the 1950s, although obviously not without important differences. According to this timetable, conservative thought will remain in ascendancy until 1990, at which time the country will find itself in the embraces of another liberal resurgency.

It is this political reality on which the economic cycles must ultimately be superimposed in order to determine whether supply-side economics, or any subset thereof, can hope to rescue the economy from the excesses of the 1970s—or whether the secular trend toward larger government, higher inflation, declining productivity, and a lower standard of living is irreversible, in which case the downward shift of the Phillips curve in 1982 was just a temporary development.

Both the 1920s and the 1950s were periods of conservative economic orthodoxy. Reduce the national debt—or at least balance the budget. Cut government spending. Once these goals have been accomplished, aim for zero inflation as the norm. Encourage profits and capital formation. And, reluctantly, use tighter monetary policy if inflation heats up even though the budget is balanced.

For some reason, however, this economic orthodoxy never did seem to produce the desired results. The 1919–29 decade, which was viewed as one glorious expansion by so many latter-day historians, of course ended in the Great Depression, and did contain three recessions. Real growth during the decade averaged a respectable but not spectacular 3.5 percent, while the unemployment rate averaged 5 percent.

It would be foolish to ignore or forget the lessons of the Great Depression, for some of the very same mistakes were repeated in 1982—such as raising taxes in the middle of a recession. Yet for practical purposes the cataclysmic events of the 1930s are rather distant from what is likely to happen to the U.S. economy for the remainder of this decade. Thus rather than relying on "ancient history" to determine how the Republican orthodoxy has affected the economy, it makes more sense to look at the postwar record. From 1947 through 1982, the country had a Democratic president for 17 years and a Republican one for 18 years; it is instructive to see how the economy has fared under each of them.

The common perception is that under the Democrats the economy grew faster as a result of stimulative fiscal and monetary policies. As a result, government spending increased faster, the deficit widened, and inflation was worse, leading to higher interest rates and worse stock market performance under the Democrats than the Republicans.

However, a brief review of the postwar statistics indicates exactly the opposite. Under the Republicans, real growth has been lower and inflation has been higher than under the Democrats. The unemployment rate has risen instead of fallen. While all major components of real GNP have grown more slowly, the biggest disparity has occurred in capital formation. Stock prices and after-tax economic profits have increased 50 percent faster under the Democrats. The level of the federal deficit has been twice as large under the Republicans, and *the annual change more than three times as large.* Finally, federal government spending excluding defense has increased 2.4 percent per year faster under the Republicans. All these statistics are summarized in table 12.1.

Some would argue that such a table is misleading because the Democrats tend to leave the economy in a shambles—high inflation rates, large budget deficits, and an economy verging on the brink of recession—and that it takes

TABLE 12.1

Comparison of Economic Performance under Democratic and Republican Administrations

Variable Name, Annual Percentage of Change	Democrats	Republicans
Real Economic Activity		
GNP, constant dollars	4.4	2.3
Capital spending, constant dollars	4.8	1.7
Unemployment rate	−0.2	0.5
Prices and Financial Variables		
GNP deflator	3.8	4.6
Stock prices[a]	7.2	4.8
Economic profits after taxes[b]	8.5	5.0
Fiscal Policy[c]		
Federal government spending excluding defense	8.8	11.2
Federal budget deficit, level	−9.7	−21.6
Federal budget deficit, change	2.0	6.5

SOURCE: Calculated by Evans Economics, Inc.
NOTE: Democrats: 1947–52, 1961–68, 1977–80; Republicans: 1953–60, 1969–76, 1981–82. All figures are percent of change, except the last two lines.
[a]Standard and Poor 500 stock price index.
[b]Profits adjusted for inventory and depreciation changes due to inflation (IVA and CCA).
[c]NIPA basis.

the Republicans most of their time in office to reverse the damage done and return the economy to its proper track. However, the only time this ever happened was under Jimmy Carter, who managed to make a mess of virtually everything he touched. When Truman left office, he turned over to the Republicans an economy with an inflation rate of 1.4 percent, an unemployment rate of 3.0 percent, and a federal budget in surplus five of the last seven years with a cumulative surplus of $34.6 billion. When Eisenhower left office eight years later, the inflation rate was virtually the same at 1.6 percent but the unemployment rate had risen to 5.5 percent—it was to soar to 6.7 percent the next year—with a cumulative budget deficit of $8.7 billion during his two terms, although it was in surplus in 1960.

When Johnson left office, the economy was thought to be in far worse shape, with the inflation rate rising to 4.4 percent. However, eight years later, Ford bragged about reducing inflation to 5.2 percent with an unemployment rate some 4 percent higher and a basically unmanagable federal deficit of $53 billion, a gift bequeathed from the biggest government spender of them all, Richard Nixon.

Similarly, it was under the Democrats that the corporate profit tax rate was reduced from 52 percent to 48 percent and then to 46 percent; and it was under the Democrats that the investment tax credit of 7 percent was introduced, although it was increased to 10 percent under the Republicans. This was their only stab at aiding the business community, though. During 1969–76 the maximum tax rate on capital gains was raised from 25 percent to 49 percent, and it was under the Democrats that it was lowered to 28 percent, although admittedly Carter and Blumenthal fought that one every step of the way.

To be sure, the election of each of the Republican presidents in the postwar period has been partially caused by the perceived ineptness of the Democrats in foreign policy. For Eisenhower, it was Korea; for Nixon, Vietnam; and for Reagan, the hostages in Iran. Yet each Republican president felt strongly that the economy was out of order and went about trying to reduce the rate of inflation and the relative size of the government sector. In the case of Eisenhower, as has been seen, orthodox fiscal and monetary policy were used. Nixon tried wage-and-price controls, a disaster compounded by his political ineptitude after Watergate. Reagan, of course, tried tax cuts without spending cuts and ended up with monetary policy pitching the economy into its most prolonged slump since the 1930s.

In spite of the wide variety of methods chosen, the fact of the matter is that *none of them worked.* Whether it was tight fiscal policy, tight monetary policy, or controls, each of these methods failed for exactly the same reason. It did not attack the principal underlying cause for the buildup of inflationary pressures, namely the lower growth of productivity. In all cases the cure was worse than the disease; the policies followed were virtually guaranteed to reduce rather than improve productivity.

This author obviously has no quarrel with the concept that a bigger government sector hampers productivity and eventually leads to higher inflation and lower real growth. However, to improve the economy it is not sufficient merely to cut back on government spending and assume everything else will magically fall into place. Those resources released must be directed into productive purposes in the private sector. Cutting back on the *total* amount of resources available is never the right way to increase productivity. Indeed, supply-side economics works poorly or not at all under the constraints of slack resources. Lower tax rates simply will not improve the incentive to look for work if fewer jobs are available. Capital formation will not be stimulated no matter how generous the tax rates if operating rates are at 50 percent or less. Thus the reduction in inflation generated by the Republicans was largely the result of higher unemployment instead of higher productivity.

Many who support the general constructs of supply-side economics have argued that these comments are unfair: how can any administration, they ask, be expected to undo the problems of the past fifteen—or thirty, or fifty—years in one or two years? The problems take time to be reversed. First the economy must undergo its recession, take its bitter medicine; then we will have an extended period of balanced, non-inflationary growth. The worst mistake of all, according to this logic, would be to try and rush the process along too soon. That would reignite another inflationary spiral and undo all of the good work.

While the economic logic behind that approach is not inconsiderable, on a realistic political scale it rates a zero. For the American voters do not approve of recessions, whatever their motive or cause, and they approve even less of recessions accompanied by record-high interest rates and apparent harsh treatment of the poor and disabled. When these events do occur, the voters always elect more Democrats.

Thus the 1954 recession wiped out the Republican majority in Congress, and thereafter government spending grew 9.3 percent per year for the next three years—over 6 percent per year in real terms—in spite of Eisenhower's determination to keep the budget in balance. When Nixon finally gained the chance which was denied him in 1960 by Ike's balanced budget and the third recession in eight years, he did not stint: after his first two years in office with token cuts and tax increases, government spending grew 11.2 percent per year from 1970 to 1976. Nonetheless, when the inevitable 1974–75 recession finally did appear, the Republicans were reduced to their thinnest ranks since the debacle of 1964. The Democrats went back into action and government spending rose 11.8 percent per year for 1977–80—leading to yet another recession.

The message is repeated over and over: if the Republicans, either by design or misadventure, cause even a brief recession through their policies, the Democrats will retake the reins and pump up the economy again. Even prolonged recessions simply do not accomplish the task of reducing the underlying rate of inflation very much for two reasons. First, they weaken rather than strengthen the underlying rate of productivity growth. Second, they are politically indefensible, and as such contain their own seeds of destruction by virtually guaranteeing that the opposition will supply the policies that will raise the growth rate, reduce unemployment—and eventually lead to more inflation.

The Reagan program did lower the underlying rate of inflation somewhat by squelching inflationary expectations, reducing the cost of government regulation, and instituting a rational energy policy. In addition, the increase in unemployment to double-digit rates also reduced the growth in wage rates, although much of that was due to lowered inflationary expectations. However, a 10 percent unemployment rate and 15 percent rate of interest was not what the voters wanted, as they showed in the November 1982 elections.

If history does repeat itself precisely, the conclusion we would draw from the first two years of the Reagan administration is that the economy would remain sluggish for much of the 1980s, and that eventually a Democratic administration would be elected on the pledge to get the economy moving again. Yet while this is indeed an odds-on bet to occur, the differences will be almost as notable as the similarities.

In the first place, the budget is so badly out of balance—and it would be so difficult to repair this imbalance with the normal tools of fiscal and monetary policy—that under present law the deficit is likely to increase indefinitely not only in actual terms but as a proportion of GNP. Since the voters have clearly indicated that they do not want their middle-class benefits cut, this points in the direction of significantly higher personal income and Social Security taxes.

Yet that hardly qualifies as a satisfactory solution. Indeed, tax rates had already been jacked up so high by inflation and bracket creep under the Carter administration that even with the existing Reagan tax cuts the average worker will find himself in the 40 to 50 percent marginal tax bracket by the end of the decade, when Social Security and state and local income taxes are included. The moves toward tax avoidance are largely irreversible and will result in even less equity in our tax code, which will further enrage and discourage those who do pay their taxes honestly.

During the 1950s, the social fabric of the country was for the most part smooth. While it is true that minority unrest was foreshadowed by the resistance toward integration in the South, these forthcoming events were dimly perceived by the general electorate.

Thirty years later, the social fabric is severely rent. While integration has for the most part been achieved throughout the nation, for most blacks it has been a hollow victory, as inner-city schools are still segregated and the black teenage unemployment rate approaches 50 percent. Concomitant with these developments, nevertheless, has been an increasingly widespread belief that the criminal justice code of this country has become perverted. This view was widespread long before it was intensified by the acquittal of John Hinckley. Indeed, California voters had just weeks earlier approved Proposition 8 for a widespread, sweeping change in that state's criminal code. Those changes included much stricter bail provisions, banning plea bargaining, ruling out the insanity defense, changing the rules for excluding evidence, and lengthening prison terms for repeat offenders. As the *Wall Street Journal* editorialized the next week:

> Politicians take note. The California voters who brought you Proposition 13 and the tax revolt are giving you another issue on a platter. Its message is simple: People are fed up with crime, and with a court system that appears to be more concerned with the rights of criminals than the fate of victims.
>
> Proposition 8 has tremendous symbolic importance . . . a society that is serious about coming to grips with crime will make sure its legal system doesn't lose its sense of proportion in protecting the rights of criminal defendants. The California election is a clear sign that voters are prepared to redress this imbalance.[1]

Thus over the past decade a widespread belief has developed among the American public that both the civil and criminal codes of justice in this country are close to becoming inoperative. With these twin pillars of society crumbling, the social fabric on which democracy rests becomes much more fragile. The aim of the average voter will not be to initiate bold, new solutions. It will be to try and return to the patterns of the past, when both real living standards and the quality of life were improving. For at least the rest of the decade, no radical new tax schemes need apply.

Thus whereas the Democratic campaigns of 1932 and 1960 were brimming with radical ideas—many of which were actually implemented—the 1984 Democratic platform will consist mainly of a return to "proven virtues." The flat-rate tax will be discussed but dismissed. Stimulus will be provided by more jobs programs and the "reindustrialization of America," which basically substitutes selective tax credits in place of market decisions to determine capital spending projects.

Someone will have to pay for these programs, because the Democrats will be at least as unwilling as the Republicans to raise the relative size of the deficit. The tax increases will primarily take the form of raising the tax rate and income base on Social Security contributions, which will be called "necessary to preserve the fiscal integrity" of the Social Security system. In addition, the plans to index the personal income tax rate scheduled will be scrapped, thus reinstituting bracket creep.

A slight increase in the rate of inflation, perhaps to 6 percent or so, will also be acceptable, since that will help fill the federal coffers more quickly. In fact, with 4 percent real growth, 6 percent inflation, and total government spending increasing at the same rate as GNP, the federal budget deficit would diminish approximately $40 billion per year. While that will still result in massive budget deficits for many years, it will at least provide the illusion that progress is being made. Productivity growth will languish at about 1½ percent, roughly half the rate of the first twenty years of the postwar period, but admittedly an improvement over the 1977–82 period. The usual Republican grumblings over such a program will be muted by the fact that profits will increase about 15 percent per year for at least three or four years under this set of economic assumptions.

It would clearly be presumptuous to predict the outcome of the 1984 elections at this date, but the preceding comments do indicate that even if the Republicans somehow manage to win the presidential race, it will be with a sharply reduced margin, and that the Democrats are all but certain to increase their majority in the House and regain control of the Senate. Such a move would essentially signal the demise of supply-side economics and a return to the more traditional fiscal policies of the past fifty years.

Thus in the end we are necessarily forced to conclude that the economic policies followed by the Reagan administration will end in failure. Not because business and personal tax rates were cut—that in itself would have stimulated saving and investment, work effort, and individual incentive, thereby lifting productivity growth back to its earlier postwar levels—but because the political realities did not permit the spending cuts necessary to make the program work. Indeed, the economy was too far from equilibrium for even the finely balanced Kennedy-Johnson economic program to have worked in 1981. First the government had to demonstrate that it could reduce the deficit and lower inflation; then the productivity-increasing tax and spending cuts could have proceeded apace. But in fact the worst possible combination of policies was followed: tax cuts with no spending cuts, and hence a monetary-induced recession which killed any chance of an investment boom. Radical surgery in the form of a flat-rate income tax receives no serious consideration from any established politician.

The tragedy of the situation is that the virtues of supply-side economics will now remain buried in the rubble for many years. The theory that the economy could be rescued by tax cuts to stimulate saving and investment—that the economy could simultaneously have higher growth and lower inflation—has allegedly been tested and found severely wanting, even though the actual supply-side theory was never implemented at all. The best chance for the economy to recover has gone by the boards, with the result that, without radical restructuring of fiscal policy, the United States will gradually follow its demise as the leading military power into the position of a second-rate economic power as well.

Notes

Chapter 1

1. Eggert Economic Enterprises, Inc., "Blue Chip Economic Indicators" (10 March 1981).

2. Eggert Economic Enterprises, Inc., "Blue Chip Economic Indicators" (10 September 1982): 8.

3. See table 8.3 for full documentation.

4. See table 10.3 for full documentation.

5. See, for example, his *Economics,* 7th ed. (New York: McGraw-Hill, 1967), p. 57.

6. For a thorough review of this material, see Robert E. Keleher and William P. Orzechowski, *Supply-Side Effects of Fiscal Policy: Some Historical Perspectives* (Atlanta: Federal Reserve Bank of Atlanta, 1980).

7. Jean Baptiste Say, *A Treatise on Political Economy, or The Production, Distribution, and Consumption of Wealth,* trans. Clement C. Biddle (Boston: Wells and Lilly, 1824).

8. Keleher and Orzechowski, *Supply-Side Effects,* pp. 33, 39.

9. For a more extended discussion of this, see Jude Wanniski, *The Way the World Works* (New York: Simon & Schuster, 1978), p. 141.

10. John Maynard Keynes, *The General Theory of Employment, Interest and Money* (New York: Harcourt Brace Jovanovich, 1965), p. 129. The exact quote is:

> If the Treasury were to fill old bottles with banknotes, bury them at suitable depths in disused coalmines which are then filled up to the surface with rubbish, and leave it to private enterprise on well-tried principles of *laissez-faire* to dig the notes up again (the right to do so being obtained, of course, by tendering for leases of the note-bearing territory), there need be no more unemployment and, with the help of the repercussions, the real income of the community, and its capital wealth also, would probably become a good deal greater than it actually is.

11. John Maynard Keynes, "Essays in Persuasion," in *Collected Writings,* 3rd ed., vol. 9 (Cambridge, England: Cambridge University Press, 1972), pp. 57–58 (orig. in *The Economic Consequences of the Peace,* ch. 6).

12. See, for example, his testimony before the Senate Appropriations Committee on January 23, 1981 (Washington, D.C.: Government Printing Office), in which he stated, "Unless some ac-

tion is taken to couple fiscal and monetary constraint . . . with some type of wage-price restraint, we will be doomed to years of slack and slow growth in the economy" (p. 202).

13. Chase Econometric Associates, Inc., long-term macroeconomic forecast.

Chapter 2

1. Dean Witter, "Economic Opinion," 3 February 1971.

2. Chase Econometric Associates, Inc., long-term macroeconomic forecast.

3. Alan Greenspan, Testimony before Senate Appropriations Committee, 28 January 1981, pp. 159–62.

4. Ibid.

5. Ibid.

6. Bruce Bartlett, *Reaganomics: Supply Side Economics in Action* (Westport, Conn.: Arlington House, 1981), p. 111.

Chapter 3

1. Robert A. Mundell, "The Appropriate Use of Monetary and Fiscal Policy for Internal and External Stability," International Monetary Fund papers, March 1962, pp. 70–77.

2. Mundell's views are best summarized in *The Dollar and the Policy Mix, 1971,* "Essays on International Finance," no. 85, Princeton University. His views are also well represented in a conference held on global inflation in Bologna, Italy, in 1971. The transcript of the entire conference has been published in *Inflation as a Global Problem,* ed. Randall Hinshaw (Baltimore: The Johns Hopkins University Press, 1972).

3. Hinshaw, *Inflation as a Global Problem,* p. 142.

4. Jude Wanniski, "It's Time to Cut Taxes," *Wall Street Journal,* 11 December 1974.

5. Editorial, "Handle With Care," *Wall Street Journal,* 27 February 1964.

6. Editorial, "Blumenthal's Ghost," *Wall Street Journal,* 12 August 1981.

7. Mundell, *The Dollar,* p. 24.

8. Ibid.

9. Randall Hinshaw, ed., *Inflation as a Global Problem* (Baltimore: The Johns Hopkins University Press, 1972), p. 150.

10. Mundell, *The Dollar,* p. 10.

11. Ibid., p. 13.

12. Ibid., p. 14.

Chapter 4

1. Robert E. Hall and Dale W. Jorgenson, "Application of The Theory of Optimal Capital Accumulation," *Tax Incentives and Capital Spending,* ed. G. Fromm (Washington, D.C.: The Brookings Institution, 1971), p. 59–60.

Notes

2. *Economic Report of the President* (Washington, D.C.: Government Printing Office, 1981), pp. 81–84.

3. Testimony Before the Senate Appropriations Committee, 28 January 1981, p. 210.

4. Ibid.

5. Editorial, "Bad News Markets," *Wall Street Journal,* 26 August 1981.

6. Eggert Economic Enterprises, Inc., "Blue Chip Economic Indicators," 10 July 1981 and 10 December 1981.

7. Eggert Economic Enterprises, Inc., "Blue Chip Economic Indicators," 10 August 1981 and 10 February 1982.

8. Dale W. Sommer, "CEO's Forecast 1982: 10th Annual Survey," *Industry Week,* 30 November 1981.

Chapter 5

1. Walter W. Heller, *New Dimensions of Political Economy* (New York: W. W. Norton & Co., 1967), pp. 105–06.

2. Ibid., p. 112.

3. *Washington Post,* 12 February 1982, p. 1.

4. Jude Wanniski, "Looking for the Right Broom," *Wall Street Journal,* 17 August 1976.

Chapter 6

1. Senate Appropriations Committee Hearings, 28 January 1981, p. 193.

2. "A New Look in Economics," *Business Week,* 22 December 1980.

3. *Senate Appropriations Committee Hearings,* 28 January 1981, p. 286.

4. "Moral Deficit," *The New Republic,* 19 May 1982: "Without that promised economic boom, the moral basis of Reaganomics simply collapses . . . the program is bankrupt, both economically and morally."

5. See Steve Rattner, "Top Officials Clash on Tax Cut Timing," *New York Times,* 23 January 1981.

6. Ibid.

7. I heard Walter Heller state this at the Senate Appropriations Committee hearings on 28 January 1981, but the statement never appeared in the record. His exact statement was "I wonder who's feeding Reagan that crap."

8. See, for example, Thomas Mayer, *Permanent Income, Wealth, and Consumption* (Berkley: University of California Press, 1972).

9. Michael Boskin, "Taxation, Saving, and the Rate of Interest," *Journal of Political Economy,* pt. 2 (April 1978): 3–27.

10. Simon Kuznets, *Uses of National Income in Peace and War* (New York: National Bureau of Economic Research, 1942), p. 30.

11. John Maynard Keynes, *The General Theory of Employment, Interest and Money,* p. 96.

12. A. Smithies, S. M. Livingston, and J. L. Mosak, "Forecasting Postwar Demand," *Econometrica* 13, no. 1 (January 1945): 1–37.

13. J. S. Duesenberry, *Income, Saving, and the Theory of Consumer Behavior* (Cambridge, Mass.: Harvard University Press, 1948).

14. Milton Friedman, *A Theory of the Consumption Function* (Princeton: Princeton University Press, National Bureau of Economic Research, 1951).

15. Ibid., p. 10.

16. F. Modigliani and A. Ando, "The 'Permanent Income' and 'Life Cycle' Hypothesis of Savings Behavior: Comparisons and Tests," *Consumption and Saving,* vol. II, ed. I. Friend and R. Jones (Philadelphia: University of Pennsylvania Press, 1960).

17. Michael K. Evans and L. R. Klein, *The Wharton Econometric Forecasting Model* (Philadelphia: University of Pennsylvania Press, 1967). Also see Mayer, *Permanent Income,* esp. table 19 (p. 237) and table 21 (p. 240).

18. Taken from testimony of M. K. Evans to Ways and Means Committee, 3 April 1981.

Chapter 7

1. Capital stock figures for 1950–79 are taken from *The Survey of Current Business,* February 1981, p. 57; those for 1980–82 are extrapolated by Evans Economics using the same method.

2. William F. Butler, ed., *How Business Economists Forecast* (Englewood Cliffs, N.J.: Prentice-Hall, 1966), p. 521.

3. See, for example, Chase Econometric Associates, Inc., "Macroeconomic Impact of Current Cost Depreciation," July 1977.

4. Senate Finance Committee Hearings, 24 July 1980.

5. This table and additional commentary also appear in the 1982 *Economic Report of the President* (Washington, D.C.: Government Printing Office), p. 124.

6. See, for example, Lester Thurow, *The Zero-Sum Society* (New York: Basic Books, 1980), pp. 97, 101.

7. See, for example, Ira Magaziner and Robert B. Reich, *Minding America's Business: The Decline and Rise of the American Economy* (New York: Harcourt Brace Jovanovich, 1982); also Robert B. Reich, "Hi-Tech Warfare," *The New Republic,* 1 November 1982.

Chapter 8

1. David L. Birch, *The Job Generation Process* (Cambridge, Mass.: M.I.T. Program on Neighborhood and Racial Change, 1979), pp. 8–9.

2. Catherine Armington and Marjorie Odle, *Sources of Recent Employment Growth, 1978–1980* (Washington, D.C.: Business Microdata Project, The Brookings Institution, 1982), pp. 4–5.

3. Birch, *Job Generation,* p. 13.

4. The figures in this section are taken from Allen H. Lerman, *Current Law and History of Capital Gains Taxation* (Washington, D.C.: Office of Tax Analysis, 15 April 1981).

5. P. L. Stern, *The Rape of the Taxpayer* (New York: Random House, 1973).

6. "Snapping Back," *Wall Street Journal,* 30 July 1979.

7. "Boom Time in Venture Capital," *Time,* 10 August 1981.

8. "The Bulls Are Back in Venture Capital," *New York Times,* 17 August 1980.

9. "Venture Capitalists Ride Again," *The Economist,* 11 October 1980.

10. Chase Econometric Associates, Inc., "An Alternative to the Fiscal Stimulus Act of 1978: A Reduction in Capital Gains Taxes," April 1978.

Notes

11. Ralph B. Bristol, Jr., "Pitfalls in Using Econometric Models: The Chase and DRI Capital Gains Estimates," *Tax Notes,* 15 May 1978.

12. "Flash and a Touch of Brass," *Time,* 25 June 1979.

13. James Tobin and William C. Brainard, "Asset Markets and the Cost of Capital," *Economic Progress, Private Values and Public Policy, Essays in Honor of William Fellner* (Amsterdam: North Holland Publishing Co., 1977), pp. 235–62.

14. Editorial, "The 40% Solution," *Wall Street Journal,* 21 October 1980.

Chapter 9

1. Richard A. Musgrave, *The Theory of Public Finance* (New York: McGraw-Hill, 1959) p. 242.

2. U.S. Department of Health, Education, and Welfare, *Summary Report: New Jersey Graduated Work Incentive Experiment* (Washington, D.C.: Government Printing Office, December 1973).

3. K. C. Kehrer, "The Gary Income Maintenance Experiment: Summary of Initial Findings" (Bloomington: Indiana University Press, March 1977).

4. M. C. Keeley et al., "The Labor Supply Effects and Costs of Alternative Negative Income Tax Programs: Evidence from the Seattle and Denver Income Maintenance Experiments, Parts I and II," SRI International (May 1977).

5. L. Hausman, "The Impact of Welfare on the Work Effort of AFDC Mothers," *The President's Commission on Income Maintenance Programs: Technical Studies* (Washington, D.C.: U.S. Government Printing Office, 1970).

6. G. C. Cain and H. W. Watts, eds., "Toward a Summary and Synthesis of the Evidence," *Income Maintenance and Labor Supply: Econometric Studies* (New York: Academic Press, 1973); J. A. Pediman and P. M. Timpane, eds., *Work Incentives and Income Guarantees: The New Jersey Negative Income Tax Experiment* (Washington, D.C.: The Brookings Institution, 1975); J. N. Morgan et al., *Income and Welfare in the United States* (New York: McGraw-Hill, 1962).

7. Keeley et al., *Gray Income,* p. 25.

8. N. B. Tuma, M. T. Hannan, and L. P. Groenfeld, "Variation Over Time in the Impact of the Seattle and Denver Income Maintenance Experiments on the Making and Breaking of Marriages," SRI International (February 1977).

9. M. Kosters, "Effects of an Income Tax on Labor Supply," in *The Taxation of Income from Capital,* ed. A. C. Harlerger and M. J. Bailey (Washington, D.C.: The Brookings Institution, 1969), p. 323.

10. L. Godfrey, ed., *Theoretical Empirical Aspects of the Effects of Taxation on the Supply of Labor* (Organization for Economic Cooperation and Development, 1975), esp. pp. 85–86.

11. Melvyn B. Krauss, "The Swedish Tax Revolt," *Wall Street Journal,* 1 February 1979.

12. It was Elvis Presley.

13. M. K. Evans, "The Effect of Changes in the Federal Tax Structure on Aggregate Supply and Economic Activity," ch. 7, pp. 91–103, prepared for Senate Finance Committee, 1980.

14. David E. Koskoff, *The Mellons* (New York: T. Y. Crowell Co., 1978), p. 237.

15. These figures also appeared in M. K. Evans, "Taxes, Inflation and the Rich," *Wall Street Journal,* 7 August 1978.

16. P. M. Gutmann, "The Subterranean Economy," *Financial Analysts Journal* (November/December 1979).

17. Edward Feige, "How Big Is the Irregular Economy?" *Challenge* (November/December 1979).

18. "Estimates of Income Unreported on Individual Income Tax Returns," IRS publication 1104.

19. Testimony of Roscoe Egger before Senate Finance Committee, 22 March 1982.

Chapter 10

1. Chase Econometric Associates, Inc., "The Economic Impact of Pollution Control: Macroeconomic and Industry Reports," prepared for The Council on Environmental Quality, August 1976, pp. 2–3.

2. See K. W. Chilton and M. L. Weidenbaum, *Small Business Performance in the Regulated Economy* (St. Louis: Center for the Study of American Business, Washington University, 1980), working paper no. 52.

3. *Economic Report of the President,* 1982, pp. 145–56.

Chapter 12

1. Editorial, "California's Crime Revolt," *Wall Street Journal,* 16 June 1982.

Index

Index

Index

Individual Retirement Accounts (IRAs), 44, 129–30, 212, 238
industrial production, index of, 59*n*
industrial sectors, key: aid to, 44, 230; capital spending in, 158–59; cutback in investment in, 76–77
Industry Week, 73
inflation, 5, 10, 17, 44, 69, 118, 142, 180; and balanced budget, 6, 7, 39–40; constrained through tight money, 48, 53–56; decline in, 76, 86–87, 100–1, 255; under Democratic and Republican administrations, 271, 272; double-digit, 19, 20–21, 27, 56; and investment ratio, 145–49, 150; in national sales tax (proposed), 263–64; parity with interest rates, 25–26, 27, 33–34, 60–66, 68–69, 185, 260; and productivity, 12f, 247, 248, 249–50, 251, 252; projections on, 26; and rate of return, 111, 112, 116; and rate of saving, 36–38; reflows and, 98, 99, 100; tax cuts and, 4, 21, 22, 50–51, 52–53, 108, 109; at time of Kennedy-Johnson tax cuts, 9, 39–40; underlying rate of, 26, 58, 68, 80, 272, 273–74; *see also* expectations, inflationary
inflation rate, 10, 18, 42, 62, 125, 223, 261; and assets of choice, 11; effect of government regulation on, 231; goal, 259, 260, 261; increase in, 43, 44, 114, 116, 118, 276; and investment decisions, 80; and profit margins, 77; projections on, 8, 28, 29–30, 111; trade-off with unemployment, 245–52
informal economy, 209; *see also* underground economy
innovation, 195–96, 237, 238
interest rates, 4, 177, 213, 274; and budget deficit, 86–87; determinants of, 57–59; and earnings/price ratio, 184; effect of decline in saving rate on, 36–38; effect of tight money on, 53–56; with flat-rate tax, 269; forecasts of, 27; Great Depression, 16; high, 161, 266, 267; and inflation, 101, 260; and investment behavior, 73, 74, 75, 76, 77, 78, 79, 80–81, 83, 256, 257–58; and investment ratio, 141, 144, 145, 148, 150–51, 157–58; long-term, 10, 11f, 34, 57, 80–81; monetary policy and, 48, 49, 51, 52, 54, 56, 60, 62, 63, 65, 66–67, 69; money supply growth and, 56–59; parity with interest rates, 25–26, 27, 33–34, 60–66, 68–69, 185, 260; projected decline of (Reagan economic program), 25–47, 48; real, 4, 26, 27, 36, 185, 269; regulated by Federal Reserve, 60–61, 62, 63, 65, 66–67, 69; and saving rate, 111, 112, 118; short-term, 34, 56, 80–81
Internal Revenue Service, 194, 195, 204, 208–9
inventory stocks: valuation of, 146
investment, 22, 56, 253; booms (postwar), 141–45; effect of business tax cuts on, 70–83; effect of high interest rates on, 69, 70–83, 256; and productivity, 138–41; and rate of

return, 110; Reagan tax cuts failed to stimulate, 157–59; stock prices and, 177–81; targeting, 159–62, 264; tax incentives for, 141–44, 150–51, 153, 161; *see also* capital spending
investment behavior, 73–83, 139–41
investment decisions: based on economic reasons, 267–68; and capital allocation, 159–60; tax avoidance and, 196–98; time lag in, 79–83, 157
investment multiplier, 179–80
investment ratio, 82 (table), 83, 138–41, 142–43, 144, 145, 149, 152, 161, 162; under flat-rate tax, 269; and productivity, 215–16
investment tax credit (ITC), 40, 70–71, 77, 78–79, 143–44, 145, 152–53, 157–59, 212, 238, 272; in Kennedy-Johnson tax cuts, 9; selling, 44, 102, 103, 154–56 (*see also* Safe Harbor Leasing)
Italy, 166; Phillips curves, 251, 253 (figure), 255 (figure); saving stimulation in, 128, 156
"It's Time to Cut Taxes" (Wanniski), 50

Japan, 125, 166; Phillips curves, 251, 253 (figure), 255 (figure); saving stimulation in, 127–28, 156; targeted investment in, 160–61
job mobility, 196
job training, 94, 218
jobs, new, 164, 165, 179, 268
Johnson, Lyndon B., 10, 18, 40, 62, 144, 272; economic policy, 18, 19, 79, 114; fiscal policy, 63; and Social Security benefits, 92–93; *see also* Kennedy-Johnson tax cuts
Joint Committee on Taxation, 181
Jorgenson, Dale, 70–71, 74, 150–51

Kaufman, Henry, 32–33
Kennedy, John F., 31, 40, 62, 77, 78, 142–43
Kennedy-Johnson tax cuts, 8, 20, 64, 65, 86, 94, 143, 197, 219, 276; differences from Reagan tax cuts, 9, 28, 39–45; effect of, 28, 85, 250; reflows and, 99–100; and saving rate, 112, 114; as supply-side cut, 17, 43, 50; and tax revenues, 198, 199
Kemp, Jack, 71, 99
Keogh plans, 212, 238
Keynes, John Maynard, 16–17, 59; consumption function, 122
Keynesian theory, 57, 70–71, 110; consumption function, 120–21, 122, 123
Keynes's Law, 18–19
Klein, Lawrence R., 123
Korean War, 10, 45, 55, 89, 142
Kosters, Marvin, 191
Kuznets, Simon, 120

Index

Index

293